Cold War Theories

Cold War Theories

VOLUME I

World Polarization, 1943–1953

Kenneth W. Thompson

Louisiana State University Press

Baton Rouge and London

To George F. Kennan

Copyright © 1981 by Louisiana State University Press
All rights reserved
Manufactured in the United States of America

Designer: Patricia Douglas Crowder
Typeface: VIP Baskerville
Typesetter: G&S Typesetters, Inc.

Library of Congress Cataloging in Publication Data

Thompson, Kenneth W., 1921–
  Cold war theories.

  Includes index.
  Contents: v. 1. World polarization, 1943–1953. 1. World politics—1945–
  2. Balance of power. I. Title.
  D843.T423   327.1'12   81-6001
  ISBN 0-8071-0876-6 (v. 1)   AACR2

Contents

	Introduction	1
	Prelude	10
Chapter One	Causes of the Cold War: Two Interpretations and a Critique	23
Chapter Two	Historic Origins of the Cold War	57
Chapter Three	America's Response: Containment Revisited	119
Chapter Four	Collective Security and the Balance of Power: NATO as the Model	155
Chapter Five	Korea: The Limits of Containment	179
	Index	215

Cold War Theories

Introduction

Because the historian stands both within and outside history, and his own era exerts upon him the powerful force of dominant trends of thought and strong-running ideological and national passion, no history can be complete. And if the effort at understanding a given period of history increases in relation to the number of permutations the explanation takes, the process of mixing and sifting is nevertheless the advantage and duty of the historian. The principle of ongoing reexamination is hardly more significant anywhere than in the evaluation of the crucial decade that saw the unfolding of the Cold War.

In the debate over the Cold War, two dominant schools of thought have emerged. The official viewpoint has tended to attribute major responsibility for the outbreak and intensification of the Cold War to the Soviet Union and in particular to Premier Stalin and the policies he pursued during the closing months and the aftermath of World War II. Official historians have tended to see Stalin as the high prophet of a rigid theology and the chief executor of the fixed and unchanging objectives of international communism. The orthodox view finds that causal relations can be sharply drawn; proponents of this view show their impatience when anyone raises the question as to whether Americans may not themselves have contributed to the deepening of the crisis. Paul Seabury, having traced the beginnings of the Cold War to the formulation of the Truman Doctrine, goes on to say, "The utility of choosing this point in time is not (as some Soviet apologists would have it) that Truman's speech was an American declaration of ideological hostilities." Indeed the defense of free people everywhere which the Truman Doctrine proclaimed was a call by American statesmen for a full turn in history and "no one in policy councils of government opposed either the decision or the bold manner in which . . . [the Doctrine] was formulated."[1] Explanations that focus on the traditional Russian quest for a security zone in Eastern Europe are beside the point. The victims of Soviet expansion lost their freedom, and for sophisticated thinkers or historians to philosophize about the motives of their oppressor is to ignore a far more simple and obvious explanation. The real issue in the Cold War was "the future character of the most advanced, effective, and powerful zone in the world. . . . The central assumption of Marxists which the Soviet leadership inherited was that they were the legatees of the European bourgeoisie whose historical task was to manage the last transitional act of a drama staged in the heart of industrial civilization."[2] Stalin was the principal manager of the grand design and only following Khrushchev's unsuccessful thrust at Berlin in 1961 was the master plan thwarted.

A similar emphasis can be found in C. B. Marshall's *The Cold War: A Concise History*, which accents even more pointedly than the Seabury book the inevitable and worldwide march of communism propelled by the aims and purposes of messianic communism. Arthur Schlesinger, Jr., writing in the late 1960s, observed: "The orthodox American view, as originally set forth by the American government and as reaffirmed until recently by most American scholars, has been that the Cold War was the brave and essential response of free men to communist aggression."[3] Professor Schlesinger himself contributed to this viewpoint both in an article in the influential journal *Foreign Affairs* (October, 1967) and in his book *The Vital Center*, as did Eric F. Goldman in *The Crucial Decade* and John W. Spanier in *American Foreign Policy Since World War II*. Participants and decision makers in the crucial American policies of the early Cold War period threw the full weight of their authority and constitutional prestige behind the official viewpoint especially in the memoirs and accounts of James Forrestal, James Byrnes, W. Averell Harriman, William C. Bullitt, Cordell Hull, Admiral William D. Leahy, and President Harry S Truman.

There is of course something arbitrary about drawing together a group of men of affairs and historians who on many of the points at issue have displayed significant differences. It is equally possible to point to other dimensions of their writings which diverge from the official

1. Paul Seabury, *The Rise and Decline of the Cold War* (New York: Basic Books, 1976), 16.
2. *Ibid.*, iii.
3. Lloyd C. Gardner, Arthur Schlesinger, Jr., and Hans J. Morgenthau, *The Origins of the Cold War* (Waltham, Mass.: Ginn and Company, 1970), 43.

viewpoint; yet certain broad political assumptions and intellectual tendencies can be traced. Most felt compelled by the arguments advanced by the Truman administration to explain and justify its actions. America following the war, endeavoring to stand on the principle of Soviet-American cooperation, had dismantled its mighty armies and had dedicated itself to building within the United Nations a system of collective security, which President Truman had described as "the cornerstone of American foreign policy." Not only had the United States been thwarted on every hand by the Soviet Union but it had found its wartime ally poised for an expansionist drive across Europe. America's former ally had broken its promises made at Yalta to respect the integrity of Eastern Europe, leading President Truman to administer a tongue lashing to Soviet Foreign Minister Molotov, in a White House meeting on the eve of the San Francisco Conference, for having made the Yalta agreements a one-way street. When Molotov protested he had never been talked to like that before in his life, Truman shot back that if Russia kept its agreements its leaders would not be lectured in that way. Ambassador W. Averell Harriman, who with James Forrestal and Major General John R. Deane had urged greater firmness by the president (with Secretary of War Henry L. Stimson and General George C. Marshall urging caution), was forced nonetheless to acknowledge: "I did regret that Truman went at it so hard because his behavior gave Molotov an excuse to tell Stalin that the Roosevelt policy was being abandoned. . . . I think it was a mistake, though not a decisive mistake."[4]

With Harriman, as with other policy makers or historians who have espoused the official viewpoint, it may be unfair to suggest that he found the United States blameless in the developing conflict with the Soviet Union. What is fair is to report that leaders of such persuasion have generally found the United States not responsible for any "decisive mistakes" leading to the Cold War. Thus Marshall D. Shulman (Columbia University's Soviet specialist who served as assistant to several secretaries of state), though prepared to recognize that American over-reactions to Soviet actions had some effect on the deterioration of East-West relations, concluded:

> It is disproportionate to argue, as some writers have done, that the abruptness of the cancellation of the Lend-Lease arrangements with the Soviet Union, the mishandling of the Soviet loan request, the severity of President

4. W. Averell Harriman and Elia Abel, *Special Envoy to Churchill and Stalin, 1941–1946* (New York: Random House, 1975), 454.

Truman's reception of Soviet Foreign Minister Molotov en route to the founding meeting of the United Nations, or other instances of United States ineptitude or inconsistency as the war drew to a close, were of a sufficient order to have created a legitimate basis of Soviet concern for its security against a western attack.[5]

Instead it was Stalin and, more directly, Andrei Zhdânov who established the Cominform, tightened Soviet controls in Eastern Europe, engineered the coup in Czechoslovakia, and incited the Communist parties of France and Italy to militant actions against their governments. Soviet leaders, especially in the first years of the Cold War, were men of "a narrowly dogmatic outlook." They were single-minded in pursuing Soviet objectives. Soviet ambition to augment its power position in the world, coupled with the ideological perceptions and expectations of Communist leaders, brought on the Cold War. According to the Marxist-Leninist world view, non-Communist regimes had been and would continue to be uncompromisingly hostile to the Soviet regime, with East-West conflict an inevitable consequence. Yet history in the Marxist design foreordained the eventual collapse of non-Communist societies and their inescapable replacement by new societies shaped in the Soviet image. "It has been this component . . . that has made Soviet dynamism more complex and less susceptible to territorial stabilization than if it simply reflected the bursting energy of a nation-state entering upon a virile state of development."[6]

In this context, it would not have been difficult to predict even in the 1950s that a reaction would set in against the defenders of the Cold War. An opposing school of thought emerged whose spokesmen were committed to prove that the United States and not the Soviet Union was largely if not primarily to blame for the Cold War. In the 1960s, a group of younger historians responding to mounting dissatisfaction with Cold War thinking in the United States and to the Vietnam War found in past and present American imperialism the determining cause of the Cold War. Their writings and interpretations were foreshadowed in the dissenting views of a little band of public figures and popular writers on international relations. Senators such as Robert A. Taft of Ohio, Claude Pepper of Florida, and Glen Taylor of Idaho had spoken out in the 1940s. James P. Warburg, an independent-minded Wall Street banker,

5. Marshall D. Shulman, *Beyond the Cold War* (New Haven: Yale University Press, 1966), 14–15.
6. *Ibid.*, 16.

had devoted the last years of his life to a tireless questioning of the assumptions of American foreign policy. Henry Wallace, President Truman's secretary of commerce and a former New Deal intellectual, criticized American policies toward Russia, as did such political commentators as I. F. Stone, Freda Kirchwey, and Vera Michels Dean, who asked as early as 1946: "Is it possible we may be expecting of Russia higher standards of international conduct than our own?"[7] Characterizing the thinking of this group, Thomas G. Patterson argued, "The Cold War critics, contrary to their detractors, were not fuzzy-minded idealists clinging to illusory hopes or out of touch with power politics. They recognized that postwar Soviet-American competition was unavoidable and that relations would not be free of troublesome debate. But they refused to accept the idea that a growing militarism, heated verbiage, and actual military skirmishes were inevitable."[8]

It is obvious in looking back that these early Cold War critics were a handful of independent-minded individuals who represented no single coherent doctrine of foreign policy. Wallace differed as significantly from Warburg as Senator Taft did from Senator Taylor. The contrast was particularly evident in 1948, when Taft supported Thomas Dewey for the presidency, Senator Pepper reluctantly backed President Truman, and Senator Taylor left the Democratic party to run as Wallace's vice-presidential candidate for the Progressive party. By contrast, the revisionist historians in the 1960s were largely drawn, as Robert J. Maddox has attempted to show, from the New Left. The revisionists challenged in the most outspoken terms the proposition of the orthodox historians that the Cold War represented "the brave and essential response of free men to communist aggression,"[9] arguing that the United States itself bore heavy responsibility for the conflict either because of the failure of President Truman and his closest advisers to continue the policies of Franklin D. Roosevelt or because the American capitalist system required overseas markets to assure economic expansion and increased production. Finally, it should be noted that the later revisionists drew on the work of earlier critics such as D. F. Fleming, whose *The Cold War and Its Origins* was described by Hans J. Morgenthau as a Cold War polemic in reverse, or Gar Alperovitz, who maintained in *Atomic Diplomacy:*

7. Vera Michels Dean, "Is Russia Alone to Blame?" *Foreign Policy Report*, XXV (March 8, 1946).
8. Thomas G. Patterson (ed.), *Cold War Critics: Alternatives to American Foreign Policy in the Truman Years* (Chicago: Quadrangle Books, 1971), 10.
9. Gardner, Schlesinger, and Morgenthau, *The Origins of the Cold War*, 43.

Hiroshima and Potsdam that the atomic bomb was used against Japan not primarily to foreshorten the war but as a political weapon in the impending struggle with the Soviet Union.

The roots of revisionism as a school of thought were more fundamental than a simple protest over specific policies of the Truman administration. The rise of the organized historical movement of revisionism coincided with a major debate on the proper objectives of the social sciences and the humanities. By the 1960s, a growing number of scholars were calling for the overthrow of scientific and value-free studies of society. Purpose as a determinant of policy analysis came to the fore and an impressive body of younger historians and sociologists prided themselves that their inquiries were not value-free but directed to undisguised social and political ends. They rejected so-called objective history, which they insisted cloaked scholarly defense and justification of American foreign policy. Historians had a duty to explain, propagate, and defend their underlying purposes, and the Cornell historian Walter LaFeber, whom some have described as "a moderate revisionist," pointed to the core of such thinking when he declared: "It is past time the revisionists believe, for the admission that for American historians history begins and ends with ideology."[10] The historian was challenged in his writings and teachings to mold the future in accordance with his ideological convictions and he was enjoined to make explicit his commitments to a given set of values.

To the present day, controversy surrounds attempts to identify and evaluate the underlying assumptions of individual revisionist historians. Robert Maddox, whose critical study *The New Left and the Origins of the Cold War* evoked a storm of protest and bitter counterattacks from those he criticized, staunchly maintained that revisionists fall into one of two identifiable groups. The "soft" revisionists tend to fix responsibility for the Cold War on individuals rather than economic forces or social institutions. They point to the results of the sharp break said to have occurred between the foreign policies of Franklin Roosevelt and Harry Truman. The latter substituted abruptly and with little warning attitudes of open hostility and belligerency for Roosevelt's more conciliatory and pragmatic approach, thus making conflict inevitable. The "hard" revisionists find the causes of the Cold War in the structure and organization of American capitalism. Not individual American presi-

10. Walter LaFeber, "War: Cold," *Cornell Alumni News*, October 1968.

dents but the spokesmen for the corporate system which required end-less expansion sought to promote capitalist hegemony in the world be-cause they had been recruited from Wall Street, large corporations, and private foundations, and from the American establishment. Whoever the president might be and however humble his background, he was subjected to certain irresistible forces; the conduct of American foreign policy, whether in Eastern Europe or Vietnam, reflects the inherent needs of a conservative, expansionist-capitalist order. Markets, not na-tional interest, have become the determinant of American policies, whether in Eastern Europe or Vietnam, cloaked in the language of an "Open Door" for the markets of all nations everywhere in the world. A small group of revisionists combine "soft" and "hard" revisionism, an example being David Horowitz, a Rutgers historian who condemns orthodox scholars for consciously promoting "the State Department line," meaning the serving of the interests of both American capitalists and the official policies of a government hostile to the Soviet Union.[11]

No one can question that revisionist historians have become a signifi-cant, articulate, and influential scholarly group successful in extending their influence down to the present. Nor can it be denied that they have furnished a necessary corrective to many of the rather too uncritical jus-tifications of recent American foreign policy. It must also be acknowl-edged that the revisionists taken as a whole constitute a relatively di-verse group whose policy recommendations hardly add up to a single monolithic doctrine on every issue in the Cold War. Underlying almost all their beliefs, however, is the concept that economic factors are the determining ones in foreign policy. Moreover, the United States in its present stage of economic development has little choice in the policies it pursues. Commerce and trade and more or less continuous economic expansion are indispensable for capitalism's survival; these in turn de-pend on favorable interventions by governments to open up new mar-kets and protect and preserve old ones. Policy makers are linked by past background and present ties to business interests by an umbilical cord that is not easily severed. Decisions by American policy makers to assist in the rebuilding of Europe following World War II were motivated pri-marily by economic considerations and particularly by vigorous compe-tition for European markets. Economic pressures have also been used to

11. David Horowitz, *The Free World Colossus: A Critique of American Foreign Policy in the Cold War* (Rev. ed.,; New York: Hill and Wang, 1975), 7.

coerce and influence the enemy, the Soviet Union, as in the curtailment of lend-lease without prior notice in May, 1945, at the end of the war in Europe.

While turning on its head the prevailing historical interpretation of American foreign policy in the Cold War laid down by orthodox historians, the revisionists have also been determined to alter American views of Stalinist Russia. If Stalin appears in certain early Cold War histories as a ruthless demon setting out with maniacal cunning to overcome the West, the revisionists find him "frank" or "sincere" or "well-intentioned" in nearly all his policies. The Soviet Union under Stalin is seen as reacting to aggressive and expansionist moves by an adversary, moves attributed not so much to evil men as to leaders compelled to follow capitalist interests by forces they are helpless to control.

Granted that revisionism has offered a healthy corrective to the neglect some orthodox historians have displayed toward powerful economic forces, it remains a mystery why important proponents of revisionism should characterize all American policy makers as mere tools of nefarious capitalists bent on worldwide exploitation. Many responsible policy makers and historians who have shown considerable sympathy for new approaches to decision making end by seriously questioning the unqualified economic determinism in revisionism. Policy makers insist there has been little evidence of slavish acceptance and support of economic interests in most of the policy discussions in which they have participated. They maintain that vital decisions in the executive and legislative branches of government are made in the national interest more often than revisionist critics know or appreciate it. General Motors or IBM are invoked rarely if at all. In twenty years with a large American private foundation, I am unable to recall a single instance in which decisions on international programs were linked to the explicit interests or the promptings of Exxon, Chase Manhattan, or any other giant business or banking concern.

It is, however, another question, and one deserving of the most exacting and imaginative historical study, to explore whether decision makers are influenced unconsciously by their backgrounds or past associations. Leaders in every sphere must be eternally vigilant and on guard against the "country club complex" which Robert M. Hutchins described over thirty years ago in his "Report on a Free and Responsible Press." We know that every large institutional group is endangered by its inwardness; it runs the risk of seeing the world through but one window and failing in its perceptions to move outside and beyond itself. We are all of us captives of our class, region, and nation. The republic is in jeopardy when any meritocracy, whether of wealth or talent, sees itself as the sole self-annointed defender of civilization and shuts itself off from opposing views. The rich and the powerful are endlessly tempted to grasp authority beyond society's mandate and their individual capacity. Wealth leads to the abuse of power but this danger is a far cry from the irresistible domination that international capitalism is said to be exerting on every foreign policy decision in the Cold War.

In summary, the orthodox historians and the revisionists alike are guilty of similar errors however much they inveigh against one another. Each group portrays a major political system as being driven by a determinism beyond its control. Each identifies an expansionist dynamic at work which makes conflict inevitable. Each views one set of decision makers as driven by an ideology which blinds them to responsible political judgments. Both choose verbs and adjectives to serve their own interpretative objectives. Thus for the official historians, the Americans and the British "restore order" in an occupied area whereas the Russians "suppress dissident elements." Revisionists merely interchange these favorable and unfavorable references. Policy makers on the "other side" are not wrong but malevolent, and it is painful if not impossible for one or the other school of thought to admit the existence of the "enemy's" legitimate national security interests whether, in a given instance, such interests are Russian or American.

Prelude

Historical interpretation is only one of the factors that complicate the task of understanding the Cold War. Of the many factors that must be reckoned with, some are a part of the human drama and others are peculiarly American. Under the first of these categories is the tendency of human nature to locate responsibility and pin the blame on someone or something. Nations no less than individuals point the finger at the authors of their discomfort, whether a stubborn leader, a misguided ally, or a threatening rival. Man's underlying assumption that some individual, group, or nation is to blame for human ills becomes cloaked in righteousness. History is written about heroes and villains and he who encroaches on my rights or causes my nation to stumble is not only misguided but evil. There is another form of history far less appealing to the masses but more likely to withstand the buffeting of time. Sir Herbert Butterfield, the late vice chancellor of Cambridge University in England, has offered it as an alternative to what he described as Whig history, the tendency to see the world through the eyes of a single party or group. Writing in the New York *Times*, Butterfield explained:

> Many of us have been brought up on a kind of history which sees the human drama throughout the ages as a straight conflict between right and wrong. Sooner or later, however, we may find ourselves awakened to the fact that in a given war there have been virtuous and reasonable men earnestly fighting on both sides. Historians ultimately move to a higher altitude and produce a picture which has greater depth because it does justice to what was thought and felt by the better men in both parties.[1]

1. New York *Times*, January 3, 1973, p. 34.

Abraham Lincoln's Second Inaugural Address is remembered for the clarity of its moral and political vision as an embattled wartime leader rose above conventional loyalty to region, creed, or group. Having made his choice and mobilized the nation's energies, Lincoln might have followed the path of most wartime leaders and become the mouthpiece for Unionists or, in Butterfield's phrase, the voice of Whig history. Instead, as he looked out on the warring parties he found that: "Both read the same Bible and pray to the same God, and each invokes His aid against the other." Lincoln's Second Inaugural Address is a model of what Max Weber called the ethics of responsibility. It resounds with an awareness of purposes higher than all the fragmentary purposes that were joined together in the "war of the states": "Fondly do we hope, fervently do we pray, that this mighty scourge of war may speedily pass. Yet if God wills that it continue . . . so still must it be said, that the judgments of the Lord are true and righteous altogether." Lincoln's harshest judgment leveled at "all the wealth piled by the bondsman's two hundred and fifty years of unrequited toil" is followed immediately in his concluding appeal to both sides:

> With malice toward none, with charity for all, with firmness in the right as God gives us to see the right, let us finish the work we are in, to bind up the nation's wounds, to care for him who shall have borne the battle, and for his widow and his orphans, to do all which may achieve a just and lasting peace among all nations.[2]

Butterfield pointed to another dimension of the historical endeavor when he wrote: "Behind the great conflicts of mankind is a terrible human predicament . . . which contemporaries fail to see . . . a terrible knot beyond the ingenuity of man to untie." If in the study of the Cold War the orthodox historians point simply to Soviet territorial expansion as provoking the brave response of the free and peaceful America, and the revisionists shift the blame to American imperialism and the insatiable demands of capitalists for worldwide economic markets, then neither side within its framework can account for the unexpected turnabouts in the tide of conflict, the forces whether national or international which controlled leaders' actions and the tragic and twisted pattern of attempts to impose restraints on the struggle. No one in either group appears ready to acknowledge the role of accident or the absolute

2. Abraham Lincoln, Second Inaugural Address, delivered at Washington, March 4, 1865.

predicaments or irreducible dilemmas which lie at the core of human conflict.

Nations joined in peaceful or not so peaceful competition are caught up in a condition of needing one another to survive but fearing one another's actions and motives. A Hobbesian fear casts its fateful shadow over states in the Cold War. As Butterfield has described it:

> There could be a United States and a Russia standing at the top of the world, exactly equal in power, exactly equal in virtue, and each could fear with some justice that the other might steal a march on it, neither of them understanding for a moment—neither of them even crediting—the counterfear of the other. Each could be sure of its own good intentions, but might not trust the other, since one can never really pierce to the interior of anybody else. Mutual resentment would come to be doubted because, on the top of everything each party felt the other was withholding just the thing that would enable it to feel secure. This situation may never exist in its purity, but the essential predicament underlies international relations generally, making even simple problems sometimes insoluble.[3]

In a confrontation such as the Cold War each side conceives its policies as designed to assure its security but "may overlook the fact that it can make its own security complete only by destroying the security of the other altogether." Both sides are caught up in what students of international politics have called the security-power dilemma and the fears and insecurities of leaders are magnified and intensified many thousand-fold by the hopes and frustrations of the man in the street. In an era when foreign policy has become everyone's business and when leaders invoke public opinion to justify or excuse actions or constraints, the dreams and the dissatisfactions and in particular the unfulfilled aspirations of the ordinary citizen are thrown into the balance of almost every important decision. Of this factor, Butterfield observes: "The key to everything . . . lies in the mediocre desires, the intellectual confusions and the wilful moods of the average man. . . . The real trouble is the moderate cupidity of Everyman—his ordinary longing to advance a little farther . . . even just his dread of a decline in his standard of living. This when multiplied by millions, can build into a tremendous pressure on government."[4] The dominant influence of these public sentiments may be traced in the statements of President Franklin D. Roosevelt, who con-

3. Herbert Butterfield, New York *Times*, January 3, 1973, p. 34.
4. *Ibid.*

tinuously explained and justified himself to Churchill and Stalin by references to the traffic that American public opinion would bear and in Stalin's repeated defense of his unwillingness to make concessions, especially on territorial questions, in his reference to the public opinion of the Ukranians and other Soviet republics. The acid test of political leadership is whether or not the leader consistently and effectively prepares Everyman for comprehending the deep dilemmas of foreign policy. It is scarcely enough to say "trust the people" and then leave their education to chance or to pass over the first principle of representative government: that leaders must sometimes act as the people would act if they possessed the same information.

This brings us around to a factor deserving of major attention: the human factor. To a large extent, the interpretation of the events of history depends upon a comprehension of the decision makers and the leaders of the groups or nations involved. It seems appropriate in a discussion of the causes of the Cold War to examine the human or leadership equation as it has affected American foreign policy. The human factor in the origin of the Cold War precedes all others and influences the drama as it unfolds.

Biographers of Franklin D. Roosevelt are generally agreed that he was the consummate politician, a Hudson Valley aristocrat who because of his early privileged life was secure in the exercise of authority and self-confident even to the point of recklessness about his political "hunches." (Secretary of War Henry Stimson often warned that the president needed to be protected against his impulsiveness.) He prided himself on his flexibility and pragmatism. "I dream dreams," he once wrote, "but am, at the same time, an intensely practical person."[5] One biographer, James MacGregor Burns, has characterized Roosevelt as "a deeply divided man. . . . He was a practical man who proceeded now boldly, now cautiously, step by step toward immediate ends. . . . He was both a Soldier of the Faith, battling with his warrior comrades for an ideology of peace and freedom, and a Prince of the State, protecting the interests of his nation in a threatening world."[6] When asked if his concept of international order resembled Wilson's Fourteen Points, he re-

5. Quoted in John L. Gaddis, *The United States and the Origins of the Cold War, 1941–1947* (New York: Columbia University Press, 1972), 27.
6. James MacGregor Burns, "FDR: The Untold Story of His Last Year," *Saturday Review*, LIII (April 11, 1970), 15.

sponded: "Oh no. Oh no. . . . Things like points, well, are principles: This is a working organization that we are talking about."[7]

It would be wrong to portray Roosevelt as an idealistic captive of a single grand design. His thinking gravitated around a clustering of independent principles which coexisted in his mind but which he seemed never to have ordered or ranked, perhaps because to him they were little more than points. High on his agenda in World War II was military cooperation with the Soviet Union. When called on to defend this policy, he answered in a press conference on February 17, 1942: "Put it in terms of dead Germans and smashed tanks." In May, 1942, he wrote General Douglas MacArthur that "the Russian armies are killing more Axis personnel and destroying more Axis material than all other twenty-five United Nations put together."[8]

Lest anyone suppose that Roosevelt's determination to cooperate militarily with the Russians was somehow the product of his being soft on communism, it must be recalled that he followed and did not lead that lifelong enemy of communism, Winston S. Churchill, in making such a commitment. On the day Germany attacked Russia, Churchill communicated Britain's determination to help in a message to Stalin. Three months earlier, in the beginning of April, 1941, because he was convinced that Germany would attack Russia, he told Maisky, the Soviet ambassador to London, that in such an eventuality Britain would come to Russia's aid. A month before the invasion, he appealed to Roosevelt, saying:

> Should this new war break out, we shall, of course, give all encouragement and any help we can spare to the Russians, following the principle that Hitler is the foe we have to beat. I do not expect any class political reactions here, and trust a German-Russian conflict will not cause you any embarrassment.[9]

When asked by his private secretary John Rupert Colville if by joining Russia he was not "bowing down in the House of Rimmon," Churchill answered: "I have only one purpose, the destruction of Hitler, and my life is much simplified thereby. If Hitler invaded Hell I would make at least a favourable reference to the Devil in the House of Commons."[10]

7. Quoted in Gaddis, *The United States and the Origins of the Cold War*, 29.
8. Roosevelt to MacArthur, May 6, 1942, quoted in Herbert Feis, *Churchill, Roosevelt, Stalin: The War They Waged and the Peace They Sought* (Princeton: Princeton University Press, 1957), 42.
9. Winston S. Churchill, *The Grand Alliance* (Boston: Houghton Mifflin, 1950), 369, Vol. III of *The Second World War*.
10. *Ibid.*, 369.

Privately Roosevelt, despite resentment in the State Department against the harsh and brazen demands the Russians had made of us for vital war materials even during the time of the Nazi-Soviet Pact, reassured Churchill through Ambassador Winant. On June 20, 1941, Churchill wrote: "The American Ambassador, who was my guest at the weekend, brought me the President's answer to my message. He promised that if the Germans struck at Russia he would immediately support publicly any announcement that the Prime Minister might make welcoming Russia as an ally." [11] When war broke out between Russia and Germany, it was the old enemy of Bolshevism, not Roosevelt, who broadcast a message to the Russians and on July 7, 1941, sent personal word to the Russians offering help and welcoming the military mission that the Russians proposed to send.

If Roosevelt was second to Churchill in taking the initiative with the Russians, he was not alone in the American government. Secretary of State Cordell Hull was ill at home when news came of the German invasion of Russia, but he called Roosevelt and Undersecretary of State Sumner Welles to urge: "We must give Russia all aid to the hilt." And in the days that followed his recuperation, Hull recounted: "I was in constant touch . . . urging that we give Russia the most vigorous assurances of all the help we could extend." [12] Such support notwithstanding, Roosevelt was more cautious than Churchill. On June 24, 1941, when he was asked at a press conference if the defense of Russia is the defense of the United States, Roosevelt advised his interrogator to ask another question such as "How old is Ann?" On June 26, he announced through Undersecretary Welles that in the future the Neutrality Act would not be invoked against the Soviet Union. Some three weeks later, he sent Presidential Aide Harry Hopkins to London to discuss with the British strategies for supplying the Russians, and then to Moscow. On August 2, the American government made a more official commitment and on August 30, Roosevelt wrote Secretary Stimson: "I deem it to be of paramount importance for the safety and security of America that all reasonable munitions help be provided for Russia not only immediately but as long as she continues to fight the Axis powers effectively." [13]

What were the reasons for Roosevelt's uncertainty and delay? Why

11. *Ibid.*
12. Walter Johnson (ed.), *The Memoirs of Cordell Hull* (New York: Macmillan, 1942), II, 973.
13. W. L. Langer and S. Everett Gleason, *The Undeclared War, 1940–1941* (New York: Harper & Brothers, 1953).

did he hesitate in saying publicly what he had promised privately to Churchill? Some writers explain his actions by attributing them to a certain ingrained tendency to deceive the people. One historian writes: "Genius of the unexpected, maestro of the improvisational, artist of the dramatic, his mind danced across the scene where his legs would not carry him. . . . Had he expended the same effort convincing the public to do what he felt was right that he spent dreaming up ways to advance clandestine projects, it probably would have been more productive." [14] Most would agree with Herbert Feis, however, who wrote: "The President had taken care not to provoke argument about coming to the aid of Communist Russia. He put off from day to day what he knew he would have to do to carry out his policy—to be sure that before qualifying Russia for Lend Lease Congress would not deny the necessary appropriation. In an attempt to clear the way he had tried to get Stalin to say something in approval of freedom of religion which might avert Catholic opposition." [15]

It is impossible to understand Roosevelt's actions apart from his preoccupation with domestic politics. On every issue it seemed, he followed a strategy of postponement and delay. "Roosevelt feared that any detailed discussion of political settlements would provoke intense controversy within the United States distracting attention from the war effort and possibly threatening the nation's willingness to assume future world responsibilities." [16] His strategy was to call for delay in the consideration of most of the pressing issues of international politics whether the question of a provisional government in France under de Gaulle, the controversy with the British over governments in occupied Italy and liberated Greece, or of Russian demands in Eastern Europe. Roosevelt was of course aware of Stalin's insistence that Poland, Finland, and the Baltic states of Latvia, Lithuania, and Estonia were part of the prewar Russian empire. He knew of the provisions in the 1939 pact with Hitler, which, when victory was achieved, would incorporate eastern Poland, the Baltic states, Bessarabia, and parts of Finland into the Soviet Union. Stalin had made no secret of his territorial aims. As early as July, 1941, the Russians announced that they intended to retain the parts of Poland they had taken two years earlier. In December of that year, Stalin asked the Brit-

---

14. James R. Leutze, *Bargaining for Supremacy* (Chapel Hill: University of North Carolina Press, 1977), 42.

15. Feis, *Churchill*, 15.

16. Gaddis, *The United States and the Origins of the Cold War*, 14.

ish government "to support his bid for all of the Baltic States and territorial concessions from Finland and Rumania" and called on Anthony Eden for immediate recognition of the Soviet Union's western boundaries as they existed prior to Hitler's attack in 1941. Stalin also proposed certain territorial rearrangements in Europe, including spheres of influence.[17] He explained that all he sought was to restore his country to its earlier frontiers.

The British had first resisted Stalin's request, thereby contributing no doubt to the 1939 Molotov-Ribbentrop Pact. At the time, both Roosevelt and Churchill rejected Stalin's demands. Later, Churchill changed his mind and announced he was willing to accept Stalin's territorial claims.[18] Roosevelt, by contrast, urged his British ally to resist and based his argument on at least three factors: concession now would violate the Atlantic Charter; Russia's fears were based on the false prospect of a resurgent Germany; the acceptance of Soviet claims would be damaging in American domestic politics. Assistant Secretary of State Adolf Berle, with his eye on American politics, had warned that a "Baltic Munich" would place the United States in a dangerous position "both morally and realistically."[19] The one-time friend of Russia but now its severest critic, William C. Bullitt, warned: "Don't let Churchill get you into any more specific engagements than those in the Atlantic Charter. . . . The treaties—if made—will be as difficult for you to handle as the secret treaties were for Wilson."[20]

Unanswered is the question of why Roosevelt did not disclose to the American people the persistent claims of the Russians for a sphere of influence in Eastern Europe. Whereas Stalin had talked in these terms, Molotov denied at the Tripartite Moscow Conference in October, 1943, that the Soviet Union "would be interested in separate zones or spheres of influence" and guaranteed that "there was no disposition on the part of the Soviet Government to divide Europe into such separate zones."[21] By promising the Russians a second front in 1942, Roosevelt wrung

17. *Ibid*, 15. See also Churchill, *The Grand Alliance*, 628–29, and Johnson (ed.), *The Memoirs of Cordell Hull*, II, 1165–79.

18. See Churchill, *The Grand Alliance*, 630–37; Churchill, *The Hinge of Fate* (Boston: Houghton Mifflin, 1950), 327, Vol. IV of *The Second World War*.

19. Berle to Welles, April 3, 1942, in Samuel I. Rosenman (ed.), *The Public Papers and Addresses of Franklin D. Roosevelt* (4 vols.; New York: Harper & Brothers, 1950), III, 539–41.

20. Presidential Secretary File (PSF), Bullitt, in Franklin D. Roosevelt Library, Hyde Park, N.Y.

21. *Foreign Relations of the United States* (Washington: Government Printing Office, 1943), Vol. I, pp. 638–39.

from Stalin a promise to postpone his demand for postwar territorial interests. By early the next year, however, the president had reluctantly concluded he could not prevent Stalin from achieving his goals in Eastern Europe. His optimism led him to his own form of wishful thinking—to believe that with the "unconditional surrender" of Germany, Soviet claims might moderate or perhaps disappear. Having united the American people in a struggle for the rights of all peoples to self-determination, he feared the divisive effects of a premature disclosure of Soviet actions against self-determination in Eastern Europe and the dilemmas thus raised for American policy. In his last State of the Union address he did point out that while power politics ought not to be all-determining, "we cannot deny that power is a factor in world politics, any more than we can deny its existence as a factor in national politics." One student of the conflict points out: "The resulting tension between the American principle of self-determination and Russian security needs became the single most important cause of the disintegration of the Grand Alliance."[22]

From the sixteenth century, security for the Russians has meant expansion. But there was something else. For Roosevelt the dominating reason for opposing Soviet territorial ambitions was the Atlantic Charter. His advisers repeatedly pointed out that the secret accords of the Allies in World War I had spread disillusionment in the United States with the idealistic principles of President Wilson. To accept the Russian demands would destroy one of the central concepts of the Atlantic Charter, that of opposing territorial changes that did not accord with the wishes of the people involved. When this point was raised with Stalin, he responded by asking if the charter was directed against Germany or the Soviet Union. Churchill, differing with Roosevelt, had from the outset viewed the charter as an "interim and partial statement of war aims designed to assure all countries of our righteous purpose and not the complete structure which we should build after victory."[23] It was simpler for the British pragmatist, long schooled in the realities of international politics, to accept, however sadly, the notion of such tentative agreements. This clashed, however, with Roosevelt's determination to postpone territorial settlements not only because of domestic politics but because of his belief that certain noble goals were indeed achievable in practice. Harry Hopkins, explaining the president's idealistic streak, told Robert Sherwood in 1941:

22. Gaddis, *The United States and the Origins of the Cold War*, 15.
23. Churchill, *The Grand Alliance*, 442.

You and I are for Roosevelt because he's a great spiritual figure . . . an idealist like Wilson. Oh—he sometimes tries to appear tough and cynical and flip-
pant, but that's an act he likes to put on, especially at press conferences.
. . . You can see the real Roosevelt when he comes out with something like
the Four Freedoms. And don't get the idea that those are any catch phrases.
He believes them! He believes they can be practically attained.[24]

Yet it would be false to paint Roosevelt as the pure idealist and
Churchill as the incorrigible cynic. Writing of the charter, the latter declared, "Considering all the tales of my reactionary, Old-World outlook,
and the pain this is said to have caused the President, I am glad it should
be on record that the substance and spirit of what came to be called the
'Atlantic Charter' was in its first draft a British production cast in my
own words."[25] It is also worth noting that when the president gave
Churchill a revised draft adding Paragraph Six on freedom of the seas
and Seven on disarmament (reminiscent of President Carter's proposal
for comprehensive disarmament in his Inaugural Address), Churchill
pointed to the absence of any mention of establishing an international
organization after the war. He suggested adding to the president's disarmament statement the words "pending the establishment of a wider and
more permanent system of general security."[26] The charge is simply un-
true that Roosevelt's thinking was from the beginning dominated by a
universalistic creed leaving the preparation and the maintenance of
peace entirely to an international organization. That this idea was in the
air and that many of Roosevelt's aides held such a view is beyond dispute.
The scholarly and religious community was active in mobilizing public
opinion to assure that the nation would not repeat its tragic mistake of
1919 in rejecting the League of Nations. But Roosevelt, although a
Wilsonian, had by the outbreak of World War II abandoned the simple
faith that a universal organization could keep the peace. What was
needed, he asserted, was not a debating society but an instrument for the
prompt and effective use of force. He declared in September, 1941: "In
the present complete world confusion, it is not thought advisable at this
time to reconstitute a League of Nations which, because of its size, makes
for disagreement and inaction. . . . For a time at least there are many
minor children among the peoples of the world who need Trustees in
their relations with other nations and peoples, just as there are many

24. Robert E. Sherwood, *Roosevelt and Hopkins* (New York: Harper & Brothers, 1948),
266.
25. Churchill, *The Grand Alliance*, 434.
26. *Ibid.*, 437.

adult nations or peoples which must be led back into a spirit of good conduct."[27]

Roosevelt was doubtful about the readiness of the American people for a full role in international organization. Remembering the fate of Wilson's League, he hesitated to commit himself to another collective security body. Therefore, he refused to approve Churchill's proposal that a statement on international organization be added to the Atlantic Charter. It would be better to wait two to four years after the close of the war before establishing a new organization; the architects of the League of Nations had moved too quickly. In the interim, the peace would be preserved by the Big Four: the United States, the Soviet Union, Great Britain and, by courtesy, China. The four policemen would disarm all other nations and, if they threatened the peace, blockade and bomb them if necessary. Throughout 1942, the president continued to avoid any personal commitment but allowed his associates to speak out privately and in public, oftentimes in disagreement with his basic thesis. By the summer of 1942, public opinion polls showed that three out of four Americans favored participation in some kind of international organization. By April 1944, the State Department produced a compromise plan intended to be responsive both to Roosevelt and the internationalists. It was to be universal, drawing on the membership of all nations who had fought against Germany and Japan but incorporating Roosevelt's idea of the four policemen, who as permanent members of the Security Council could exercise the right of veto. Approval was assured, the president believed, both by the Senate and the Soviet Union. Throughout the debate he warned against expecting too much. "Let us not forget," he said in his State of the Union Address, January 6, 1945, "that the retreat to isolationism a quarter of a century ago was started not by a direct attack against international cooperation but against alleged imperfections of the peace." How vain these warnings were was all too evident in the wild applause which greeted Secretary of State Hull on his return in the autumn of 1943 from the Moscow Conference of Foreign Ministers when he told the Congress: "There will no longer be need for spheres of influence, for alliances, for balance of power, or any other of the special arrangements through which, in the unhappy past, the nations strove to safeguard their security or to promote their interests."[28]

Having warned against utopianism and perfectionism, Roosevelt

27. Quoted in Gaddis, *The United States and the Origins of the Cold War*, 24.
28. *Congressional Record*, November 18, 1943, pp. 678–79.

himself was to be their victim not so much with regard to a new international organization as with American-Soviet relations. The bedrock of his attitude and the sources of his working assumptions are not difficult to understand. He kept in mind throughout the wartime period that the two great powers would have to live together in the postwar world. In a speech on October 21, 1944, to the Foreign Policy Association, he declared: "We either work with the other great nations or we might some day have to fight them. And I am against that." In achieving his ends, he misjudged his ability to influence Stalin and disregarded the words of advisers such as Berle and Bullitt.

In part, though, Roosevelt may have been more realistic than his more hard-line advisers since he recognized the limits of American power. As the war drew to a close, he worried, as had Churchill, about the risk of a separate peace between the Soviet Union and Germany which would have left Britain and the United States with an altogether different military task.[29] He doubted whether the American people would accept the sacrifices necessary for pursuing a more aggressive American policy. He believed mistakenly, as it turned out, that Soviet military assistance was essential in the Far East. His thinking was to some extent influenced by contemporaries in the American intellectual and political community who prophesied that the United States and the Soviet Union would draw closer together in their political and economic systems and make future conflict unlikely. And he was suspicious if not hostile to political converts such as Bullitt who "had gone to Moscow in 1933 an enthusiastic supporter of the Moscow regime, but in one of the abrupt shifts from admiration to hatred which characterized his life, he soon became anti-Soviet."[30]

Yet Bullitt was as wrong on one side as Roosevelt was on the other, telling Roosevelt in August of 1943: "Hitler's aim was to spread the power of the Nazis to the ends of the earth. Stalin's aim is to spread the power of the Communists to the ends of the earth. Stalin, like Hitler, will not stop."[31] (One remembers Stalin's claim to the contrary: Unlike Hitler, I know when to stop.) Persistent anti-Communists such as Bullitt alien-

29. Professor Vojtech Mastny analyzes the evidence of contacts between Germany and the Soviet Union, especially in 1942–1943, in an important article, "Stalin and the Prospect of a Separate Peace in World War II," *American Historical Review*, LXXVII (1972), 1365–88, and his book, *Russia's Road to the Cold War* (New York: Columbia University Press, 1979), 73–74. See also William Stevenson, *A Man Called Intrepid* (New York: Ballantine Books, 1979), 381.

30. Gaddis, *The United States and the Origins of the Cold War*, 54.

31. Bullitt to Roosevelt, August 10, 1943, in Roosevelt MSS, PSF: "Bullitt".

ated Roosevelt as much by their tactics as their ideas. Bullitt engaged in a smear campaign against Sumner Welles which brought about the under-secretary of state's forced resignation in an episode which was a har-binger of McCarthyism.[32]

Roosevelt, however, also erred and his failures may be accounted for by political and ideological factors. He fell prey in the end to his own skills as an American politician. He imagined somehow that he could ca-jole, flatter, wheedle, and maneuver Stalin as he had many American politicians whom he had influenced. So great were his political skills do-mestically that on numerous occasions he intervened with constituents on behalf of beleaguered congressmen. As with scores of other success-ful American politicians, he found himself in an alien environment when he moved out into international politics. His failures were not as total as Chamberlain's, who believed he could talk with Hitler as to a Bir-mingham businessman, but there was one common element: the illusion that know-how in domestic politics or business was readily transferable to the international scene. Ideologically, he was handicapped by an al-most pathological aversion to British imperialism, which led him to favor Stalin in certain disputes with Churchill and to confuse a fairly amiable personal relationship with Stalin with genuine political cooperation. The question that must be asked is not the one that specialists in demon-ological thinking ask: Was Roosevelt (or for that matter Truman or any other American leader) an evil and misguided man, but instead, what were the political and moral assumptions which guided his thinking and that of mainstream American policy makers and were there alternative assumptions and principles then and now which might provide today the basis for another approach to foreign policy? This question will be a central issue as we examine in detail the origins and causes of the Cold War.

32. Gaddis, *The United States and the Origins of the Cold War*, 54.

Chapter One

Causes of the Cold War

Two Interpretations and a Critique

The Official Historians on Causes

The official historians of the Cold War without exception have pointed to a causative relationship between communism and the Cold War. They have found that national leaders of Communist states have been propelled by the dynamic dialectic of Marxism-Leninism. The words of Marx and Engels in the *Communist Manifesto* provide a living text for Communists throughout the world: "The Communists everywhere support every revolutionary movement against the existing social and political order." The orthodox view on the controlling role of communism was forcefully stated by David Rees, who found that the origin of the Cold War "stems from the events of 7 November 1917, with the successful storming of the Petrograd Winter Palace by Trotsky's Red Guards, followed by Lenin's fateful words uttered the next day to the Second All-Russian Congress of Soviets: 'We shall now proceed to construct the social order.'"[1] A year later in December, the German Marxist Rosa Luxembourg prophesied: "The struggle for socialism is the most gigantic civil war world history has ever known, and the proletarian revolution must provide the tools for civil war."[2]

The severity of the clash between communism and the guardians of the existing international order was due to the fact that Soviet leaders were men disposed toward a narrowly dogmatic outlook holding to their own brand of "a rigid theology." The ideological perceptions and expectations of the Communist leadership constituted a primary cause of conflict rather than a secondary and intensifying cause. Even a neutral his-

1. David Rees, *The Age of Containment* (New York: St. Martin's Press, 1967), 1.
2. Quoted *ibid.*

torian in the orthodoxy-revisionism debate was led to conclude: "As in the French Revolution, the ideological challenge added yet another justification to the age-old motives that have always caused nations to ravage each other: pride, greed, distrust and fear."[3] The fact that American foreign policy crystallized around the democratic creed of President Woodrow Wilson made it possible to speak, as Trotsky did, of Lenin and Wilson as the "apocalyptic antipodes" of our time. Because of Marxist dogma, Communist leaders saw the non-Communist world in a state of inherent antagonism toward Communist aims and purposes. "Stalin must have assumed that there had always been a Cold War, which would continue after the defeat of Hitler as before."[4] The Soviet Union was caught up in an inevitable conflict from which, in Khrushchev's words, it could not free itself without "a political earthquake."

The basic causes of the Cold War viewed in this light can be found in two epic events in 1917: America's entry into World War I and the Russian Revolution. President Wilson's declaration to the Congress of April 2, 1917, that "peace must be planted upon the tested foundations of political liberty" collided head on with Leon Trotsky's proclamation to the Congress of Soviets following the revolution: "Either the Russian Revolution will create a revolutionary movement in Europe, or the European powers will destroy the Russian Revolution."[5]

Some official historians have of course not been oblivious to the weight of Russian national power as a mighty vehicle for carrying Communist doctrine to the ends of the earth. Whatever the dynamics of the Communist creed, it would hardly have posed a threat to the world in the hands of a weaker protagonist. Napoleon at St. Helena had prophesied that the world would soon be either an American republic or a Russian absolute monarchy. Sainte-Beuve, in a paraphrase of Louis Adolphe Thiers, December 19, 1847, predicted:

> Europe has had its day. There are now but two nations—the first is far-off Russia, still barbarian, but large and . . . worthy of respect. Sooner or later old Europe will have to come to grips with this force of youth, for, as people say, Russia is young. The other nation is America, an intoxicated, immature democracy that knows no obstacles. The future of the world lies between

---

3. André Fontaine, *History of the Cold War: From the October Revolution to the Korean War, 1917–1950* (New York: Vintage Books, 1970), I, 12.

4. Louis J. Halle, *The Cold War as History* (New York: Harper & Row, 1967), 50.

5. Quoted in John Reed, *Ten Days that Shook the World* (New York: Vintage Books, 1960), 190.

these two great nations. One day they will collide, and then we will see struggles the like of which no one has dreamed of.[6]

André Fontaine, drawing on the insights of Sainte-Beuve and Thiers concludes: "There would have been no Cold War had there not been, in mid-century two—and only two—sufficiently large and populous powers that were confident enough in the worth of their beliefs and weapons to contest which would assume world leadership, without either's being able to prove a decisive superiority."[7] Whatever the motives underlying American foreign policy, America following World War II confronted a great power which the French diplomat, the Marquis de Custine, had described as early as 1839 as "essentially a nation of conquest, rendered greedy by privations" which "expiates in advance through humiliating submission at home its desire to exercise tyranny abroad."[8] Russia, to paraphrase Dostoevsky, had never reconciled itself to playing second fiddle.

The expansion of Russia and the United States had not occurred overnight. In 1800, Russian territory spread out from Warsaw to Manchuria and constituted one-sixth the land area of the world. By 1850, the territorial boundaries of the United States extended from the Atlantic to the Pacific. By 1890, the population of the United States exceeded that of Germany and France combined. Following World War I, the Russians expanded to the west. The history of Russian imperialism led one British writer to observe: "The Cold War has its origins in the struggle for power in Central Asia between the rival imperialisms of Britain and Russia in the nineteenth century."[9] The struggle which was forecast by nineteenth-century political prophets was not of a continuation of Russo-British conflict but one involving two emerging great powers destined to become the dominant forces of mid-twentieth-century international politics. In de Tocqueville's words: "There are on the earth today two great people, who from different points of departure, seem to be advancing toward the same end. . . . All other peoples appear to have attained approximately their natural limits . . . but these two are growing." For de Tocqueville, the conclusion inevitably followed that: "Their points of departure are different, their paths are divergent; neverthe-

6. Quoted in Fontaine, *History of the Cold War*, 11.
7. *Ibid.*
8. Marquis de Custine, *La Russie en 1839* (Paris: Librarie d'Amyot, 1843), IV, 354.
9. Desmond Donnelly, *Struggle for the World: The Cold War and Its Causes* (New York: St. Martin's Press, 1965), 10.

less, each seems summoned by a secret design of providence to hold in his hands, some day, the destinies of half the world." [10] It was the objective power/political situation and historic Russian and American behavior and interests that led to conflict and rivalry—a contest which would have occurred even if Karl Marx had never written the *Communist Manifesto.* The two countries were destined to confront one another as competing centers of power had done throughout the history of the European state system. The clash of massive Russian and American concentrations of power was no accident of history but a necessary and predictable result of forces that were in a certain sense beyond the control of individuals and ideologies. What in fact came to pass would have come to pass regardless of the ideological label attached to the authoritarian regime that governed Russia. "What the Revolution of 1917 did was simply to reinvigorate the traditional principle of authoritarianism in Russia. It replaced a decadent and enfeebled authoritarian dynasty with a new, vigorous, and ruthlessly determined dynasty. . . . The Cold War, then, represents an historical necessity to which the Communist movement is incidental rather than essential." [11]

However much the official historians may recognize the importance of national power, international rivalries, and cultural divergences, they have tended to look elsewhere in substantial measure for an explanation of root causes of the Cold War. Thus Dexter Perkins could write: "In reality . . . we can see that there existed a deep divergence between the views of Washington and . . . of Moscow. That divergence lay in the ideological sphere." [12] If the conflict between East and West had been primarily one between competing national interests, it might have been composed. (Interests can be compromised but not ideals.) It was the political dreams and ideological aspirations of men on both sides of the Iron Curtain which presented major obstacles to any kind of settlement. "The revolutionary faith that had been kindled into flame in the great revolution of 1917 still burned brightly in Russia." [13] The leaders of that revolution fought the Second World War believing that the struggle would lead somehow to the breakdown of the bourgeois world order and to the spreading of the Communist design particularly throughout Europe. Nor were their expectations unrealistic as reflected in an Amer-

10. Quoted in Halle, *The Cold War,* 10.
11. *Ibid.,* 11–12.
12. Dexter Perkins, *The Diplomacy of a New Age* (Bloomington: Indiana University Press, 1967), 17.
13. *Ibid.*

ican intelligence agency forecast of Russia's postwar position. The Soviet Union would be the dominant power in Europe with the defeat of Germany.

Such intelligence estimates led other American authorities, more anxious about the possibility of another world war than the resolution of the ideological conflict, to conclude that postwar relations with the Soviet giant must be predicated on the building of an "era of good feeling." "President Roosevelt and the American government did not aim at reestablishing a balance of power in Europe to safeguard the United States; they expected this security to stem from mutual Russo-American goodwill, unsupported by any power considerations. This reliance upon mere goodwill and mutual esteem was to prove foolish at best and, at worst, might have been fatal."[14]

However, the interpreters who held to the view that the threat to European security would result from the Soviet Union's supplanting Nazi Germany were divided among themselves as to the fundamental cause of that threat. Some saw the threat as arising primarily from a shift in the balance of power which a determined commitment by the West could restore. A vacuum of power in Europe had opened up as a result of the conduct and conclusion of World War II. The Australian Chester Wilmot, who served as a combat correspondent in the Middle East and thereafter in the South Pacific Theater and whose book *The Struggle for Europe* has been described as a classic worthy of a place alongside the writings of Churchill's *The Second World War* and the most important book on the military and political struggle for Europe, set forth his purpose as an endeavor "to explain how the present situation came about; how and why the Western Allies while gaining military victory, suffered political defeat." Wilmot explained that from the perspective of the 1950s: "I have tried to show not only why Hitler was overthrown but also why Stalin emerged victorious; how Russia came to replace Germany as the dominant power on the Continent; and how Stalin succeeded in obtaining from Roosevelt and Churchill what he had failed to obtain from Hitler." The chief virtue of Wilmot's approach lies in the fact that more than any other writer he focused on the close interrelation between strategy and diplomacy, between military events and their political consequences. He wrote: "In the summer of 1944 the Western Allies had it in their power, if not to end the war against Germany that year, at least

14. John Spanier, *American Foreign Policy Since World War II* (New York: Praeger Publishers, 1973), 23.

to ensure that the great capitols of Central Europe—Berlin, Prague, and Vienna—would be liberated from Nazi rule by the West, not the East." While Hitler's object in the German offensive in the Ardennes in the winter of 1944 was military, it was also political in seeking to divide the Grand Alliance and make possible a compromise peace with the Western Allies that would thereafter enable Germany to resist Russian expansion into "the heartland of Europe." Hitler in following this course weakened his Eastern front, allowing the Russians to advance from the Vistula to the Oder on the eve of the Yalta Conference. "This strategic situation reacted directly on the diplomatic discussions of that historic conference, for Stalin, having overwhelmed his enemies in the field, was able to outmaneuver his allies at the conference table." [15]

Stalin's military strategy from the early 1940s was geared to his post-war ambitions. Even in the dark years of defeat with the Germans in the western suburbs of Moscow, Stalin never lost sight of political objectives. On December 4, 1941, at the height of a lavish dinner party in the Kremlin for the Polish prime minister, General Sikorski, Stalin turned to him and said: "Now we will talk about the frontier between Poland and Russia." [16] The Soviet design for control in Eastern Europe was as evident in the negotiations between Molotov and Ribbentrop in Berlin in 1939 as in Stalin's negotiations with Roosevelt and Churchill in 1945 in Teheran and Yalta. What had changed by 1945 was Stalin's power and capacity to carry forward with little resistance Russia's historic imperial ambitions.

In his diplomacy, he bided his time awaiting the results of Soviet military strategy. At Teheran, Stalin had postponed a full discussion of Russia's overall territorial ambitions, but he did discuss the western boundaries of Russia with Churchill and privately with Roosevelt. Preliminary agreement was reached on the boundaries with Poland. [17] He urged that the major western offensive be directed through France, not the Balkans. By the time of Yalta, negotiations went on with the shadow of the Red Army extending into all of Eastern Europe except Greece. Stalin appeared in the last nine months of the war less interested in speeding the defeat of Hitler than in assuring Russian domination in

15. Chester Wilmot, *The Struggle for Europe* (New York: Harper & Brothers, 1952), 11, 12, 13.
16. Stanislaw Mikolajczyk, *The Pattern of Soviet Domination* (London: Sampson, Law, Marston, 1948), 25.
17. Charles E. Bohlen, *Witness to History* (New York: W. W. Norton & Co., 1973), 151–53.

the heart of Europe, capturing Warsaw, moving up the Danube through Bucharest and Belgrade to Budapest, conquering Poland and turning from the seizure of Berlin, which lay within his reach, to the capture of Vienna. He resumed the attack on Berlin only when the Americans were in sight of the German capital and simultaneously persuaded General Eisenhower to hold back the western advance to Prague. It was military strategy in World War II and not the diplomacy of Yalta which created power vacuums on either side of Russia into which it irresistibly expanded.

Historians dispute whether or not in its early postwar expansion the Soviet Union became overextended. Thus "it is not clear that Stalin wanted to extend his dominion as far West as possible . . . since he knew that the area over which he could maintain effective control was limited."[18] Prime Minister Churchill observed that some Western leaders, "blinded by illusions that affect us all," believed Russia would not continue the war once she had regained her frontiers. It was, moreover, a common opinion that the Western Allies would have to persuade Russia not to relax her efforts. By 1949, those who had held to this view discovered that "the western boundary of the rapidly expanding Russian empire . . . [had] advanced to a line four-fifths of the way from Russia's pre-war boundaries to the boundaries of Holland, Belgium and France."[19] For Western leaders, the dominating question was how much farther would the Soviet Union expand?

On the side of the Western Allies, three other factors contributed to the creation of a power vacuum in the heart of Europe. One was the doctrine of "unconditional surrender" propounded by Churchill and Roosevelt and their Combined Chiefs of Staff at the Casablanca Conference in January of 1943. On the final day of the conference, January 24, President Roosevelt announced the Allies' intention to continue the war to the end of achieving the "unconditional surrender" of Germany, Italy, and Japan and suggested as an aside that the conference might be called the "Unconditional Surrender Meeting." The president later mentioned to Harry Hopkins that this phrase had "popped into his mind" as he was talking. Roosevelt absolved Churchill from all responsibility for the statement, but the prime minister in reply to Robert Sherwood's question replied: "I heard the words 'Unconditional Surrender' for the first time from the President's lips at the conference. . . . I would not myself have

18. Halle, *The Cold War*, 80.
19. *Ibid.*, 84.

used these words, but I immediately stood by the President and have frequently defended the decision."[20]

Controversy and debate have surrounded the question whether Roosevelt and Churchill discussed the 'unconditional surrender principle' in advance. Churchill, in *The Second World War* (Volume IV, *The Hinge of Fate*) acknowledged that the subject must "have cropped up in my official talks with the President" and further had been considered by the War Cabinet. Yet the words were not contained in an official joint communique which Churchill considered had superseded anything said in oral conversation. Nevertheless, Churchill conceded that both he and Ernest Bevin were probably in error when on July 21, 1949, both declared neither they nor the cabinet had been consulted before Roosevelt made his statement.[21] Defense of the policy then and now has been necessary because by unconditional surrender the Allies probably cut off the chances of diplomatic maneuver and hardened resistance within Germany. Before Casablanca, Goebbels had written in his diary: "The more the English prophesy a disgraceful peace for Germany, the easier it is for me to toughen and harden German resistance." Roosevelt's aim was to deny before the bar of world opinion and not least to the Russians the possibility of the Western Allies seeking a separate peace; little thought was given to the effect of enemy resistance.

Robert Sherwood challenged the view that Roosevelt had made the statement on the spur of the moment; instead it represented a deliberate and well-considered position designed in part to avoid postwar Germany's charging the Allies with a breach of another war's "Fourteen Points." Roosevelt explained at the time that the Americans had called the Civil War General Ulysses S. Grant "Old Unconditional Surrender" and as he spoke this image came to mind "and the next thing I knew, I had said it."[22] Hopkins wrote, however, in his description of the conference that Roosevelt spoke from notes which contained the sentence: "Unconditional surrender means not the destruction of the German populace, nor of the Italian or Japanese populace, but does mean the destruction of a philosophy in Germany, Italy, and Japan which is based on the conquest and subjugation of other peoples." Sherwood summed up his defense of "Unconditional Surrender" saying: "Whether it was

20. Robert E. Sherwood, *Roosevelt and Hopkins* (New York: Harper & Brothers, 1948), 699.
21. Churchill, *The Hinge of Fate*, 686–88.
22. Sherwood, *Roosevelt and Hopkins*, 699.

wise or foolish, whether it prolonged the war or shortened it—or even if it had no effect whatsoever on the duration (which seems possible)—it was a true statement of Roosevelt's considered policy and . . . he restated it a great many times."[23] It was a reaction to the policies of the French Generals Darlan and Peyrouton and reflected a fear that other Allied leaders might negotiate a separate peace with the Germans or the Japanese. It was a clarion call in behalf of Allied victory and an assurance to Stalin that inability of the Allies to open a second front in 1943 was not a sign of the weakening of Western resolve to fight to the finish.

To this argument, the critics of "Unconditional Surrender" replied that no one responsible for the ominous words had fully weighed or considered their effect on the German people or the German armed forces. In his haste to avoid the "escape clauses" of a subsequent peace settlement brought about by a repetition of the Fourteen Points which might invite exploitation by another Hitler, Roosevelt spoke with the ghost of Woodrow Wilson at his shoulder. The point of view was not unreasonable in the light of past experience. However, "it was one thing to form this resolve in secret for ultimate enforcement; it was quite another to proclaim it to the enemy in advance. . . . The Nazis were now able to command conviction when they said to the nation, 'It is you, as well as we, that they want to destroy.'"[24] The critics maintained that the Casablanca statement was both unnecessary and unwise. No one doubted that Hitler would fight on, as he once said "until five past midnight," but unconditional surrender, coupled with the Morgenthau Plan for the total destruction of German industry and the indiscriminate mass bombing of cities, guaranteed popular resistance by Germany to the end. Stalin had drawn a sharp distinction between the German people and the Nazis. A similar distinction reiterated again and again by Roosevelt might have lent support to the opposition within Germany.

Yet there was a more fundamental issue at stake than German resistance. The foremost critic of unconditional surrender has insisted: "The carrying out of Roosevelt's principles ensured that the war against Germany would continue beyond the stage of military decision to the point of political collapse, and would not end until the Russian and Anglo-American armies met in the heart of the continent."[25] There was something peculiarly American about unconditional surrender. It reflected

23. *Ibid.*, 696–97.
24. Wilmot, *The Struggle for Europe*, 123.
25. *Ibid.*, 173.

32 Cold War Theories

the American determination to wage war to total victory. It was a formula more appropriate to General Grant and the beleaguered garrison at Fort Donelson in Tennessee, and to apply it *carte blanche* "to the contestants of a world struggle—contestants so varied in national character and martial ardour as Germany, Italy, and Japan—[was] . . . both illogical and dangerous."[26]

Whereas Stalin doubted the wisdom of unconditional surrender, it worked to his advantage in at least two respects. It "increased the 'proletarianisation' of the people of Germany and Central Europe and thus made them more susceptible to Communist influence." Secondly, the necessity of enforcing a peace based on unconditional surrender "meant that the Red Army, having advanced to the Elbe, would have a lawful reason for staying there and for maintaining what would amount to occupation forces in the countries through which its supply lines ran."[27] It may be unfair to claim, as did some British writers, that the postwar situation in Europe was at least partly the result of American immaturity in world politics. Yet Churchill in the last eighteen months of the war sought without success to persuade the Americans that the war should be fought for the dual purpose of defeating Germany and forestalling the emergence of the Soviet Union as a mighty power in the center of Europe. For his pains he was rebuked by the American secretary of state and only in Greece and Yugoslavia was he successful. In all this a traditional American attitude asserted itself—that war as an instrument of the national interest was somehow morally wrong. The American creed carried with it a requirement that "the United States if driven to war in self-defense or to uphold the right, should seek no national advantage or aggrandisement. . . . Her aim should be Victory, nothing else. Since America fights for no political objective, except peace, no political directives should be given to American commanders in the field."[28]

A second factor related to the first which helped shape the postwar world was the curious ambivalence of Americans toward Britain and British imperialism. Roosevelt more than once in wartime conferences saw himself as functioning as a go-between or honest broker between Churchill and Stalin. He had become a legendary figure in Britain, "the best friend we have ever had" to the ordinary man in the street. Intimates reported, however, that the American and British leaders were

26. *Ibid.*, 122–23.
27. *Ibid.*, 714.
28. *Ibid.*

never wholly at ease with one another. Churchill never lost sight of Roosevelt's superior position as head of state equivalent to the King, whereas the prime minister was merely head of government. Roosevelt, when assistant secretary of the Navy in World War I, had traveled to London and met Churchill for the first time at a banquet. "Churchill, already an eminent statesman had apparently failed to take much notice of the young American official and had promptly forgotten this encounter, but Roosevelt remembered it clearly." [29] Churchill was impressed with Roosevelt's political acumen and his patience and skill in breaking the American tradition of isolationism. Both were continuously aware of the pressures of their home political constituencies and the tides of public opinion within their respective states. Roosevelt complained of political constraints, but Churchill was equally a prisoner of the British empire. The Americans questioned the niggling qualifications that Churchill introduced into the Atlantic Charter which began "with due respect for . . . existing [imperial] obligations." Harry Hopkins observed at the Atlantic Conference in 1941 that whereas Roosevelt appeared to be completely on his own, Churchill exchanged more than thirty communications with the War Cabinet in London. The British cabinet never regarded the Atlantic Charter as a formal state paper and Churchill sought in a speech before the House of Commons to draw a distinction between Europe and the colonial peoples of Asia, saying: "At the Atlantic meeting we had in mind, primarily, the restoration of the sovereignty, self-government and national life of the States and nations of Europe now under the Nazi yoke. . . . [This] is quite a separate problem from the progressive evolution of self-governing institutions in the regions, and people which owe allegiance to the British crown."

If Churchill and Roosevelt had one persistent overriding difference, it was on the issue of British imperialism. Americans from the time of their independence from Britain in 1776 had nurtured a deep and abiding antipathy toward colonialism whatever its forms. Every young American who went to school with a liberal schoolmaster learned that British imperialism was the remnant of a world order whose demise he must seek to hasten. When Britain in 1940 was threatened with destruction by a far more evil imperialism, the Americans under Roosevelt's guidance came to its aid. But even a common language and heritage and a recognition that Britain remained the last bulwark of freedom and of Western civilization could not erase from American consciences a dis-

29. Sherwood, *Roosevelt and Hopkins*, 351.

taste for traditional imperialism. In discussions at the Atlantic Conference, Roosevelt made this concern explicit, saying: "I can't believe that we can fight a war against Fascist slavery, and not work to free people all over the world from a backward colonial policy."[30] Anticolonialism was in the air. To many Americans, the ideas of empire were archaic and medieval and out of tune with moral progress. Cordell Hull wrote: "We had definite ideas with respect to the future of the British Colonial Empire, on which we differed with the British. It might be said that the future of that Empire was no business of ours; but we felt that unless dependent peoples were assisted toward ultimate self-government and were given it . . . they would provide kernels of conflict."[31]

Churchill's response to Roosevelt was much quoted on both sides of the Atlantic. At Mansion House on November 10, 1942, he was unequivocal: "I have not become the King's First Minister in order to preside over the liquidation of the British Empire." His characterization in the same speech of Roosevelt as the "greatest American friend we have ever known" was intended to conceal the fact—and succeeded in doing so—that his declaration was aimed at the president. What could not be concealed was the failure of the two leaders in preliminary meetings before such conferences as the one at Yalta to create a united front. Roosevelt appeared determined to avoid leaving the impression with Stalin that Russia was faced with an Anglo-American alliance united against it. Roosevelt spoke on more than one occasion of the necessity of his mediating between Churchill and Stalin. He labored to prevent Anglo-Soviet differences, viewing himself as "the Good Neighbor of the World." He joined Stalin on occasion in twitting Churchill and played along with the former's shocking statement at Yalta that 50 to 100 thousand German leaders must be executed after the war, a statement which caused Churchill to leave the conference room in high dudgeon. When Churchill and Roosevelt stopped at Malta to discuss the agenda for the Yalta Conference, the British delegation found that the Americans were less uneasy about the dangers of postwar Soviet actions than those of Britain. Whatever its merits (and it was to be vindicated in certain areas), American anticolonialism drove a wedge between the Americans and the British and may have dulled American sensitivity to the perils of Soviet imperialism and the need for early resistance.

30. Elliott Roosevelt, *As He Saw It* (New York: Duell Sloan and Pearce, 1946), 37.
31. Walter Johnson (ed.), *The Memoirs of Cordell Hull* (New York: Macmillan, 1948), II, 1477–78.

The third and perhaps the most significant factor which influenced the shape of the postwar world was Roosevelt's supreme self-confidence in his skills of personal diplomacy in dealing with Stalin and his idealistic faith that a new international order would reduce the effects of national rivalries. In his Inaugural Address, following an unprecedented election for a fourth term, he proclaimed: "We have learned to be citizens of the world, members of the human community. We have learned the simple truth, as Emerson said, 'The only way to have a friend is to be one.'" Americans and Russians had joined together in winning the war. The American and Russian soldiers had developed trust and affection for one another. Because both the United States and the Soviet Union were large and satisfied states rather than hard-pressed and resource-poor nations seeking "lebensraum" (living space), they suffered no basic conflicts of national interests. In June, 1944, Roosevelt allegedly told the Polish leader Mikolajczyk, "Stalin is a realist, and we mustn't forget, when we judge Russian actions, that the Soviet regime has had only . . . [limited] experience in international relations. But of one thing I am certain, Stalin is not an Imperialist."[32]

Roosevelt had felt constrained on the Polish question by the pressures of an election year, but with the election behind him he promised to serve as a moderator and bring about a settlement. There were few problems, he prophesied, that he and Stalin could not settle on a man-to-man basis. Nor did his most important advisers disagree, as when Hull declared that the United States "must and could get along with the Soviet government,"[33] or when Hopkins wrote on August 1, 1945, six months after the Yalta Conference:

> We know or believe that Russian interests, so far as we can anticipate them, do not afford an opportunity for a major difference with us in foreign affairs. We believe we are mutually dependent upon each other for economic reasons. We find the Russians as individuals easy to deal with. They like the United States. They trust the United States more than they trust any power in the world. I believe they not only have no wish to fight with us, but are determined to take their place in world affairs in an international organization, and above all, they want to maintain friendly relations with us.[34]

Furthermore, General Eisenhower wrote: "In the past relations of America and Russia there was no cause to regard the future with pessimism."

32. Mikolajczyk, *The Pattern of Soviet Domination*, 65.
33. Johnson (ed.), *Memoirs of Cordell Hull*, 1467.
34. Sherwood, *Roosevelt and Hopkins*, 922.

Again Eisenhower explained: "In his generous instincts, in his love of laughter, in his devotion to a comrade, and in his healthy, direct outlook on the affairs of workaday life, the ordinary Russian seems to me to bear a marked similarity to what we call an 'average American.'" (Anyone who served in the European Theater of Operations knows that General Eisenhower was not alone in holding to such beliefs.) Finally, it was said of Russia and the United States that "both were free from the stigma of colonial empire building by force."[35]

And yet contemporary observers of the postwar scene and the statesmen who followed Roosevelt and Churchill were confronted by the yawning gulf which grew up between the apparent optimism of Roosevelt, Hopkins, and Eisenhower and the harsh reality of Soviet behavior. The millions of Americans who had believed and trusted their leaders could hardly be satisfied with the explanation that had Roosevelt lived he and Stalin would have cooperated and the situation would have been different. The official historians stepped into the breach and provided the answer. They helped reconcile expectations and events. It was messianic communism and the utter ruthlessness and cruelty of its leader and high priest that accounted for the Soviet march into Europe. One particularly able orthodox historian, writing with the benefit of hindsight, pictured Stalin as: "The grim monarch—for monarch he may be called—who dominated the Russian scene, filled with suspicions of his allies, and without scruples as to means, looked forward, at the least, to the extension of Russian power, and of the Communist faith."[36]

For Americans the intensity of the struggle stemmed from a persistent latent antagonism to communism. The same historian wrote: "No political and economic philosophy . . . has ever aroused in the United States so deep a distrust as has Communism. The totalitarianism of the right, repulsive as it was to democratic idealists, left standing a large part of the economic order." Communism by contrast gave offense to almost every important element in American society. "The business classes could hardly fail to view with intense repugnance a system of economic organization which regards them as superfluous, as exploiters, as the source and root of all economic evil."[37] Liberals were affronted by communism's contempt for the individual and its reckless destruction of hu-

---

35. Dwight D. Eisenhower, *Crusade in Europe* (New York: Doubleday & Company, 1952), 457, 473–74.
36. Perkins, *The Diplomacy of a New Age*, 17.
37. *Ibid.*, 17, 18.

man freedom. The religious community protested the disappearance of religious freedom in the Soviet Union. Labor unions resisted the attempts of Communist strategists to bore from within and capture the labor movement by bold promises to end social and economic grievances. Even diplomats who had greater knowledge and longer memories of Soviet-American relations could call to mind the more sordid aspects of these relationships: Stalin's cynical bargain with Hitler for the partition of Poland, the Soviet invasion of Finland in 1939, the absorption of the Baltic states in 1940/41 and the churlish reaction of Russian leaders to Anglo-American warnings of Hitler's plan to invade Russia. Even in an "era of good feeling," diplomats such as Averell Harriman, Charles Bohlen, and George F. Kennan, who were in close touch with Russian leaders, reported increasing difficulties and signs of a growing rift leading them to alter what had been a more optimistic viewpoint.

Beyond the reactions of separate groups there was a more fundamental and recurrent condition of American life which played a part in the drastic shift of attitudes and expectations. The turbulent events and secular trends of the twentieth century produced a cyclical pattern in American history. The early decades of the century saw the nation struggling to find itself, combatting bigness, rallying to the call of progressives and populists, joining a "war to end war" only to repudiate Woodrow Wilson's crusade for a "League to Enforce the Peace." Then in the twenties the nation, reeling from its abortive internationalism and the demands of "the strenuous life," sought a return to normalcy, regrouping and seeking to reconstitute itself. The pendulum was to swing once again and the late twenties and the thirties ushered in a grim depression overcome only by a determined national effort, and another world war. It should not have been surprising that victory in war brought with it a vaulting sense of triumph and a certain euphoria over prospects for peace. Then came the Cold War, the Russian advance into Europe and the specter of communism threatening to undo the peace and order which Americans had helped to achieve through sacrifice and force of arms.

The writings of the official historians were especially credible and carried weight both because of the swing of the pendulum after Roosevelt and the resulting shift in the national mood and because of the actions of the world's most powerful Communist state. Many Americans, including some who had embraced Russian troops at the end of World War II, became conscious for the first time of the threat of the

Soviet Union. Suddenly with the outbreak of the Cold War, Americans became aware, as George F. Kennan wrote:

> . . . for the first time, of the horrible reality of the postwar world—of the fact that this earnest and upright partner was not there at all, and that in his place there was only another one of these great inexplicable monsters, more formidable this time than all the others, sitting astride the resources of half the world . . . sitting there . . . like some graven image . . . committed to the encompassing of our ruin, inaccessible to our words and reasoning, concerned only for our destruction. And now it suddenly occurred to many people what dangers could reside in the association of the dominant portion of the physical resources of Europe and Asia with a political power hostile to ourselves.[38]

Strong words and unambiguous explanations were needed if Americans were to understand how this horrible reality had come about despite a multitude of wartime assurances and promises. The early years of the Cold War were not a time to speak of fear and mistrust, of military strategy divorced from political objectives, and of the divergence of the American ideal of national self-determination from Stalin's stated conviction that "friendly" states could only be Communist states. The argument of a handful of interpreters that the source of Russian mistrust went back to the postponement of the Second Front from 1942 to 1943 to 1944 and a capitalist decision to allow ideological foes to exhaust themselves was far too subtle and remote to account for the sudden crisis. A comprehensive and all-out accounting was required and this was the major contribution of the first wave of historical writing on the Cold War. The worldwide threat of Communist expansion provided the answer. What Professor Joseph Schumpeter wrote of the intellectual satisfaction and political purpose afforded Communist believers by the Marxian theory of imperialism may also be ascribed to the effort of official historians to account to Americans for the sudden eruption and basic cause of the Cold War: "A series of vital facts of our time seem to be perfectly accounted for. The whole maze of international politics seems to be cleared up by a single powerful stroke of analysis."[39]

Yet a reaction was to set in before a decade and a half had passed. The revisionists were to challenge the orthodox historians on the causes of the Cold War. The climate of opinion in the nation was to change

38. George F. Kennan, *Realities of American Foreign Policy* (Princeton, N.J.: Princeton University Press, 1954), 27.
39. Joseph Schumpeter, *Capitalism, Socialism, and Democracy* (New York: Harper & Brothers, 1947), 51.

again. The late 1950s and the 1960s were influenced by a shift from ideological confrontation to competitive coexistence. External forces and changes in the pattern of Soviet-American relations fed back new perspectives into the interpretation of the causes of the Cold War. It was no longer credible for scholars and observers to explain the Cold War by writing of a great inexplicable monster threatening our ruin. The pendulum had swung in writings on the Cold War.

The Revisionist Historians on Causes

Walter LaFeber, who has been described as a moderate revisionist and is one of the ablest historians writing on the Cold War, begins his account of the twentieth century's thirty-year war by observing: "The Cold War has dominated American life since 1945. It has cost Americans a trillion and a half dollars in defense expenditures, taken the lives of nearly 100,-000 of their young men, ruined the careers of many others during the McCarthyite witch-hunts, led the nation into the horrors of Southeast Asian conflicts, and in the 1940s triggered the worst economic depression in forty years." [40]

In comparing the Cold War with earlier struggles for power it would be difficult to exaggerate the scope and magnitude of the conflict, its intensity or its duration. Not only has this one all-encompassing struggle penetrated every corner of the globe with consequences on every continent but by the mid-1980s it will have dominated the lives from birth of millions of forty-year-olds in Asia, Africa, Europe, and Latin America, as well as in America and Russia. One perceives the differences between the nature of conflict in the late eighteenth and in the twentieth centuries in reading Edward Gibbon's account in 1781 of Britain's wars with its American colonies and the coalition made up of France, Spain, and Holland: "The balance of power will continue to fluctuate, and the prosperity of our own or the neighboring kingdoms may be alternately exalted or depressed; but these events cannot essentially injure our general state of happiness, the system of arts, and laws, and manners." Then Gibbon, looking out over Europe and North America, added, "In war, the European forces are exercised by temperate and undecisive contests." [41] The temperate contests of the eighteenth century that could not injure

40. Walter LaFeber, *America, Russia, and the Cold War, 1945–1975* (3rd ed.; New York: John Wiley and Sons, 1976), 1.
41. Edward Gibbon, *The Decline and Fall of the Roman Empire* (New York: Modern Library Edition, 1932), II, 93–94, 94–95.

the happiness and manners of the majority of Europeans resulted from the commitment of European states to the maintenance of a balance of power. That balance or system of equilibrium among neighboring states depended in turn on the intellectual and moral unity of Europe. The peace settlement of 1783 justified Gibbon's faith in Europe as a single republic whose inhabitants had respect for mutual survival and a common level of political and cultural understanding. Later Arnold J. Toynbee wrote: "In the American Revolutionary War, Great Britain was eventually defeated by an overwhelming coalition of opposing forces; but her opponents did not think of crushing her." France did not seek the return of Canada, which had been taken by Britain during the Seven Years' War and ceded to the British Crown in the peace of 1763. France's sole objective had been the restoration of the balance of power upset by Britain's victories in three successive wars, which led Toynbee to conclude: "Great Britain, let off with the loss of her thirteen colonies, could congratulate herself, in Gibbonian language, upon having survived, without shipwreck, a fluctuation in the Balance of Power . . . in which no essential injury had been done to the general state of happiness of a polite society which was the common spiritual home of the subjects of King George and the subjects of King Louis."[42]

Professor LaFeber and other historians writing in the late 1960s and 1970s could hardly have described the struggle with the Soviet Union as temperate and polite; nor would they have claimed the participants shared an underlying moral consensus. Its costs were too great in human lives and material devastation. Each side feared the other was seeking its destruction. Revisionist writers have pointed out that American policy makers during World War II saw little to choose between the evils of a "Communist dictatorship" and a "Nazi dictatorship." The Democratic senator from Missouri, Harry S Truman, spoke for fellow congressmen in 1941 when he declared: "If we see that Germany is winning we should help Russia and if Russia is winning we ought to help Germany, and that way let them kill as many as possible, although I don't want to see Hitler victorious under any circumstances."[43] LaFeber has characterized the moral disunity resulting from a half-century of Russian-American enmity in these words: "Possessing drastically different views of how the world should be organized, unable to cooperate during the 1930s against

42. Arnold J. Toynbee, *A Study of History* (London: Oxford University Press, 1939), IV, 149.
43. New York *Times*, June 24, 1941.

Nazi and Japanese aggression, and nearly full-fledged enemies between 1939 and 1941, the United States and the Soviet Union finally became partners because of a shot-gun marriage forced upon them by World War II."[44]

By the late 1960s, students of the Cold War and in particular the revisionists were calling for a fundamental reexamination of the causes of the struggle. Few if any denied that a profound moral gulf separated the antagonists; no one suggested that international conflicts, as in Gibbon's era, were marked by temperate and undecisive contests that could easily be resolved. The United States itself could scarcely be described, especially in the late 1960s, as a polite society, and in the 1950s Khrushchev had warned that the Communists would bury their rivals.

Social critics and protest leaders caught up in a debate over the nature of American society and its underlying values charged that the nation had been led astray, and their criticism was not limited to American foreign policy. Young people coming of age within an affluent society proclaimed they were betrayed by the compromises and concessions of their parents' generation and the contradictions between values professed and values practiced. Civil rights spokesmen warned that the nation had become a nation of two societies—one rich, powerful, and privileged and the other made up of minorities lacking in hope and deprived of constitutional rights and equal opportunity. Scholars were divided between those who called for scientific detachment and value-free analysis and others who demanded the defense of ideology and purpose.

Intertwined with all the other sources of discontent was the rancorous debate over the Vietnam issue growing more embittered as the conflict dragged on and sharpened in focus by the values, fears, and self-interest of young people unwilling to commit their lives in a protracted and unpopular war. The pathos of the struggle was hardly lessened by democracy's inherent limitations in sustaining and justifying a limited war (exaggerated no doubt by an emerging consensus among journalists and well-respected voices from the mass media proclaiming that America and its ally, South Vietnam, were losing the war because we had chosen the wrong side in a revolutionary civil conflict in Asia). It was argued that had we been more faithful to the American heritage and to our birthright we would have aligned ourselves with the forces of

44. LaFeber, *America, Russia, and the Cold War*, 7.

revolutionary change; instead the United States was resisting social and political change around the globe and had become an uncompromising defender of the status quo.

Of fundamental importance to the conflicting interpretations of the Cold War was the fact that the social and intellectual climate in the United States in the 1960s contrasted markedly with that in 1945. The historical situations to which writers responded were essentially different. Following World War II the United States had disarmed itself both emotionally and militarily. It rapidly dismantled one of the mightiest armies the world had ever known. American leaders such as Roosevelt, Hull, and Hopkins sought to prepare the nation to live at peace with the Soviet Union within and outside the United Nations. Then suddenly and with little warning the bright dream of a peaceful world was shattered. Our Communist ally became our principal adversary in Eastern and Central Europe, Greece and Turkey, Iran, and most of all in certain countries of Western Europe. Now a quarter-century later, the underlying consensus on which America's postwar foreign policy had been based was weakened by important changes in the moods of Soviet and American policy and fragmentation within the Communist and non-Communist worlds, the spread of neutralism and nonalignment in the Third World and the seemingly irreparable Sino-Soviet division. In the 1970s detente replaced confrontation as the rallying cry of policy for East and West; leaders from the two camps carried on negotiations at "the Summit."

Despite these well-publicized advances, raw conflict persisted within and outside the United States. Violence erupted in the ghettoes during the years from 1965–1968. Washington and Capitol Hill became the scene of hostile encampments and intermittent riots. Three tragic political assassinations followed one another in all too rapid succession—those of John F. Kennedy in 1963 and Martin Luther King and Robert F. Kennedy in 1968. President Lyndon Johnson confided to a political biographer his deep-seated fear that he would be overrun by events and forces that were out of control, much as he remembered once fearing that stampeding cattle would overrun him and his grandmother when he was a small boy. In January, 1968, the Vietcong forces launched their TET offensive, reaching into the center of Saigon, and by the end of March President Johnson had announced he would not run for reelection in November. (There is significant evidence from LBJ's closest associates, that his decision not to run was influenced more by reasons of health than Vietnam). Because of demonstrations and riots, six thousand armed troops were flown into Chicago to garrison the Democratic National Convention in its nominating of a presidential candidate. The American empire, much like the British empire which preceded it, was weakened from within and on its periphery as well, where it was challenged not only by the Soviet Union and China but by Japan and the European Common Market. The Third World and its urgent problems though largely ignored in the early 1970s seemingly lay beyond the reach of American military and economic power.

How were Americans to account for the sudden and precipitous decline of American influence and power and the loss of unity at home and abroad? How could we have become so powerless when we had been so powerful? In electoral politics, the popular response was to blame the Democrats, although this judgment apparently convinced no more than a tiny plurality of voters as reflected in the .7 percent margin of victory in 1968 of Richard Nixon over Hubert H. Humphrey. (Ironically it was America's foremost liberal who suffered the most grievous attacks from the radical left.) The other response came from those who called for a major reorientation and redirection of thinking about the American national purpose and the causes and conduct of the Cold War. Statesmen and historians each offered prescriptions, one for an immediate and the other a more basic reordering of action and thought.

Policy makers who responded to the crisis in confidence did so by seeking to bring American commitments and power into balance and drawing back where the United States had been overextended. The source of the problem was not new but had been discussed since 1947 with the promulgation of the Truman Doctrine. Not only had World War II destroyed German and Japanese power but it had ended the reign of the British and French empires. Postwar America attempted in 1945 to substitute itself not just for one but every disappearing center of power and ultimately to follow a strategy aimed at bringing about the decline and disintegration of Communist ideology and power. As Walter Lippmann warned at the time, the United States was becoming dangerously overextended in far-flung commitments beyond its natural limits. The Cold War as viewed by Lippmann was the result of East-West confrontation with no buffers between the great powers. We had miscalculated the limits of American power, our national resources, and our potential for influence in the world. The Nixon Doctrine, whereby the United States announced its intention to give military assistance only to those nations who resolved to defend themselves—but not to fight their wars—symbolized a fundamental change of perspective. As for the Cold

War, what mitigated the struggle in the 1970s was less any transformation in Soviet messianic foreign policy or its uses of totalitarian power than strong and compelling forces at work inside the United States. Fears continued that the Soviet Union was seeking to rule the world. However: "Having coexisted successfully with an allegedly expansionist Russia for a full generation, countless Americans by 1970 were ready to accept the conclusion that their leaders had overestimated the Soviet danger."[45] Much as American leaders and the people after World War II had become war weary, the public or substantial segments of it had grown restive about the Cold War after twenty-five years of unremitting political strife.

This pragmatic response of policy makers to the realities of the Cold War had merit but did not go far enough for the revisionist interpreters. They looked for a more universal explanation of the causes of the conflict and the conditions of peace. William Appleman Williams, the most powerful and influential expositor of the new school of revisionist historiography, announced that the Cold War was "in reality only the most recent phase of a more general conflict between the established system of western capitalism and its internal and external opponents."[46] Revisionism offered not a palliative nor simply more flexibility and efficiency in the pursuit of traditional policies; it called for breaking free of prevailing assumptions, habits, and beliefs. It demanded cutting to the bone or scraping the marrow of well-established concepts and perspectives. It diagnosed a radical cause of the Cold War and a radical way out. American foreign policy, according to Williams, had been governed politically by warm and generous humanitarian impulses to help other peoples and by a commitment to national self-determination, or the rights of societies everywhere to govern themselves. Economically, however, the United States espoused a contradictory principle, that "other people cannot . . . solve their problems and improve their lives unless they go about it in the same way as the United States."[47] America's economic expansion and its quest for free markets clashed with the demand for the political and economic independence of other peoples. Because of the irresistible pressures of American capitalism and the power of economic elites in the shaping of foreign policy, the United

45. Norman A. Graebner, *Cold War Diplomacy: American Foreign Policy, 1945–1975* (New York: D. Van Nostrand Company, 1977), vi–vii.
46. William Appleman Williams, *The Tragedy of American Diplomacy* (2nd ed.; New York: Dell Publishing Company, 1972), 10.
47. *Ibid.*, 13.

States pursued a policy of imperial anticolonialism rationalized in the language of humanitarianism and national self-determination but motivated by the quest for free markets essential to America's prosperity and well-being.

The causes of the Cold War, therefore, as seen from the revisionist perspective are more economic than political. A few American leaders, including Roosevelt, recognized but failed to resolve the contradiction between an American foreign policy based on respect for national self-determination around the world and an open-door strategy for protecting America's interest in free markets. By 1945, they had "internalized . . . the theory, the necessity and the morality of open-door expansion." Revisionists maintained that it was not their intention to apportion praise or blame or "to say that the United States started or caused the cold war." The real issue was the more subtle one of who had possessed preponderant power when conflict erupted in 1945. According to Williams, the United States had "from 1944 to at least 1962 a vast preponderance of actual and potential power." The resulting question concerned "which side committed its power to policies which hardened the natural and inherent tensions and propensities into bitter antagonisms and inflexible positions."[48] Given its preponderant power, the United States can scarcely claim that it was forced to pursue its chosen policies. Revisionists contended that "the discretion available to [American] policy makers did not demand the specific policies adopted after April 1945 that led to the Cold War."[49] Failure to explore alternatives was due primarily to the framework within which postwar foreign policy was approached. "The United States used or deployed its preponderance of power wholly within the assumptions and the tradition of the strategy of the Open-Door Policy."[50] It gave first priority to American markets and ignored Soviet security needs or Russia's staggering losses of human and material resources. "Stalin's effort to solve Russia's problem of security and recovery short of widespread conflict with the United States was not matched by American leaders who acceded to power upon the death of Roosevelt. The President bequeathed them little, if anything, beyond the traditional outlook of open-door expansion."[51]

48. *Ibid.*, 206 and 207.
49. Athan Theoharis, "Roosevelt and Truman on Yalta: The Origins of the Cold War," *Political Science Quarterly*, LXXXVII, No. 2 (June, 1972), 210–41.
50. Williams, *The Tragedy of American Diplomacy*, 208.
51. William Appleman Williams, "Open Door Policy and the Cold War," in Norman A. Graebner (ed.), *The Cold War: A Conflict of Ideology and Power* (2nd ed.; Lexington, Mass.: D.C. Heath and Company, 1976), 47.

A small group of diplomatists and political columnists had criticized certain American policy makers, notably Secretary of State Hull and President Truman, for rejecting spheres of influence on moral grounds. Revisionists joined columnists and diplomats in challenging this moralistic attitude, as when LaFeber observed: "Since becoming a major power, the United States had viewed anything resembling Stalin's fence as incompatible with American objectives." However, whereas diplomatic analysts attributed dominant American attitudes to faulty political perceptions, revisionists found their source in fears that regional hegemony by Russia would restrict United States trade and commerce and plunge America into a worse depression than that of the late 1920s and 1930s. Moreover, the maintenance of American exports at prewar levels would not suffice; the flow would have to be tripled if economic production were to reach capacity and this required expanded markets in Europe and in the rest of the world. The concept of governments friendly to the Soviet Union on its western borders would not preclude foreign trade. Hence the United States accepted this concept in the Declaration of Liberated Europe. But Communist states under Soviet domination falling within the Soviet zone of influence would never provide a firm basis for the guarantee of free markets. A Soviet sphere of influence was in basic contradiction to an American open-door policy and the basic incompatibility of Soviet and American interests so defined became the underlying cause of the Cold War.

The focus of revisionists on the economic causes of the Cold War fell on fertile soil in the America of the 1960s. A generation of students spawned on radical or Marxian philosophies of history, nurtured by the writings of Herbert Marcuse, Eugene Genovese, and Gabriel Kolko, and convinced that the consumerism of American culture resulted from the high-velocity requirements of the system of economic production, had only to project their thinking on to the international scene to comprehend the meaning of revisionism. Marcuse had taught that capitalism sought constantly to generate new demands for new products in order that expanded economic production be maintained. The success of the industrial machine required an ever-accelerating turnover of new products and new styles substituted for older products and designs in order to preserve the required momentum of the economic process. Crass materialism had its roots in rapidly changing tastes and needs artificially stimulated by mass advertising and hucksterism. The children of middle class families in the sixties grew ever more cynical of the workings of the economy. They came to believe that interruption of the cycle of research and development, along with the high cost of promotion for mass sales and the acceleration of product obsolescence in order to make necessary the repetition of the cycle, would lead to the breakdown of the economic system, to economic depressions, and economic decline.

Although this version of economic history offered a rather melancholy picture of basic economic motivation, it helped to explain a process which for three decades had failed to satisfy deeper human needs and aspirations. In the 1930s and 1940s the parents of the children who were to find themselves in the vanguard of the youth revolution of the 1960s had looked to economic advancement and improved standards of living as *the answer* to the malaise of the depression era. Having moved in the 1950s from depressed areas to the more affluent suburbs, upwardly mobile families found that despite a dream abundantly realized they remained alienated and dissatisfied in the brave new world. One of the explanations for their distress which attracted a wide following, especially among the young, was that the economic system subordinated man's deeper human and spiritual needs to the narrowly material requirements and kaleidoscopic functioning of the existing modes of production.

The conclusions to be drawn from national experience extrapolated onto the world scene were not difficult to imagine or construct. The tragic legacy of war in numerous conflict-ridden nations was hunger, pain, and chaos. Two vast international conflicts within the space of thirty years had caused or accentuated economic and human devastation which spread to the far corners of the earth. Before the guns of war had been silenced, civil strife and internecine conflict in Europe and Asia replaced the struggle between the Axis and the Grand Alliance. The United States, by comparison, emerged from World War II imcomparably the richest and strongest nation in the world, conscious of its augmented strengths and capable of playing a decisive role in postwar reconstruction. Its objectives as viewed by the revisionists were deceptively simple. "Essentially, the United States' aim was to restructure the world so that American business could trade, operate, and profit without restrictions everywhere."[52] On this there was consensus and the assumptions which followed set limits to choice in foreign policy. "American business could operate only in a world composed of politically reliable and stable capitalist nations, and with free access to essential raw materials." To attain its goals the United States was determined to dis-

52. Joyce and Gabriel Kolko, *The Limits of Power: The World and United States Foreign Policy, 1945–1954* (New York: Harper & Row, 1972), 2.

mantle prewar structures, ending economic restrictions and building a new system of world trade. Britain's sterling bloc and a global structure of Commonwealth preferences had to be weakened in the name of anti-colonialism and a new internationalism; Europe's economic rivalries and the economic nationalism of prewar Germany had to be supplanted by a unified international capitalist system. To institutionalize worldwide economic cooperation, wartime planners in the United States mapped out plans for a network of new international economic organizations. "The United States' ultimate objective at the end of World War II was both to sustain and to reform world capitalism."[53]

The conviction which dominated social and economic reformism in the 1930s within the United States was writ large in America's wartime and postwar economic goals. Much as anxiety and despair had been attributed largely to economic distress domestically, war and conflict were assumed to have resulted primarily from economic rivalry and barriers to free trade. The international community was mobilized to break up exclusive trading blocs and other impediments to the free exchange of commodities and raw materials. Economic internationalism, however, barely concealed American self-interest as Assistant Secretary of State William L. Clayton made plain when he declared: "So, let us admit right off that our objective has as its background the needs and interests of the people of the United States. . . . We need markets—big markets—around the world in which to buy and sell."[54] In prophetic words, the assistant secretary continued," We are today net importers of practically all the important metals and minerals except two—coal and oil. Who knows how long we can go without importing oil?"[55] In the present and more so in the future, America needed reliable and profitable world markets.

The American drive for markets and free trade led inescapably to the conclusion that certain forms of national development and state control were inimical to the worldwide economic design of the United States. State socialism and state ownership anywhere conflicted with America's national and worldwide economic interests and values. Expansion of open-door policies was a necessity for a prosperous America. The shadow of the Great Depression haunted postwar planners. America's share of prewar trade had been reduced in part by the rise of exclu-

53. *Ibid.*, 2, 11.
54. *U.S. Department of State Bulletin*, November 24, 1946, p. 950.
55. *Ibid.*, 952–53.

sive trading blocs. During seven years of the post-1929 decade, the United States suffered a negative balance of trade; adverse exchange restrictions and rival cartels controlled one-half of the world's trade. To reform the international economic order, Article VII of the Lend-Lease Agreement of February, 1942, which the British, whose exclusive trading rights were challenged, reluctantly accepted, foreshadowed the implementation of America's postwar economic blueprint and was followed in rapid succession by the establishment of the International Monetary Fund and the International Bank for Reconstruction and Development, so organized that the United States would be able to maintain a voting majority within the new organizations. The mechanisms of international trade and development were no longer to be left to chance but would be controlled by American interests.

For revisionist thinkers, the larger economic and political objectives of the United States for the postwar world were determining factors in the Cold War. They were designed to build a "world restored" on a globe swept by the winds of change. World War II was "a cataclysm that ripped apart the moorings and foundations of a world already gravely wounded by the prior war."[56] Following World War I, there was a liberal world order for European states to restore. After World War II, "only the United States was in a position to resist those larger forces of change, upheaval, and revolution that the war had unleashed."[57] To mold such a world to their interests, interventionism became the characteristic mode of American and Soviet diplomacy—American intervention endeavoring to revive the Right and Soviet intervention hoping to control and dominate the Left. Unlike the post–World War I period, "the local forces with which the United States aligned itself were far weaker than an ascendant Left growing amidst the frustrations and hunger of the peoples of Europe and Asia." If left to themselves, Europeans and Asian societies would have moved in directions inimical to American interests. The economic imperatives of American policy led to a shoring up of rightist and capitalist regimes and a prevention of victory by leftist groups. To reverse the worldwide trend of social revolution brought about by the collapse of prewar social and economic systems and to forestall Soviet advances, American diplomacy was "marked by the interacting themes of containment, stability, and counterrevolution." Without the counterweight of American influence, "the transformation of Euro-

56. Kolko, *The Limits of Power*, 30.
57. *Ibid.*

pean and Asian societies in unknown and undesirable ways—from Washington's viewpoint—was certain." The revisionists maintained that "only in Eastern Europe was such a strategy impossible, if only because there the security interests of the Soviet Union clashed with the restorative policies of the United States, and the breakdown of traditional societies was too profound for the casual support the Americans might, at best, be able to give to them." Intervention in Asia employing selective assistance to countries in which Right and Left were more evenly balanced proved more feasible but led by an irresistible logic to *démarche* in the Vietnam War. The Cold War, as revisionists viewed it, "was far less the confrontation of the United States with Russia than America's expansion into the entire world—a world the Soviet Union neither controlled nor created." Washington was unable or unwilling to distinguish between "the Left in Greek mountains or northern French mine fields and the dictates of the Kremlin, and it was hardly prone to attribute the dynamism of local radicals to the decline of capitalism."[58]

The revisionists coupled their indictment of American foreign policy for its worldwide capitalist and counterrevolutionary design at the expense of sound political estimates with an even harsher judgment of American elitism. In this they were again supported by the spirit of the times, the antiestablishment views of Vietnam protest groups and the writings of men such as C. Wright Mills, professor of sociology at Columbia University and author of *The Power Elite*. It was argued historically that policy since the days of President William McKinley had been shaped by a handful of "insiders." The decision to acquire the Philippines at the end of the war with Spain had been made by a small group around the president. Military intervention in China was carried out by executive order. President Theodore Roosevelt took full responsibility for the decision to seize the Panama Canal without the advice or knowledge of anyone, saying: "I took the Panama Canal." President Woodrow Wilson intervened with force against the Bolshevik revolution without congressional authority and President Franklin D. Roosevelt deftly brought the United States into World War II despite a fundamentally divided American public. Wartime secrecy accentuated elitism and President Truman won support for America's counterrevolutionary policies after World War II by forming political alliances with a small group of congressional leaders and announcing policies which it was expected everyone but defectors from American patriotism would naturally sup-

58. *Ibid.*, 30 and 31.

port. The decision to intervene in Korea was made without public discussion and was justified as a necessary police action based on a congressional commitment to the United Nations to provide troops to resist aggression anywhere in the world. The Central Intelligence Agency carried the retreat from responsible self-government one step further, deposing premiers, installing counterrevolutionary governments, and planning and executing the abortive invasion of Cuba at the Bay of Pigs. Interventionism reached its fateful climax in Santo Domingo and the "Vietnam Civil War." While secrecy begun in wartime undergirded the initiation of such American policies, the impetus to act without public debate was reinforced by a deep-seated popular aversion to any foreign involvement which threatened individualism, private property, and a free market economy at home. The foundations of public resentment of elitism go back in American history to the rise of Jacksonian Democracy in the 1820s. The setbacks and errors of postwar American foreign policy were caused, according to the revisionist criticism, by "the elite's self-isolation from the nature of reality, by its loss of the power of critical thought, by its exaggerated confidence in American economic strength and military might, by its own arrogance and self-righteousness, and by its messianic distortion of a sincere humanitarian desire to help other peoples." [59]

When asked to explain how the elite had drawn to itself such power and become isolated from wider criticism, revisionists responded that top government officials are recruited largely from a narrow sector of American life representing big business, corporate law, and large-scale financial interests. Gabriel Kolko found that "of the 243 men who during 1944–60 held the key positions in the State, Defense or War, Treasury, and Commerce Departments, plus other relevant executive agencies dealing with foreign and military policy, their multiple government careers meant that they accounted for at least 678 posts, most of which were at the highest policy-making level." [60] Big law, banking, and investment firms accounted for 36 percent of key positions and another 25 percent were monopolized by men from industry, utilities, and other business and commercial firms. All but eight of fifty-seven American secretaries of state have been lawyers. It is also significant that from the three-fifths of public servants who occupied top policy-making posts in foreign affairs described above, 16 percent left government on comple-

59. Williams, *The Tragedy of American Diplomacy*, 8.
60. Gabriel Kolko, *Main Currents in Modern American History* (New York: Harper & Row, 1976), 321.

tion of their services for positions in business. (The proportion moving from high military ranks to related business enterprises was considerably higher.) These practices led the Carter administration on assuming office in 1977 to exact commitments from certain high-level appointees not to accept positions in related corporations seeking government contracts for the two years immediately following their government service.

The strength of the revisionist viewpoint and its appeal in the late 1960s lies partly in its self-contained character and its seeming coherence and inner consistency. The time was ripe for an alternative view of the causes of conflict with the Soviet Union. Enough water had passed under the bridge so that the first crush of Soviet-American confrontation was but dimly remembered or known only as history by a new generation. The anti-communism consensus, which once appeared firm, had begun to dissolve. Americans were asking for the first time if their early postwar leaders had not themselves been guilty of a brand of "rigid theology" progressively relaxed, first, by President Eisenhower and more significantly in the Nixon-Kissinger policy of detente. Moreover, revisionism enjoyed certain points of credibility with the silent majority in American society. Elitism was an obvious facet of foreign policy formation in the United States, no less than in Britain and the Soviet Union. Lawyers and businessmen, foundation officials, and members of the Trilateral Commission founded by David Rockefeller and of New York's Council on Foreign Relations moved in and out of government with undeniable consistency whether Republicans or Democrats occupied the White House.

Yet the full weight of revisionism would not have been felt had the nation been spared the trauma of Vietnam. The judgments of history are inextricably bound up with the facts of success or failure. Historians who passed the first favorable verdict on President Truman's foreign policy were influenced by the success of the Marshall Plan and signs that containment was effectively turning back Soviet expansionism. Yet by the 1960s and 1970s Truman and his successors were viewed by some as "architects of illusion" and revisionists were claiming that "responsibility for the way in which the Cold War developed . . . belongs more to the United States." They insisted "there were at least three issues, which, if they had been decided differently, might have spared the world the worst moments of the Cold War."[61] The first was believing, as Truman

61. Lloyd C. Gardner, *Architects of Illusion: Men and Ideas in Foreign Policy, 1941–1949* (Chicago: Quadrangle Books, 1970), 317.

did, that the United States could use economic leverage to impose drastic changes in Russia's policies for Eastern Europe, making American aid contingent on Soviet good behavior before the outstanding issues of reparations, peace treaties for the satellite countries, and American policy for Germany had been negotiated. The second was the failure to offer the Soviets a firm guarantee of German disarmament accompanied by the dismemberment of German power and an explicit security treaty in early 1945. The third was turning to "majoritarian diplomacy" in pursuit of the Baruch Plan in the United Nations rather than following Secretary Stimson's advice and approaching Soviet leaders directly on the control of atomic energy. Behind all three of these errors in policy were miscalculations that went back to elitist commitments to "America's economic supremacy." The rediscovery of Brooks Adams' book with this title, with its prophecy that the United States and Russia would confront one another not as two rival nations but two powerful conglomerates of economic power provided early Cold War leaders with signposts for the future. After twelve years of depression and war, American capitalists desired an open world. "Washington turned a deaf ear to the Soviet complaint that the United States enjoyed its own 'sphere of influence' in Latin America and the Pacific."[62] It saw itself as having inherited world leadership from Great Britain and this in practice meant the moral and political defense of world capitalism. Given its mission, the United States was destined to clash with an alien economic system centered in Moscow and to oppose its advance wherever their claims overlapped.

An Alternative View on the Causes of the Cold War

The clash between the official and revisionist interpretations of the Cold War leaves little room for compromise. Each in its own way sounds a note of final truth and moral absolutism. Both orthodoxy and revisionism err by seeking to reduce the complexities of international political rivalry to simple and unequivocal realities. They ignore proximate differences. They leave little room for nuance and human choice. Whatever the uniqueness of a given historical situation, men tend to act according to the roles larger historic forces assign them. Thus, for the revisionists to assert that the Truman Doctrine and the Marshall Plan "were the two sides of the same coin of America's traditional program of open-

62. *Ibid.*, 319.

door expansion"[63]—for example—is to oversimplify. The Marshall Plan was fashioned in response to a systematic cataloguing of needs by sovereign nation states within a developed and well-defined region struggling to restore viable societies from the wreckage and devastation of war. The Truman Doctrine was a global declaration by an American president pledging himself and his nation to come to the defense of freedom anywhere in the world. If political distinctions have any meaning, the two foreign policy actions rest on fundamentally different objectives. Yet political distinctions are the missing ingredients in the two prevailing views of the Cold War.

By contrast, a third and alternative view of the Cold War discovers the causes of conflict primarily in the objective situation of two great powers following World War II and in certain historic patterns and perspectives of Russian and American politics and foreign policy. In 1945, the two countries, each dominant over half the world, confronted one another as other competing centers of power had done throughout the history of the European state system. That confrontation was inherent in their power and would have occurred regardless of their ideological motivations; it will likely continue even if ideological conflict should abate in the 1980s or thereafter. Yet it was also true that the conflict was sustained and made more intense by the fusion by Stalin of Russia's traditional interests with communism and the misunderstanding by the West of the nature of the threat to its interests, compounded by Stalin's misunderstanding of the political and intellectual foundations of the West's response to his policies.

The alternative explanation of the causes of the Cold War takes as its first datum the expansion of Russian power, whatever the motivating force, into Eastern and Central Europe following fast on the heels of President Roosevelt's firm assurance to a joint session of Congress on his return from the Yalta Conference that Soviet-American cooperation would "spell the end of the system of unilateral action, the exclusive alliances, the spheres of influence, the balances of power, and all the other expedients that have been tried for centuries and have always failed." (Roosevelt's assurance was strikingly similar to that in Secretary Cordell Hull's address to Congress on November 18, 1943, following the Moscow Conference.) Having given itself over to what proved to be an excess of faith in the independent force of a new international organization for making and preserving the peace, the United States was thrown back

63. Williams, *The Tragedy of American Diplomacy*, 269.

with a vengeance to all those ancient practices by which states had historically sought to keep the peace. To attribute all this to economic motivations would be to judge mankind's behavior on too narrow a scale. Economic determinism ignores the idea of the irreducible dilemma which lies in the very geometry of human conflict or the seemingly inevitable clash of two powerful political forces engaged in the spread of a particular political system or a national ideology which they sought to make universal.

It is possible from this third perspective to view the Cold War in a political framework conscious of the tendencies and forces at work in international politics. From this viewpoint, it is necessary to recognize that the Cold War is full of pathos, persisting problems and conflicting values, misunderstandings and misperceptions, and, in this, is close to the universal human drama. The conduct of the Cold War seen in this framework requires learning to live with adversity and ambiguities, disputes over means and ends, actions and overreactions. It requires an awareness not only of power but of the limitations of national power outside a country's own jurisdiction, a lesson both the proponents of official and revisionist history would appear not to have learned or to have subordinated to another design. For whether the official historians call on the United States to oppose foreign revolutions or the revisionists to champion and defend them, both groups fail to recognize that the United States, like all great powers before it, can act effectively only as it follows its own national interest and has the power to support the actions it chooses. The first rule of statecraft concerning revolutions remains: "Intervene we must when our national interest requires it and when our power gives us a chance to succeed."[64] It is as fallacious to call on the United States to pursue a worldwide policy of intervention based on indiscriminate anti-communism as it is to require intervention in support of national revolutions intermingled with local or national Communist movements wherever they emerge and whether or not foreign policy objectives or national interests require it. Orthodox and revisionist historians alike are misled by their exaggerated estimates of national capacity and interests.

The cause of the Cold War in its beginnings revolved around the question of whether or not Russia would seek to extend its power westward into Europe thus threatening the security of the Atlantic states.

64. Hans J. Morgenthau, *A New Foreign Policy for the United States* (New York: Praeger, 1969), 128.

Peace or war depended not on a resolution of the ideological struggle but on "whether the borderland between Russia and the Atlantic states . . . [was] settled by consent or by pressure, dictation, and diplomatic violence."[65] That borderland began with Finland in the North, extended through Poland, the Danube nations, the Balkans, and included Germany. If the interests of the United States and Russia were incompatible in this region, there would be no lasting peace. If all the parties recognized their common interest in a European settlement, peace could be maintained. It was in Europe that the Cold War began. Conflict here was the cause of the Cold War viewed within a political framework. This assumption sets apart those who espouse an alternative view of the causes of the Cold War from both the official and the revisionist historians, and its consequences are apparent in the choice of foreign policies for a succession of early Cold War conflicts that constitute the origins of the struggle.

To place primary emphasis on the geographical locus and center of the conflict is not to deny one version of official historiography. The Four Freedoms and the Atlantic Charter were to be the foundations of a world order established by the peace settlement. Russia accepted the Atlantic Charter with some reservations. All these principles and the Declaration on Liberated Europe were disregarded and violated in the countries under Soviet occupation. The United States and the United Kingdom addressed a few notes of protest to Moscow but did nothing serious for the defense of the ideas and pledges which were supposed to be the cornerstone of a worldwide public order after the war. Did this passive Western attitude contribute to the outbreak of the Cold War? The revisionists do not speak much about this topic; the official historians give it more attention. It deserves mention alongside any statement about the geo-strategic focus of the Cold War. It will be examined in the discussion that follows.

65. Walter Lippmann, *United States Foreign Policy, Shield of the Republic* (New York: Pocket Books, 1943), 107.

Chapter Two
Historic Origins of the Cold War

The debate over the causes of the Cold War serves to illuminate certain fundamental issues essential to an understanding of *why* the conflict came about but leaves largely unexamined questions of *how* and *when* the struggle broke out and was intensified. A discussion of historical approaches helps the student of Soviet-American relations to construct a general framework of assumptions and principles without providing a systematic review of those particular events and foreign policy disputes which made bitter adversaries of wartime allies. If the task of generalizing about causes is fraught with complexities, the quest for historical meaning amidst the maze of rapidly shifting events is equally demanding. Yet any comprehensive review of East-West conflict must focus on the concrete if general propositions are to have validity. The unfolding story of the deepening conflict between Russia and the United States can be traced along a line of successive crises in which enmity and hostility supplanted apparent friendship. Historical theories are the architect's broad design; historical research carries forward the building of the structure of both peaceful and warlike relations which resulted in what came to be called the Cold War.

The Beginnings of the Cold War

Historians looking back on the beginnings of the Cold War would appear to disagree on the starting point. For certain historians, the year 1917 was a major turning point in world history, marking the entry of the United States into World War I and the Russian Revolution. Others focus on 1939/40, which brought on World War II and foreshadowed the impending East-West crisis. A secret protocol of the Molotov-Ribbentrop Pact concluded in August of 1939 and a supplementary accord added a month later provided that Finland, Estonia, Latvia, Lithuania, and eastern Poland were to fall within the Soviet orbit. By September of 1939 Russia had occupied eastern Poland. In the summer of 1940 the Red Army moved into Estonia, Latvia, and Lithuania and these countries then became a part of the Soviet Union. Failing in its invasion of Finland in 1939, the Russians accepted a cession of Finnish territory which it hoped would protect Leningrad from future encroachments. Soviet advances in 1939 and 1940 and the commitments Russia obtained from Hitler's Germany signaled its intention to expand westward, which culminated in the pursuit by the Red Army of Hitler's defeated forces to a point one hundred miles west of Berlin. The evidence seems clear that Stalin at an early date resolved to bring the Baltic states, eastern Poland, and Bessarabia within his expanding empire however much the fulfillment of his aims were to be postponed by the defense of the Russian homeland from 1941 to 1944. Thus the seeds of the Cold War from a strategic standpoint were planted in 1939 and 1940.

In 1941 Germany invaded the Soviet Union and the stage was set for the most costly and fateful struggle of the Second World War, which resulted in the loss of twenty million Russian lives. Growing differences emerged between Stalin and Roosevelt over their planned launching of a second front, which Stalin felt was being unnecessarily delayed. It could hardly have escaped his notice that American senators (including Harry Truman, destined to become his country's thirty-third president) had seemed to welcome the heavy loss of both Russian and German lives as serving American interests. (See p. 40) The decisions which might have been made by Western leaders to avert the Cold War were postponed and sacrificed to the single objective of winning the war. In public such men, responsive to the groundswell of popular liberal opinion, tended, whether from reasons of conviction or political and diplomatic necessity, to minimize the growing conflicts between the Soviet Union and the United States. In private, the possibility that the Western powers would have to someday confront a Soviet threat to the balance of power in Europe was always present in the minds of leaders such as Churchill. However, Churchill's efforts to persuade others that an invasion of Europe from the southeast might thwart Russian expansion to the west was opposed by the Americans on grounds of military expediency. The war took its frightful toll; war-weariness reduced the capacity of the strongest leaders to examine alternatives. Roosevelt had occupied his high office since 1933 and it was said that as the war neared its end he and Churchill initialed important agreements which neither had the time or strength to review. On the American side not only was military strategy conducted as an end in itself independent of political objectives but the best of its leaders were seized by that most fateful disease of American public administration—the approaching of decisions as if they existed in watertight compartments and the ignoring of their interconnectedness with one another. By 1943 the possibility of a peaceful world after the war had been undermined by the formation of an unstable equilibrium of power in Europe. After that, it was too late to prevent the Cold War.

From the perspective of other respected historians, however, 1945 was the great divide. By then the division of Europe had been largely determined. The divergence between Soviet aims in Eastern Europe and America's resistance broke out in public controversy. In 1944, the Russians had moved into eastern Poland and then the Balkans as the Americans crossed the Rhine. On April 25, 1945, Soviet and American armies met at the Elbe near the German town of Torgau, but by July the American and British armies had withdrawn one hundred miles in agreement with the Russians, reflecting, it now seems, supreme unconcern with the threat of early Russian expansionism.

The far-reaching devastation of Europe and Russia stood out in stark relief against the unscarred American landscape. The gross national product of the United States had expanded exponentially, but the industrial power of Germany and Japan, lying between the two superpowers, had been crushed. The United States had announced its intention at the Yalta Conference in February of 1945 to withdraw its troops from Europe two years after the defeat of Germany; postwar American leaders set out to dismantle the mightiest army in history, reducing its forces from 12 million to 1.5 million men. In May of 1945 the United States had 3.5 million men organized into 68 divisions in Europe, supported by 149 air groups. By March of the following year American forces abroad numbered 400,000 troops with 6 battalions in reserve in the United States. The Soviet Union, by comparison, kept its armed forces largely intact at a level of 5 to 6 million men, 50,000 tanks, and 20,000 aircraft and at the same time embarked on the building of a navy which, in the production of submarines, was to outnumber the combined navies of the world. Certain revisionist writers have pointed out that the United States, while dismantling some segments of its powerful wartime military machine, held others at a constant level and accelerated atomic research and production efforts. Revisionists further argue that the strength of the Red Army was an effect and not a cause of postwar territorial arrangements. Yet oftentimes in history appearances are more important than statistics; from the standpoint of power politics American military strength appeared to be on the decline in 1945 and 1946.

Furthermore, diplomacy and military strength are interlocked and interdependent and the decline of its armed strength reacted adversely on America's postwar negotiating ability. Throughout the war, President Roosevelt had resolutely avoided being drawn into agreements that might determine the shape of the postwar world. In part he was influenced by domestic politics and the fear of hostile coalitions of Americans with East European backgrounds. In part he possessed supreme confidence that in a more peaceful world he could through his political skills and tact lead and cajole Stalin to accept terms more favorable to America. Thus one of the deep ironies of postwar diplomacy is the fact that no peace treaties were written and no bargains struck while the power position of the United States was at its zenith. Because Roosevelt passed from the scene, because Soviet appetites increased with military and political successes, because the hoped for era of good feeling was stillborn and because mutual fears and suspicions deepened, the more favorable political atmosphere which the American wartime president had awaited never came. In this respect, military decisions and the disposition of forces had significance far beyond the sheer numbers and logistics of military power which have preoccupied military writers. This fact made inevitable the responses of quite moderate leaders and diplomatists whose thinking in the period from 1945 to 1947 hardly resembles their approach either before or after these critical years. It is in this setting that the most recent criticisms by popular writers such as Daniel Yergin of diplomatists such as George F. Kennan and Charles Bohlen must be examined. It has long been a tendency of contemporary historians to question the judgment of their predecessors in the light of a new set of circumstances. It is tempting for critics to overlook the fact that the United States showed restraint in responding to the Soviet Union for an eighteen-month period from the Japanese surrender on September 12, 1945, to the adoption of the Truman Doctrine on March 12, 1947. Only when repeated diplomatic overtures, some of which may well have been misplaced, were rejected by the Russians did it turn to a policy of containment.

A more complete account of the origins and outbreak of the Cold War must also pay heed to the impact of actions by American leaders which may have hastened the conflict. To throw the spotlight on them is not to say categorically that they ushered in the Cold War. The student of the Cold War must probe every source which may explain how a traditional great power rivalry deteriorated into a bitter ideological conflict in which compromise was equated with treason. Moreover, the political judgments of Americans are no more infallible than those on the Russian side; serious mistakes of timing and action may well have contributed to a hardening of attitudes.

One such judgment concerns the way in which the cancellation of the Lend-Lease Agreement was carried out. On May 8, 1945, President Truman signed a decree announcing a sharp curtailment of supplies going to the Allies. The American Foreign Economic Administrator, Leo T. Crowley, saw fit to interpret the presidential decree so literally that within the hour ships on the high seas had put about and returned to unload their cargoes in American ports. The timing could not have been more alarming to the Russians, who at Yalta and other wartime conferences had requested long-term postwar credits for postwar reconstruction and considered the first American response to have been favorable. Not surprisingly, Stalin, meeting on May 27 with Harry Hopkins, pointed to this action as demonstrating "that the American attitude toward the Soviet Union had perceptibly cooled once it became obvious that Germany was defeated . . . as though the Americans were saying the Russians were no longer needed."[1] Ambassador Harriman, who increasingly had urged greater firmness in dealing with the Russians and had proposed closer scrutiny of assistance not intended for use against Japan "while avoiding any implication of a threat or any indication of political bargaining," was visibly disturbed by Crowley's action. (Stalin subsequently confirmed Harriman's judgment, saying, "If the refusal to continue lend-lease was designed as pressure on the Russians in order to soften them up then it was a fundamental mistake.") Truman, who had never intended that supplies already en route to Russia should be returned, countermanded the order, but the diplomatic damage about which Harriman had warned had been done. In foreign policy, the style and manner in which action is taken may often be more important than the action itself, a lesson which future leaders were to ignore at their peril.

A similar issue arose in connection with Russia's request for a loan which Secretary of State James Byrnes on taking office in July of 1945 placed in the department's "Forgotten File." On January 3, 1945, the

1. Robert E. Sherwood, *Roosevelt and Hopkins* (New York: Harper and Brothers, 1948), 893–94.

Russians had requested a $6 billion loan with interest of 2-1/4 percent. Stalin offered as a quid pro quo substantial Russian orders of capital equipment to be placed in the United States. Simultaneously, Secretary of the Treasury Henry Morgenthau renewed a Treasury proposal for a loan to the Soviet Union of $10 billion at 2 percent interest over thirty-five years, to be used for the purchase of American products with repayment to be made through Russian exports of strategic war materials. President Roosevelt preferred to delay any promises of financial aid until after the Yalta Conference and cautioned that any loan should be used to gain concessions in bargaining on other matters. State Department officials opposed the Treasury proposal both for reasons of domestic politics and the fear that imports of Russian materials would have damaging effects on American petroleum and mining interests. These officials pointed out that not only was congressional legislation unlikely but that such a loan would encourage countries whose development was based on state socialism and who would receive more advantageous terms than would private investors. On January 27, 1945, the State Department authorized American officials in Moscow to inform the Russian government that the Americans were studying the matter of long-term credits for postwar projects but congressional action was required and a considerable delay was anticipated. At Yalta the foreign ministers gave the question only cursory attention and the three wartime leaders appear not to have discussed the matter at all. The debate continued between American officials in the Treasury and State Departments, intensified by opposition by certain diplomats to the Morgenthau Plan for Germany. In filing away the Soviet request, Secretary Byrnes noted that "our Treasury officials were not always the cold-hearted, glassy-eyed individuals all bankers are supposed to be."[2] Leaving aside the issue of timing, the premise which underlay the initial support for the loan by men such as Harriman and Morgenthau was subordinated by Secretary Byrnes to other criteria. That premise as made explicit by Harriman assumed that a strong Russian economy would make Soviet leaders more willing to pursue friendly relations with the United States and that financial aid would prove an instrument of peace.

A third issue which led to Soviet-American dissension was that of reparations. As early as September, 1941, Stalin had raised the question: "What about getting the Germans to pay for the damage?" Remembering the major thesis in J. M. Keynes *Economic Consequences of the Peace*

2. James Byrnes, *All in One Lifetime* (New York: Harper & Brothers, 1958), 310.

that Germany's unfavorable economic position after World War I had spurred on the rise of Hitler, neither the Americans nor the British had much enthusiasm for reparations. Roosevelt before the Yalta Conference had stated: "We are against reparations." Yet he was ambivalent, favoring at one time the Morgenthau Plan for the dismemberment of Germany prompted by memories of his introduction to German arrogance as a young school boy and his witnessing as assistant secretary of the Navy the reluctance of American and German officials in 1919 to allow the American flag to be displayed alongside the German one for fear of offending German pride. Stalin pressed the issue, however, reciting the harsh facts of wartime devastation facing the Russians. Not only were 25,000,000 Russians homeless as a result of the war but 4,700,000 houses, 1,710 towns, and 70,000 villages had been destroyed. Other statistics of war damage which included 65,000 kilometers of railway tracks damaged, 15,800 locomotives, and 428,000 freight cars destroyed or rendered ineffectual, and millions of livestock ravaged were less important than the symbolic importance attached to reparations. What became central to the Soviet design for the postwar world, however, was peripheral to the American blueprint. It has been argued that "the Russians could never understand the nature of American concern for Eastern Europe; similarly, the Americans could never comprehend the emotional intensity the Russians attached to reparations."[3]

For Stalin, who in other respects appeared conciliatory at Yalta, the issue of reparations had acquired a symbolic importance and represented as much a "test case" for the Russians as the Soviet domination of Eastern Europe became one for America. It is of course true that America's response to Soviet control of Eastern Europe only gradually emerged. Soviet domination was the result of wartime strategy. After the Soviet military successes in 1943 in Stalingrad and Kursk, President Roosevelt is said to have told Cardinal Spellman in early September of that year that most of Europe would become a Soviet sphere of influence.[4] From a prewar American perspective, Danubian Europe was primarily a British concern, although later in the armistice agreements and at Yalta and Potsdam, America accepted a greater share of responsibility. It would be difficult to show that Soviet domination of Eastern Europe was ever seriously challenged. At the same time, public protests increased and even

3. Daniel Yergin, *Shattered Peace: The Origins of the Cold War and the National Security State* (Boston: Houghton Mifflin, 1977), 64–65.
4. See Robert V. Gannon, *The Cardinal Spellman Story* (Garden City: Doubleday, 1962), 222–25.

though these efforts can be seen as an exercise in futility, they did reflect growing American concern. An alternative approach proposed by George F. Kennan would have been to "divide Europe frankly into spheres of influence—keep ourselves out of the Russian sphere and keep the Russians out of ours." Instead: "We have refused to name any limit for Russian expansion and Russian responsibilities, thereby confusing the Russians and causing them constantly to wonder whether they are asking too little or whether it was some kind of trap."[5]

The dispute over reparations rested on the conflicting if not incompatible objectives of the wartime allies. The Soviet Union took its stand on the principle of compensation for damages. The Western allies warned in Churchill's words that they would not "be chained to a dead body of Germany." If Germany became an economic wasteland, the task of its reconstruction would fall primarily to America and Britain. Roosevelt at Yalta, with Hopkins' prompting, had accepted as a basis for further discussion the figure of $20 billion in reparations, half for the Russians with the understanding that such reparations would be in goods, production, and equipment, not cash. Roosevelt assumed that these transfers could be accomplished without creating economic disruption in Germany, but the British remained skeptical that this was so.

From the beginning of the discussion of reparations, the concern of the British particularly had been that Germany must pay for its own recovery and development needs. If reparations were too severe and if Germany's industrial capacity was destroyed and its natural source of food supply from East Germany, which had been its breadbasket, cut off, Britain or the United States would have to pay for Germany's recovery. Stalin's proposal had been for the removal of a substantial fraction of German industrial plants and equipment in the Soviet zone plus one-quarter of the industrial complex in the other zones of West Germany. The British and Americans argued that Germany's non-military industries must be maintained at a level which would enable the country to achieve a standard of living comparable but not superior to that in other European countries and that reparations should not in future years be demanded out of current production. Even before it became clear that the Soviet proposal which Roosevelt at Yalta had accepted as a basis for discussion had been tabled by the Americans, the Russians set out within their zone to dismantle and remove German industry without informing

5. Quoted in Charles E. Bohlen, *Witness to History* (New York: W. W. Norton & Co., 1973), 175.

their allies. Simultaneously, shipments of food from East Germany were halted. One year after Germany's surrender, the United States suspended action on demands for further West German reparations to the Soviet Union. The reparations issue on which it at first appeared that Soviet and American leaders at Yalta had reached a tentative agreement thus contributed to the origins of the Cold War.

In retrospect the failure on both sides to deal realistically with the issue of reparations in the months between Yalta and General Lucius B. Clay's decision of May 3, 1946, to halt deliveries of reparations from the American zone to the East is perhaps more important than the competing explanations offered to account *for* that failure. Two moderates on the issue of Soviet-American relations describing the controversy came to opposing conclusions on the fate of reparations. George F. Kennan downplayed the issue: "It was silly to suppose that we could collaborate effectively with the Russians on such a program." Reparations, as he saw it, was bound to be a matter of "catch as catch can." "The Russians could be depended upon to do just as they pleased in the area under their occupation, and would not be inhibited in this respect by any agreement with us." Kennan quoted Ambassador Harriman as informing Washington in a wire on April 6, 1945, that he had "no reason to doubt that the Russians are already busy removing from Germany without compunction anything (repeat anything) which they find it to their advantage to remove."[6] To expect any early resolution of the issue as Kennan and Harriman saw it was unrealistic.

By contrast, Daniel Yergin has portrayed President Roosevelt as willing to gamble and as displaying vision and political courage at Yalta in retreating from his early opposition to reparations. "Roosevelt was a realist; he knew that everything depended upon implementation of the accords, and that, in turn, would depend upon intentions and future alignments."[7] He sensed that the question of reparations was bound up with Stalin's "Second Revolution," the industrial revolution within Russia, and recognized that it promised to be a "test case" in Soviet-American relations. After Roosevelt's death the American position on reparations, lend-lease, and economic aid were integrated into an overall bargaining stance in which the United States sought leverage in pushing the Russians to implement other decisions arrived at during the Yalta

6. George F. Kennan, *Memoirs, 1925–1950* (Boston: Little, Brown & Company, 1967), 260.
7. Yergin, *The Shattered Peace*, 65.

Conference. The $20 billion figure was downplayed and, as part of a tougher policy, new advisers such as former president Herbert Hoover and the American oilman Edwin Pauley were enlisted by President Truman. In response to their influence, reparations guidelines were made as restrictive as possible and the economic problems of Western Europe and Germany received precedence over those of the Soviet Union.

Thereafter, anxiety and suspicion became the controlling forces. On the American side, it was assumed that the Russians had a well-ordered plan for reparations dominated by political concerns. In fact, it was evident on both sides that a unified approach was unlikely, given the struggle going on within the respective governmental bureaucracies. For the American government, State Department planners including Ambassador John G. Winant, the American representative on the Anglo-American-Soviet European Advisory Commission established by the Moscow Conference of Foreign Ministers in October of 1943 following the surrender of Italy, had urged tripartite decisions on all issues of occupation policy by the Allies. Stalin expressed his strong dissatisfaction because the Soviet Union was not invited to participate in the Italian armistice negotiations. The tripartite European Advisory Committee was supposed to discuss such matters in the future. This apparently satisfied Stalin. Winant had warned: "If we present the Russians only with *faits accomplis* . . . we can only expect to learn of their actions and policies in Eastern Europe in a similar manner." Secretary of State Hull, influenced by the spirit of Roosevelt's tactics of delaying political solutions, instructed Winant to avoid any discussion of overall political issues. It was feared that premature American commitments would hamper efforts at building a postwar collective security system and that secret arrangements once made public would foster isolationism.

The major obstacle to tripartite discussions, however, even on the more limited questions of the surrender and occupation of defeated countries, resulted from bureaucratic infighting in Washington between the European Advisory Commission and the Working Security Committee created in December, 1943, made up of representatives from the State, Navy, and War Departments and charged with responsibility for drawing up instructions for Ambassador Winant. Particularly War Department representatives, chosen from officers from the department's Civil Affairs Division, saw occupation policy as a purely military matter. Some State Department officials expressed the belief that negotiating with the CAD was every bit as difficult as negotiating with the Russians.

Early in 1944, the State Department submitted specific recommendations to the Working Security Committee on the economic treatment of Germany including reparations. The Joint Chiefs of Staff, after holding the documents for two months, refused to accept the plans because military operations had not proceeded to the point where economic proposals could be considered. Late in July, 1944, the State Department group tried again. Once more the Joint Chiefs held the proposals for two months and then suggested they be resubmitted to the WSC, on which there was "military representation." By the fall of 1944, the reparations issue had become hopelessly ensnarled with debate over the Morgenthau Plan for Germany and was not discussed again until the Yalta Conference. The military, while not engaging in policy making itself, nevertheless shaped the course of future events by preventing anyone else from making policy.

Within its monolithic structure, the Soviet Union for its part was experiencing a similar division of opinion. At the highest levels of the Soviet government, two groups were in contention. A "Special Committee for the Economic Disarmament of Germany" under the chairmanship of Georgi Malenkov, fearing a too rapid German recovery, pushed for its own version of the Morgenthau Plan, a pastoralization scheme for postwar Germany. An opposing group composed of top military officials as well as Andrei Zhdânov, the most militant Soviet ideological leader, and Anastas Mikoyan, minister of foreign trade, argued for "Reparations for Fulfillment of the Five Year Plan." When the Reparations Commission met in Moscow in the summer of 1945, the difficulties of negotiations were further compounded by the fact that the Americans spoke in terms of commodities and goods, such as railway engines and steel, and the Russians insisted on talking about dollar values. The Russians when questioned were unclear about the base on which dollar value might be calculated and the Americans were concerned with the manipulation of price levels to serve Russians ends. A Russian economist at the conference when queried in private by the number two American delegate, the economist Isador Lubin, on the arbitrary formulation of dollar valuations answered, pointing toward the Kremlin: "Those people up there are just like you Americans—capitalists." A political officer of the Red Army told a former high official of the East German government, "that is where the enemy lives . . . our own reparations gang."[8]

8. Quoted *ibid.*, 98, 97.

On both sides the discussion of reparations had become more and more intertwined with serious internal differences over military and economic policies. Add to that the impact on American thinking of the exploding of the first American atomic bomb with a resulting toughening of American policy on all issues, and the resolution of the reparations deadlock becomes increasingly unlikely.

By the summer of 1946, the Russian position on reparations had hardened and American policy was turned in other directions by the beginnings of a commitment to a more permanent division of Germany. Earlier in 1946, General Clay and a few of his associates had held out hope that a Four Power agreement might still be possible. William Draper in his oral history observed that Soviet-American relations within Germany were positive in the first year of occupation. Looking back officials continued to consider France as the villain paralyzing Four Power control—a point forgotten as the Soviet Union emerged as the main obstacle to agreement. General Clay noted that some Americans had an "exaggerated impression of the scale of removals" of capital equipment from the Russian zone of Germany. More importantly, however, key American officials, admittedly lacking in knowledge of the internal workings of the Soviet regime, failed to realize that when Soviet Foreign Minister Molotov spoke of German disarmament he meant the payment of reparations as well as the dismantling of the German military capacity. For the Americans, German disarmament and Secretary Byrnes' proposed twenty-five year Four-Power security treaty guaranteeing German demilitarization were entirely separable from the issue of reparations. Molotov's adamant stand on the latter was not only heavy-handed but probably reflected severe pressure on him from within the Soviet bureaucracy. American officials grew increasingly convinced that reparations was part of an overall Soviet master plan to expand into Western Europe by forestalling economic recovery in Germany. Yet Americans were in error when they assumed that reparations and recovery were incompatible. Germany's industrial capacity had expanded during the war, the infrastructure of its economy was largely intact and 80 percent of heavy industry in the British and American zones was functional after the war. It was capable of making transfers to the Soviet Union. Russian leadership, however, must assume a significant responsibility for the reparations debacle.

Historians have described the Soviet policy for transfer of German industrial capacity as a failure in a dual sense. First, it was conducted in a willful, erratic, and poorly coordinated manner reflecting contradictory Russian views on whether to remove factories and equipment on a massive scale from within the Soviet zone or to permit German recovery to progress to the point that reparations might be drawn from current production. Soviet policy makers vacillated between the two alternatives and never chose between them. There was also debate over the question of which agencies of Soviet bureaucracy should administer reparations. Second, reparations ran counter to another important Soviet objective, namely that of preventing the emergence of an independent German state that would be drawn inescapably into the orbit of Western Europe. By putting reparations first, Soviet leaders helped bring about what they feared most, namely the unification of West Germany.

Yet the observer of contemporary history is hardly justified in assigning blame exclusively to Soviet policy makers. Participants in the Moscow meeting of the Council of Foreign Ministers which opened on March 10, 1947, described the conference as marking the end of an era. It came at a time when the United States was shifting from private to public diplomacy. It followed statements by responsible American officials that it was futile to sit down with the Russians to solve outstanding problems. It occurred in the wake of the adoption of the Truman Doctrine and foreshadowed the establishment of the North Atlantic Treaty Organization. It signaled a conscious American retreat from concessions and compromise. The aim of the principal American representatives, George C. Marshall and John Foster Dulles, was to advance the cause of the German and Austrian peace treaties.

The Russians for their part, however, made it clear that reparations was first on the Soviet agenda. In fact, Molotov announced, "The Soviet Government does not conceal the fact that it wants reparations from Germany nor does it conceal the amount which it wants." Soviet leaders recited the now familiar litany of wartime destruction in the Soviet Union comparing it with conditions in the United States. The wholesale removal of industrial plants from the Soviet zone of Germany had not reduced the anguish of overall devastation and famine in regions within Russia such as the Ukraine. Although a few American participants urged "some current reparations to buy economic unity" in Germany, they were overruled and on March 31, General Clay, the principal spokesman for this minority viewpoint, sensing defeat, left Moscow with Secretary Marshall's approval. Those who remained held firm in resisting what Dulles called the Soviet "process of exhaustion." Marshall, who had concluded that Soviet demands were intended to bring about the disintegration of Europe, held one final meeting with Stalin on April 15 and the die was cast.

At that meeting Stalin returned to the central issue for the Russians, reminding Secretary Marshall of the American promise at Yalta of $10 billion in reparations. The Russian people, he observed, had been informed of the promise and now the Americans were taking a different view and were opposing all future reparations. The Soviet Union could not abandon its goal and its leaders argued that the burden for Germany spread over twenty years would not be excessive. As it became clear that agreement was impossible, Stalin described the resulting impasse as not "so tragic." "Differences had occurred before on other questions and as a rule after people had exhausted themselves in dispute they then recognized the necessity of compromise."[9] He urged patience and *Pravda* announced that "the Conference marked the beginning of the solution of the German problem."

The American appraisal of the conference was far less sanguine. Marshall saw in Stalin's words a prophecy that the Soviet Union would await the collapse of Western Europe. Thereafter, America girded itself for the Cold War and Mr. Dulles on returning to the United States explained in a speech at the New York Council on Foreign Relations on April 29, 1947, that "the Soviets have a world plan to overthrow capitalism wherever it may be and to substitute police states." To at least one observer, "the Moscow Council marked for the Americans the final rejection of Franklin Roosevelt's tentatively optimistic approach to postwar Soviet-American relations."[10]

The task of evaluating contending interpretations of Soviet-American relations and their implications for the issue of reparations is complicated yet further by the absence of authoritative documentation on Soviet foreign policy. Whereas the student of the Cold War is weighed down by an abundance of literature on American foreign policy, his judgment of Soviet behavior suffers from the paucity of readily verifiable data. Moreover, historical interpretation, as we have seen, is grounded on the well-established and strongly held views of individual historians. Daniel Yergin's interpretation of the course of the negotiations on the reparations issue is shaped by his standing as a moderate revisionist holding to the view that Roosevelt's successors were lacking in the flexi-

9. Quoted *ibid.*, 300.
10. *Ibid.*, 301.

bility and resourcefulness the president had displayed in dealing with the Russians. Other historians whose thinking parallels for the most part that of orthodox writers are more inclined to appraise "the tragic impasse" of which Stalin spoke as resulting solely from Soviet expansionism and imperialistic aims. It is difficult, faced with the contending ideologies of historians, to reach a final verdict on conflicting interpretations when historical evidence takes second place to the influence of the major schools of thought.

It is less difficult to affirm with confidence that the long delays, the confusion, and the uncertainty over policy on both sides served to make reparations a major stumbling bloc to East-West accord. As early as 1943, State Department planners sought to hammer out the broad outlines of a postwar policy on Germany and in particular the question of compensation for war damages. Soviet ambitions and the Russian style of presenting demands unquestionably contributed to the stiffening of American resistance. The delaying policy of American leaders, including Roosevelt, who postponed political decisions while the military phase of the conflict continued, magnified the difficulties. Perceptions of intentions were faulty both in Moscow and Washington and bureaucratic wrangling increased and heightened the misperceptions. The Americans in all likelihood underestimated the importance the question of reparations had for the Russians and interpreted Germany's needs in the light of Allied mistakes in the period after World War I. Historical parallels are always fraught with risks, and to avoid the economic and political consequences of the too harsh policy for Germany in the period between the wars, American policy makers may have fallen prey to underestimating the seriousness of the Soviet proposals. In any event, the failure to resolve the dispute over reparations almost certainly affected Soviet-American relations and hastened the day when a mere great-power rivalry became the Cold War.

Soviet-American Attitudes and the Cold War

Robert Jervis, in his important study of attitudes and misperceptions in international politics, cites a statement by President Theodore Roosevelt in 1904 that the kaiser "sincerely believes that the English are planning to attack him and smash his fleet, and perhaps join with France in a war to the death against him. As a matter of fact, the English harbour no such intentions, but are themselves in a condition of panic terror [sic] lest the Kaiser secretly intends to form an alliance against them with France or Russia, or both, to destroy their fleet and blot out the British Empire from the map. It is as funny a case as I have ever seen of mutual distrust and fear bringing two peoples to the verge of war." [11] Mutual fear and national insecurity about the intention of rival states have frequently been a more likely cause of conflict than have actual policies. It is part of the basic security-power dilemma that rivalries become overlaid with reinforcing misunderstandings as each side sees in the other not only a potential menace but, because of misperception, an active and diabolical enemy. Then conflict and sometimes war inevitably follow.

George F. Kennan points up the operation of this kind of misperception in the building up of the Cold War. In the eyes of the leaders of the Western Allies, the establishment of NATO was a necessary defensive move taken belatedly as a means of resisting Soviet expansion. Soviet leaders, however, were totally unconvinced that the Western response was basically defensive or related to actual Soviet intentions. In Kennan's words: "The Kremlin leaders were attempting in every possible way to weaken and destroy the non-Communist world. . . . They would not have been surprised if [this] . . . had been made the touchstone of Western reaction. But why, they might ask, were they being accused precisely of the one thing they had *not* done, which was to plan, as yet, to conduct an overt and unprovoked invasion of Western Europe?" [12] The fact that Kennan's warning was ignored and pushed aside in discussions of the creation of NATO demonstrates how difficult it is for statesmen to recognize that their actions may inadvertently appear threatening to others and may lead to a deepening of the crisis.

Attitudes about another country's foreign policy oftentimes mirror the prevailing images within the perceiving country. Because a tiny minority of revolutionary leaders had produced the Russian Revolution in 1917, some Soviet leaders were misled into thinking that all Europe was on the verge of revolution because a handful of social revolutionaries were generating protests within a few Western European states. Lenin's prophecy that communism would spread into Europe through Asia was a reformulation of Marx's prediction concerning revolutionary conditions in Europe and helped influence Soviet policies for national liberation in the Third World. That prophecy assumed that revolutions were more likely in rural societies than they were in the industrial states of

11. Robert Jervis, *Perception and Misperception in International Politics* (Princeton N.J.: Princeton University Press, 1976), 74.
12. Kennan, *Memoirs, 1925–1950*, 336.

Europe. The failures of Soviet policies in Nasser's Egypt and Nkrumah's Ghana, culminating each time with the expulsion of Soviet advisers, are traceable to faulty perceptions of objective circumstances within a Middle Eastern and an African country, however hostile their national leaders may have been to European colonial regimes. In assuming those countries were in a prerevolutionary situation, Soviet leaders erred because they filtered what they observed through a set of their own preconceptions that bore little relationship to conditions actually existing in these countries.

American leaders for their part have exaggerated the prospects for the early triumph of democracy and freedom around the world matching in this way Soviet misperceptions of the Third World. The theologian Reinhold Niebuhr warned in the early years of the Kennedy administration against assuming that the threat of communism in Asia could be equated with that of communism in Europe. For Niebuhr, the former drew its strength from identification with national revolutionary movements whereas the latter appeared as a clear threat to national independence. It would be folly, therefore, to suppose that American policies which had enjoyed a modicum of success in Europe could be transferred wholesale to Asia and Africa. "The sober fact is that the peoples of the world desire national freedom, but have no knowledge of, or desire for, individual freedom except as it has validated itself as a servant of justice and community."[13] Because of American misperceptions, we became the most assiduous propagators of the idea that the whole world wanted our political freedom. Niebuhr wrote in the mid-1960s: "A series of essays on 'the National Purpose' recently published expressed a remarkable compound of both moral pretension and political parochialism, the two weaknesses of the life of a messianic nation."[14] He criticized particularly one essayist's claim that "for all its areas of blighted hope, the world now counts many constitutional democracies as it once counted only the United States."[15] To this claim Niebuhr responded: "Obviously the history of democracy in the world is not adequately portrayed in this lyrical account." To say that democracy was thriving around the world was misleading as the statement of a mature people, but this was not its most damaging feature. Stemming from such a misperception is the

---

13. Reinhold Niebuhr and Alan Heimert, *A Nation So Conceived* (New York: Charles Scribner's Sons, 1965), 150.

14. *Ibid.*

15. John K. Jessup *et al.*, *The National Purpose* (New York: Holt, Rinehart and Winston, 1960), 83.

more profound danger that we may fall prey to the illusion that with
only a slightly increased effort on our part economically and militarily
we can bring primitive agrarian societies into the same stage of development that Western nations have needed centuries to achieve. "We really
ought not to be so sure of the uniqueness of our virtue."[16]

Perception is impaired, moreover, not only by exaggerated concepts
of national virtue and capacity but by leaders who make foreign policy
an exercise in ideological justification. Such leaders portray peoples and
nations as conducting their relations based on the professed superiority
of a particular political system or economic dogma. Interpreters of foreign relations take satisfaction from the explanations of the international behavior of states they have discovered in "communism," "democracy," "imperialism," or "world order." They are comforted by the
simplicity and greater sense of assurance which political doctrine seems
to provide for analyzing and forecasting the course of foreign relations.
Yet for most of international politics, certainty and the self-fulfilling
prophecy of ideologies which realize their ends in practice or explain
away failures as deviations from the norm are remote possibilities. Not
only is reality more complex than ideology but change is the first law of
the political universe. Yesterday's friends become tomorrow's foes and
enemies are transformed into trusted allies reflecting the shifting patterns of power relations and the convergence or divergence of interests.
Within the same political system the balance of forces is unexpectedly
redistributed. Stalin's Russia yields to Khrushchev's Russia and the latter
to the technocrat's Russia. The battleground for foreign-policy decisions
even within monolithic political systems pits "hawks" against "doves,"
militarists against diplomatists, and ideologues against political realists.
No fixed ideology can rid the world of the human equation or the influence of dominant personalities or leaders.

The uncertainties of forecasting another nation's foreign policy are
compounded by the network of intricate and essentially unpredictable
relations that constitute the changing international system. Complexities increase with the number and variety of political actors. For American secretaries of state, a policy for the Cold War has necessitated sound
policy judgments of the intentions and capabilities of the Soviet Union,
but increasingly even the most successful estimates of Soviet intentions
have proven to be inadequate. For secretaries early in the Cold War estimates of Soviet behavior may have sufficed, although it is noteworthy

16. Niebuhr and Heimert, *A Nation So Conceived*, 151, 152.

that before proceeding with the Marshall Plan its founder called on individual European nations to come forward with a detailed plan of their own for European recovery specifying their own needs and interests. For Secretary of State Henry Kissinger, coping with the Soviet Union was, until his final year with Presidents Nixon and Ford, the overriding concern. In 1975 Kissinger was called upon in the Seventh Special Session of the United Nations General Assembly to formulate an overall program for meeting the needs and concerns of the developing countries. By 1976, the requirements of office necessitated that the secretary set out on travels to Latin American and African countries which he had previously neglected. And the maze of competing demands and conflicting perceptions Americans are required to weigh on the world scene has its counterpart within the United States. The foreign policy problem for any secretary of state involves balancing the claims and demands of domestic as well as foreign groups and sooner or later such demands exceed the limits of human imagination and understanding. The perception of and response to claims of friends and foes at home and abroad have proven the Achilles heel of every responsible policy maker. Secretary Marshall, having resisted the spread of communism in Europe, was denounced for the loss by America of China to the Communists. Secretary of State Dean Acheson was pilloried by one group in American politics for being "the Red Dean" ostensibly soft on Communists and by another group for being too intractable and uncompromising in relations with the Soviet Union. Some say this was because he was strongly pro-Soviet during World War II and in the first months after the war and then his attitude changed radically. While this may be true, his critics attacked him primarily because of his support for Alger Hiss, which had a touch of posturing about it, and because it was said he played a part in the loss of China. Secretary Kissinger was condemned for prolonging the war in Vietnam while at the same time suffering attacks from the right wing of his own party for pursuing a policy of detente—a word that a Republican president chose during the 1976 presidential election to remove from the American political vocabulary. As the Cold War became more complex and multifaceted and spread into continents earlier spared the intense rivalry of great-power struggles, the question of mutually incompatible perceptions became an ever more central problem.

Yet the debate over what were to be the controlling perceptions of the Cold War had its origins in the beginnings of the struggle and shaped the course of the conflict. The most responsible American interpreters and critics debated the nature of the threat from the Soviet Union and the means available for responding to the challenge. Another group of writers, including the theologian Reinhold Niebuhr, saw the threat as complex and many sided. Official historians saw it in the rigid goals of communism; Soviet apologists pointed to American policies as the real menace. Writing in 1953, Niebuhr in words reminiscent of statements of orthodox defenders of American policy asked, "What makes Communism so evil and what are the sources of its malignancy?"[17] In his earlier writings, Neibuhr identified the source of the world crisis with the weaknesses of the old liberalism commonly expressed in a false optimism which appeared to embrace the collectivism and catastrophism of Marxism and was full of illusions about the prospects of working with Communists in labor or liberal groups. In a biographical sketch, he wrote: "My first major work, entitled *Moral Man and Immoral Society*, was not uncritically Marxist, but it does reveal a failure to recognize the ultimate similarities . . . between liberal and Marxist utopianism."[18] The utopian illusions of communism made it more dangerous although not more evil than past tyrannies or imperialism. "According to these illusions every policy of Marxist propaganda and class conflict . . . hastens the day of historical climax when an ideal class society will emerge."[19] These misconceptions, in Niebuhr's view, enable Communists to pose as "the liberators of every class or nation which they intend to enslave." For Niebuhr, writing early in the Cold War, communism was more dangerous, therefore, than nazism, which could not have conquered Poland or even China by internal movements. "The fact is that . . . utopianism is the basis of the evil in Communism as well as its greatest danger. It provides a moral facade for the most unscrupulous political policy, giving the Communist oligarch the moral warrant to suppress and sacrifice immediate values in the historical process for the sake of reaching so ideal a goal."[20]

Yet for Niebuhr, change and not Communist utopianism was the first law of Soviet foreign policy. While recognizing the influence of Soviet ideology, he was not prepared to see it as the primary determinant of Soviet policy or the sole touchstone for measuring the Soviet threat. By the late 1950s and 1960s, he came to recognize that the Soviet system,

17. Reinhold Niebuhr, *Christian Realism and Political Problems* (New York: Charles Scribner's Sons, 1953), 33.

18. Charles W. Kegley and Robert W. Bretall (eds.), *Reinhold Niebuhr: His Religious, Social, and Political Thought* (New York: Macmillan, 1956), 8.

19. Niebuhr, *Christian Realism and Political Problems*, 36.

20. *Ibid.*, 37.

despite its ideological fervor and willingness to sacrifice every other value to its utopian purposes, had within it seeds of change which for him made coexistence thinkable. For one thing, the notion that the Soviet goal was the conquest of the world through its ideas and power, if that had indeed been its goal (and even in the early stages of the Cold War, Niebuhr had challenged the too simple view that communism like nazism was bent on world domination), was likely to be overtaken by necessities and events. Niebuhr saw that Western democracies, especially in "the dark continents," confronted the Soviet Union from positions of weakness. The conflict in these areas was not simply a clash between democracy and communism. Where technical civilization, which for Niebuhr was a prerequisite to a political system which functioned through fluid equilibria of power, was beyond the present competence of new societies, tightly controlled political and economic systems such as communism, promising rapid advance, were bound to enjoy certain temporary advantages. Moreover, "high and sometimes extravagant living standards (those of our own nation particularly) will seem vulgar to nations who are anxious to escape the most abject forms of poverty and of injustice prevalent in pre-industrial societies."[21]

Recognizing that the short run has ways of continuing into the long run and that the moral and political hazards of democracy would persist for years and possibly generations to come, Niebuhr nonetheless had faith that democracy was an enduring alternative to tyranny. As early as the 1950s, he predicted:

> But in the long run, the form of government which had its inception in the revolt of western middle classes against the aristocratic and feudal forms of agrarian civilizations can achieve a moral validity beyond the peculiar conditions which gave it birth. It can do this for many reasons but chiefly because it is not under the necessity of proving that the morally ambiguous instruments of social cohesion and social coordination: government, property, and social hierarchy are either in accordance with a cosmic or divine order, as the traditional ideology of government asserted, or are in the process of disappearing on the other side of a revolution, as the revolutionary ideology asserts.[22]

It was not only that Niebuhr believed that the moral and political resources of democracy were superior but that after the promised revolution, the failure of revolutionary Communist regimes to deliver on

21. Reinhold Niebuhr, *The Structure of Nations and Empires* (New York: Charles Scribner's Sons, 1959), 235.
22. *Ibid.*

utopian and Marxist "scientific" promises would diminish their apparent advantages in the Cold War. The processes of history which Marx had claimed were destined to vindicate the Marxist prophecy have in fact led to its refutation—a refutation which would be the more damaging and embarrassing because of its claim to represent a scientific and cosmic design of history.

Looking ahead, there were other factors in Niebuhr's view which made Soviet communism more likely to accept a world of "live and let live" in the future. For one, alternate centers of power were bound to grow up within the Communist world system. He foresaw the possibility of a Sino-Soviet division and he also anticipated internal struggles for power within the Soviet regime. He may have overestimated the prospects for a significant dispersion of power within that regime when he wrote later in the 1950s:

> It is significant that Khrushchev who for the moment seems to have the undisputed dominance in the Soviet hierarchy of power, found it necessary and possible to appeal from the apex of the pyramid of power, the 'presidium,' to the central committee, which supported him against the adverse majority in the presidium. . . . But the fact of his appeal to the central committee and the fact that the Polish leader Gomulka, came to power in Poland against Russian pressure because the Polish central committee gave him the victory over the Stalinists, proves that the central committees of Communist parties may be in a category analogous to the Whig aristocracy in the House of Commons and Lords in the eighteenth century.[23]

Niebuhr's optimism and his perception of the internal relations of Soviet governing elites was qualified elsewhere when he spoke of "the bare possibility" of the extension of freedom throughout the system through rivalries among the various oligarchies and through the augmented power of the Central Committee. There were also limitations to the possibility of change in the rise of technicians and experts within the Soviet Union and the granting to them of privilege and position in exchange for their contributions to significant scientific developments such as guided missiles and earth satellites for the Soviet armory of power. It nevertheless should be acknowledged "that the 'New Class,' which is not exactly identical with the political oligarchies but which has achieved a significant position in the Communist hierarchy, may ultimately provide the leaven for the lump of despotism."[24] It would be uto-

23. *Ibid.*, 263.
24. *Ibid.*, 237.

pian to expect that scientists on a large scale would risk their privileged position by challenging the ideological foundations of the Communist system; Niebuhr did not live to see the full emergence of such scientists as Andrei Sakharov or the physicist Yuri Orlov. What he foresaw, nonetheless, was the release of dynamic factors within the Communist system "which may lead to the same consequences as the dynamic factors in the culture of the West in the seventeenth to the nineteenth century."[25] He forecast a continuing struggle between "the utopians" in the system and "the realists" with the outcome remaining in doubt. Of one thing, however, Niebuhr despite his caution was never in doubt. The survival of mankind depended on which group ultimately prevailed. The utopians in any given situation would sacrifice every competing value, including the value of human survival, to the triumph of the Communist creed; the realists as practical men would more likely live with uncertainty, accept limitations, and seek coexistence in a pluralistic world.

However much a theoretical discussion may appear to depart from an historical review, Niebuhr's perception of the nature of the threat and the prospect for possible relaxation of tension can appropriately be set forth in any discussion of the beginnings of the Cold War. His perspective, as well as those of writers and diplomatists such as Walter Lippman, Hans J. Morgenthau, and George F. Kennan, provides an alternative view of the origins and evolution of the Cold War. For Niebuhr the risks and hazards of the Cold War were no less ominous and terrifying than for statesmen responsible for the early fateful decisions on Cold War policy. The full pathos of the conflict was for him even greater than for defenders of American atomic superiority because of his profound awareness of the possibility of mutual annihilation—a possibility which even certain Russian leaders came to see would mean the end of civilization with no distinction between victor and vanquished or capitalism and communism. He found little comfort in the moral and political prescriptions of the proponents of disarmament. As with Germany and France before World War II, Russia and the United States could not agree because one sought to change and the other to preserve the status quo. The call from men such as Bertrand Russell for rationalism and disinterested science offered little hope, as Niebuhr saw it. Statesmen, however wise or misguided they might be, carried responsibility for their nation's interest which no independent scientist was called on to exercise. Policies of capitulation or unilateral disarmament provided no

25. *Ibid.*

viable answer to the underlying problems of the Cold War. Nations are expected by men such as Lord Russell to sacrifice themselves, but *this* is not the way they have behaved historically. Even Dr. Kissinger's alternative of limited nuclear war enunciated in his early writings obscured the possibility of a limited war's spilling over into total nuclear war once the symbolic and psychological line between limited or conventional and nuclear warfare had been crossed. Thus Niebuhr disposed of the then fashionable and popular approaches to the limitation of conflict at the beginning of the Cold War.

Nevertheless, Niebuhr, representing an alternative view of the conflict, anticipated the prospect of relaxation of tension as historical developments modified antagonisms and changed power relations within and between the great power systems. He placed his faith in history and the erosion of crusading zeal more than in explicit political settlements. Such settlements if they came were more likely to be tacit than explicit. For this there were historical analogies in the decline of monarchical absolutism in Europe and the passing of the era of wars of religion. Niebuhr discovered early signs of a more democratic, less totalitarian regime in Russia stemming from an increase in the power of the Central Committee and the broadening of the scope of educational opportunities. While his views were not ideological in the sense of perceiving the Communist ideological system as a monolithic autonomous force determining foreign policy, Niebuhr gave weight to factors resulting from institutions and ideology. He put stress on the living political system. Two conditions, however, which boded ill for change within Communist states fell under this category: the unquestioning identification of the real with the ideal (only Islam among earlier despotisms made this identification; both Stoic and Christian thought had conceptions of an ideal justice that transcended existing political realities) and the absence in the system of strong sources of power not dependent on state bureaucracy, as with the rising middle classes throughout modern Western history. Nevertheless, Niebuhr's political predictions have been at least partially realized in the sense that it has been shown that "systems built on revolutionary ardor are particularly subject to development as revolutionary enthusiasm abates and the oligarchy acquires a sense of responsibility for the preservation of order and the adjustment of interest." Generational changes were likely to draw out some of the fanaticism and fury from Soviet aims and policies and "reduce the communist system to more or less the same dimensions which are universally manifest

in the traditional communities of history." [26] Although it would not eliminate the peril of war, Niebuhr believed historical change would make
accommodation more likely. And in the last years of his life, he espoused
the belief of a similar process in other Communist or socialist states with
the rise of second- and third-generation revolutionary leaders.

Such a perception, however much historians and policy makers may
debate it, offered a corrective to two prevailing and popular views, the
one that emerging conflicts leading to heightened tension made war
possible if not inevitable and the other that changes in the economic policies of America and of capitalism constituted the only route to the preservation of peace. It is essential in the discussion of successive crises in
the Cold War that alternative conceptual approaches be kept continuously in view and that their application be considered in the resolution
of conflict. We shall return repeatedly in this study to examine the significance and meaning of the differing perceptions of the origins and
development of the Cold War.

Soviet Policies and the Beginnings of the Cold War

Historians identify the first skirmishes in the Cold War as occurring in
the summer of 1945. They can be plotted along a chart of mounting
conflict beginning with the Polish question and ending with the creation
of NATO. More fundamental than any single crisis, as we have seen,
were the consequences of the postwar European balance of power, the
main lines of which were taking form before the Yalta Conference and
were largely fixed by the end of the war. Toward the close of 1944, Eastern Europe lay defenseless before the onslaught of the Russian Army
sweeping across Rumania, Bulgaria, and Hungary. Soviet strategy had
subordinated military to political purposes, holding the advance of Soviet forces to Berlin until substantial parts of the Balkans, of Poland, of
Hungary, and Czechoslovakia had been conquered. The Allies under
General Eisenhower invaded Europe in mid-1944, but after liberating
Rome and Paris their advance was slowed by Germany's last-ditch resistance at its borders and in December in the Ardennes Forest. Only in
March, 1945, a month after the Yalta Conference, had American troops
crossed the Rhine, but by then the fate of Eastern and Central Europe
had been decided. American military leaders had remained preoccu-

26. *Ibid.*, 285, 286.

pied with their triumphs in Western Europe and the Western Pacific. In Greece, Yugoslavia, and Albania, partisan armies under Communist leadership influenced the postwar settlement, but elsewhere in Eastern Europe it was Russian troops, not indigenous Communists—a minority element smaller than the number of Communists in France and Italy combined—who determined the future of Eastern Europe. Only Greece (because of Churchill's temporary spheres-of-influence agreement with Stalin) and parts of Finland (because of American sympathy for that brave little country) remained free of complete Soviet or Communist domination. By the convening of the Yalta Conference in February, 1945, the division of Europe was a fact. The three wartime leaders by then confronted a *de facto* situation which two of them might seek to change but which was an indisputable political reality.

The fate of Poland constituted not only the central issue at Yalta but: "There is a sense in which the Cold War, like World War II, began with flesh-and-blood in Poland."[27] It was, as Churchill saw it, the "most urgent reason for the Yalta Conference,"[28] and its consideration foreshadowed the first of the great postwar crises between East and West leading to the breakdown of the Grand Alliance. An almost continuous debate has been waged by critics and defenders of the conference as to its character and meaning. Controversies surround the three participants and their policies. Historians disagree concerning the full extent of the Soviet grand design for postwar Poland.

As we have seen, Stalin long before the conference had made clear his demands concerning Soviet postwar boundaries, demands that resembled but were not limited to the historic claims of tsarist Russia. Poland, as Stalin reiterated time and again, was not only a matter of honor but of life and death to the Soviet Union. It served as the corridor along which hostile armies moved into Russia for almost a thousand years, twice in the last thirty years with invasions by German troops. Yet it should also be noted that Stalin approached the creation of a satellite regime for postwar Poland with caution and some hesitation. He may have remembered the failures of the Polish satellite regime organized by Moscow in 1920 or the abortive regime imposed on Finland in 1939. He may also have recognized that his actions, however successful, would almost certainly arouse alarm among the Western Allies. He may have perceived that his quest for a friendly Polish government and for har-

27. Louis J. Halle, *The Cold War as History* (New York: Harper & Row, 1967), 65.
28. Winston S. Churchill, *Triumph and Tragedy* (Boston: Houghton Mifflin, 1953), 366, Vol. VI of *The Second World War*.

mony among wartime allies were two incompatible aims. It would seem, according to this portrayal of Stalin's thinking, that he hoped he might reach an agreement with the Polish democratic group in London comparable to the one he had achieved with Finnish leaders which would be acceptable to the Allies.

Such a comparison ignores the fact that the political importance of Poland and Finland are quite different from the Soviet viewpoint. Insofar as Communists in Poland were concerned, Stalin waited until late July, 1944, as Russian troops crossed the Curzon Line into Poland, to establish officially the Committee for National Liberation, to administer occupied Polish territory. (The Curzon Line was the tentative Polish-Soviet border proposed by the Allied Armistice Commission in 1919.) A month later, the committee installed itself in Lublin as the temporary capital of Poland and by the beginning of 1945 it had become the "Provisional Government" of the country. By then it was clear that two governments of Poland existed and, whatever their respective merits, the one within Poland would inevitably enjoy political advantages over the government-in-exile in London. The fact that Moscow gave support to one regime and Whitehall and Washington to the other made inevitable the first major disagreement between East and West and the ushering in of the Cold War. Primarily but not exclusively because of the Polish question, Yalta became a watershed between the era of wartime cooperation and the first sorties of the Cold War.

The Yalta Conference convened February 3, and ended February 11, 1945. (See Chapter I.) Poland was discussed at no fewer than seven of the eight plenary sessions. More time and effort was devoted to and more debate engendered on questions of Poland's future boundaries and government than to any other issue. Stalin defined the Soviet national interest in the most unequivocal terms, narrowing from the outset the possibilities of negotiation on the essentials. Churchill had pointed out that for Britain the question of Poland's future was one of honor. "Honor was the sole reason we had drawn the sword to help Poland," he declared, and Roosevelt, disclaiming any direct national interest in so distant a place, went on to appeal for Soviet magnanimity to help the six or seven million Poles in the United States to save face. A one-sided settlement of Polish boundary questions would alarm American Poles and cause the Polish government exiled in London to "lose face." Churchill joined Roosevelt in this appeal and reminded the Soviets that over 150,000 Poles were fighting valiantly in Italy and on the Western front to defeat the Nazis.

The roots of the conflict went back to the early 1940s. Britain's stake in a Polish-Soviet understanding took form in 1941, following the German invasion of the Soviet Union, although Britain had also made overtures to Russia just before the signing of the Nazi-Soviet Pact in 1939—a pact which contained assurances that the Polish-Soviet boundaries would follow the Curzon Line. At the request of the Soviets, Foreign Secretary Anthony Eden undertook to mediate with General Waldyslaw Sikorski, then premier of the Polish government-in-exile in London. The Russians had called for the reestablishment of an "ethnographic" postwar Poland and the creation of a Polish National Committee and a Polish army in the Soviet Union. The London Poles recited a catalogue of grievances inflicted on Poland in 1939, including the Nazi-Soviet Pact to partition Poland; the Soviet invasion and annexation of Eastern Poland; 200,000 prisoners of war taken and still held by the Russians; and the deportation of 1,000,000 civilians. Before the London Poles would accept an understanding with the Soviets, they demanded the release of all Polish prisoners, recognition by the Soviets of the Polish government-in-exile rather than a national committee, and restoration of the Polish-Soviet boundary to the *status quo ante* existing before World War II.

The persisting boundary dispute between Poland and the Soviets virtually paralyzed discussions of Poland's future throughout most of the war years. The Soviets consistently demanded frontier adjustments which would recognize "ethnic balance," asking in effect for all of Poland east of the Curzon Line including Western Belorussia and the Western Ukraine. The London Poles were adamant in refusing to cede Polish territory in the East, demanding for themselves German territory in the West. The British sought with growing impatience to lead the Poles to consider some reasonable solution of the dispute.

The impasse continued throughout the war years. Long and rancorous negotiations ensued with Soviet envoys pressing for the security of their troops operating against German forces in Polish territory and refusing to recognize prewar boundaries. The most the Russians were prepared to offer was "friendly relations" and an implicit promise based on trust to release the Polish prisoners. Both for the London Poles and the Soviets, however, trust was the missing ingredient. Nevertheless, under strong pressure from Britain, the Poles signed a Mutual Assistance Pact with the Soviets on July 31, 1941, in which the two parties agreed in effect to disagree. Mutual suspicion and distrust on both sides was fed by disputes ranging across such issues as the size and command of the Polish Army in Russia; the protection of lines of communications for the

Red Army by the Poles or lack thereof; alleged espionage by Polish relief administrators serving Polish deportees within the Soviet Union; and the fate of 8,000 Polish Army officers captured in 1939 and still held in prisoner-of-war camps in Russia.

On April 13, 1943, Berlin Broadcasting announced finding in a deep pit near the Katyn Forest the bodies of 10,000 murdered Polish officers, an accusation substantiated in general terms by the research of an American scholar, J. K. Zawodny, in his study *Death in the Forest*. Zawodny found that 15,000 Polish soldiers were murdered in one military operation and 4,443 bodies of Polish officers were discovered in the Katyn area. The question of Soviet guilt was conveniently obscured when the Poles and the Germans at the identical hour called for investigation by the International Red Cross, leading to the charge of Polish-Nazi collaboration by *Pravda*. On April 25, 1943, the Soviet Union broke off relations with the Poles. The following month, the Soviet Union made known that the Union of Polish Patriots, a group of Polish Communist refugees in Russia, had been assigned responsibility for forming a new Polish army on Russian soil, thus foreshadowing Soviet support for the Communist regime in Poland. The Poles continued, despite British threats and arguments, to press their claims in the boundary dispute. At the Teheran Conference in the fall of 1943, Churchill directly and Roosevelt by offering no objections accepted the Curzon Line as the Polish-Soviet frontier.

When the Red Army crossed the old Polish frontier in the East on January 4, 1944, the new Polish premier in London, Stanislaw Mikolajczyk, announced that the Polish underground would cooperate with the Red Army. So deep seated was the distrust that the Soviets interpreted this announcement as an implied threat by the Poles to claim sovereignty over Western Belorussia and the Western Ukraine and probably to disrupt communication lines of the advancing Red Army. Stalin promptly charged that Mikolajczyk's action proved that no grounds existed for cooperating with the Polish government-in-exile. Churchill, anticipating likely Soviet action within Poland, pressed Mikolajczyk to accept the Curzon Line in return for compensation to Poland within Germany up to the Oder River. Otherwise, he maintained the Russians would install their own satellite regime in Poland and the London Poles would lose all chance of a role in the governance of postwar Poland.

When Mikolajczyk visited Roosevelt on June 6, 1944, hoping to enlist his support, the president equivocated, saying that he and Churchill were not agreed on the division of Poland, concealing his agreement at

Teheran to the Curzon Line and raising the hopes of the London Poles by saying he would try to mediate the boundary question at the proper time. (Roosevelt, fearing domestic political consequences, had postponed the Mikolajczyk visit for more than six months.) Mikolajczyk left Washington convinced that the United States would support Poland strongly and in the end successfully, whereas Roosevelt's delaying tactics had been designed primarily to prevent American Poles from making the boundary dispute an issue in the presidential election of 1944. For Roosevelt the crux of the matter involved both considerations of domestic politics and the president's well-known position of delaying all postwar political settlements until the end of the war. With the Red Army driving across Poland, the issue for Churchill was a renewal of Polish-Soviet relations to prevent the displacement of the Polish government-in-exile by the Russians. British policy was direct and explicit, while American policy was one of studied ambiguity. In the end the British, having failed to influence Polish leaders in London, washed their hands of the matter and Churchill and Eden broke off their contacts with Mikolajczyk.

Interpretations of the agreements at Yalta and the diplomacy which preceded them reflect the influence of prevailing schools of thought concerning the Cold War. Orthodox and revisionist writers view the crisis from quite differing perspectives. In judging the Polish crisis, orthodox historians understandably turned to the first three articles of the Atlantic Charter put forward in the statement of common principles by Churchill and Roosevelt in August of 1941, and accepted five months later by the Soviet Union. The articles stated:

> FIRST. Their countries seek no aggrandizement, territorial or other;
> SECOND. They desire to seek no territorial changes that do not accord with the freely expressed wishes of the people concerned;
> THIRD. They respect the right of all peoples to choose the form of government under which they will live; and they wish to see sovereign rights and self-government restored to those who have been forcibly deprived of them.

Measured against the three articles, Soviet policy must be condemned unequivocally. More than once during the war, Roosevelt had expressed his conviction that the charter's principles were binding, but Churchill referred to them as not "a law, but a star." (Stalin for his part was evasive about their relevance.) Because of the charter, Poland before and after Yalta became a symbol for most Americans not only of a violation of a solemn international agreement but of the waning ability of Great Britain, the Soviet Union, and the United States to work together. The government and people of the United States were disturbed because the Soviet Union appeared to be moving unilaterally to establish its own government in Poland without the participation of Britain and the United States. Americans, except for the Polish community, prided themselves on having a detached view on Poland. The United States had no special interests in Poland and was prepared to accept any government which the Polish people desired and which was at the same time friendly to the Soviet Union. However, the Polish citizenry should be given the right through free elections to choose its own government and Poland should be genuinely independent.

This basically was the American position, a position which the Soviet Union as it achieved military successes against the Germans and as it augmented its power became increasingly less willing to accept. In late 1941, Premier Sikorski had met with Stalin, who told the Polish leader he foresaw only minor changes in the Polish-Soviet frontiers, indicating specifically that Russia had no thought of annexing the Polish industrial center of Lwow. Churchill and a few Polish leaders maintained that a political understanding was then possible under which the Polish government-in-exile would return to Poland, but, whatever their private views, neither Sikorski in 1941 nor Mikolajczyk, his successor, were able to persuade their cabinets in London to accept a boundary agreement.

After the Soviet victory at Stalingrad in January, 1943, it was too late for the settlement Sikorski had been promised and Stalin by then was confident of his ability to dictate the terms of postwar territorial arrangements. Roosevelt and Churchill were to learn that when Stalin used adjectives such as "friendly" or "democratic," they meant different things to the Russian than to the democratic leaders. In Arthur Schlesinger, Jr.'s words: "While the West saw the point of Stalin's demand for a 'friendly government' in Warsaw, the American insistence on the sovereign virtues of free elections . . . created an insoluble problem in those countries like Poland (and Rumania) where free elections would almost certainly produce anti-Soviet governments."[29] So long as the threat of a Nazi victory hung over the Soviets, they were forced to conceal their true aims. A question enveloped in historical perplexity is why in 1945 when the tide had turned and Soviet victory was in sight, the Soviet Union should have accepted the Declaration on Liberated Europe

29. Lloyd C. Gardner, Arthur Schlesinger, Jr., and Hans J. Morgenthau, *The Origins of the Cold War* (Waltham, Mass.: Ginn and Company, 1970), 63–64.

and an agreement on Poland pledging that "the three governments will jointly" act to assure "free elections of governments responsive to the will of the people." Professor Schlesinger provides three possible answers: "that the war was not over and the Russians still wanted the Americans to intensify their military effort in the West; that one clause in the Declaration premised action on 'the opinion of three governments' and thus implied a Soviet veto; . . . that the universalist algebra of the Declaration was plainly in Stalin's mind to be construed in terms of the practical arithmetic of his sphere-of-influence agreement with Churchill the previous October."[30]

As the threat of a Nazi victory diminished or disappeared, the Soviet need for cooperation with the Allies on Poland also was reduced. As one orthodox historian perceived events: "The Soviet Union, feeling itself menaced by the American idea of self-determination and the borderlands diplomacy to which it was leading . . . began to fulfill its security requirements unilaterally."[31] Although Roosevelt had urged Stalin to abstain from any major decision on Poland before the Yalta Conference and in particular not to recognize the Lublin group since only a small part of Poland had been liberated, Stalin proceeded on the last day of 1944 to declare it the Provisional Government of Poland. The ideological requirement that the Polish state be friendly and therefore Communist took priority over Allied unity. The Polish question at Yalta became the testing ground between East and West as to whether or not cooperation was still possible. It dominated the discussions of the Big Three and their foreign ministers from the first hours to the close of the conference. It was the one most conspicuous issue at Yalta on which the president and prime minister could not tell what new claims might confront them.

The fate of Poland and the limitations on the course of American action planted seeds of guilt in the United States and led on to McCarthyism. The pendulum in public reactions made its accustomed arc from euphoria to pessimism. "In 1945, the Yalta Conference was hailed as the dawn of a new era of peace and understanding. Five years later, it symbolized, for many people in the United States, the folly of trusting or seeking to reach accommodation with the Soviet Union."[32] *Yalta* became

30. *Ibid.*, 64–65.
31. *Ibid.*, 65.
32. Athan G. Theoharis, *The Yalta Myths* (Columbia, Mo.: University of Missouri Press, 1970), 1.

a code word in American politics standing for what was possible and impossible in relations with the Soviet Union.

Orthodox historians were to assert that major responsibility for the loss of trust rested with the Soviet Union, which showed contempt for the Atlantic Charter, moved unilaterally to attain domination in Poland and throughout Eastern and Central Europe, and failed to honor wartime commitments. Revisionist historians, by contrast, including Athan G. Theoharis, found that criticism of Yalta was based as much on the desire of conservatives to discredit President Roosevelt as on the shortcomings of his policies at Yalta or upon wholly unexpected Soviet actions. "During the 1930s, by assailing New Deal priorities and personnel, economic conservatives had sought directly to stymie the enactment of legislation regulating the banks and the securities industry, providing for minimum wages and social security, and creating the Tennessee Valley Authority, the Rural Electrification Administration, and the National Recovery Administration." [33] Conservatives challenged the president's use of executive power and from 1939 through 1945 leveled similar criticism at his conduct of foreign policy. The questioning of Yalta became intertwined with domestic politics. By concentrating on foreign policy decisions such as the Yalta Conference, conservative critics of the Roosevelt administration broadened their political following and retained the support of that segment of the public who had opposed New Deal principles and policies from the start. The source of the mounting criticisms of the Yalta decisions could be found, therefore, not as much in the agreements themselves as in a hostile political climate within the United States.

Revisionists, because of the politics of Yalta, have undertaken to draw a distinction between the conference itself and the political myths surrounding it. The aim of the Big Three at Yalta was to resolve a set of complex military and political problems. Their goal was to bring the war to an end as rapidly as possible and to avert postwar divisions that might prevent the building of a durable peace. In pursuing these ends, Roosevelt, though the leader of the world's most powerful nation, found himself negotiating from weakness in two respects. First, "the position of Soviet armies in 1945 created natural advantages for the Soviet Union. . . . Second, . . . he did not know whether the congressional leaders, particularly the Republican congressmen and press, would accept his

33. *Ibid.*, 2.

leadership or Yalta's spirit of compromise and concession,"[34] however essential accommodation might be to a lasting peace.

Within Eastern Europe, circumstances favored the Soviet Union and not only because of the power of the Red Army. During the war native Communists had operated within the region under the guise of national resistance leaders. Many had been exiled to the Soviet Union because of the repressive policies of right-wing military governments and had returned as members of so-called 'democratic and anti-fascist forces. "During the 1920's and 1930's, governments of Eastern Europe (Czechoslovakia . . . excepted) had outlawed all opposition parties. This lack of operational political parties having a national political base forestalled automatic use of democratic procedures after liberation."[35] (This statement regarding opposition groups is strongly contested by respected East European scholars in the United States.) Because of the weakness of prewar democratic forces and the strength of the Red Army, the creation of broadly based interim regimes whose election would be supervised and observed by a tripartite commission representing Britain, the Soviet Union, and the United States was the most the Western Allies could expect. Change was inevitable and almost certainly would be radical by comparison with the prewar order.

The revisionist framework for evaluating the negotiations and bargaining at Yalta rested on the proposition that "Stalin went to Yalta with two approaches. . . . One was based on receiving a large loan from the United States. . . . [His] alternative was to obtain, by agreement or by self-exertion, economic reparations from Germany and a strong strategic position in eastern Europe." Roosevelt for his part was limited by conservative opposition at home and Soviet power in Eastern Europe. "America went to Yalta . . . guided by little except a sense of mission to reform the world [and] a growing fear of postwar economic crisis." Roosevelt was not naïve but he "did not understand the nature and workings of a modern complex industrial economy." He failed at Yalta, according to the revisionists, because he misunderstood the one pressure he might have brought to bear on Stalin. "Short of war, economic aid was the one effective tool he had in negotiations with the Soviets. But he never used it." The Soviet Union was amenable in 1945 to some kind of an agreement with America, an agreement which would not have sacrificed Soviet influence in Eastern Europe nor acquiesced in every American pol-

34. *Ibid.*, 11, 12.
35. *Ibid.*, 15.

icy. But as the revisionists saw it, the thesis is false that the Soviet Union emerged from World War II "with a determination to take over eastern Europe and then embark upon a cold war with the United States." Not until 1947 and 1948 were the Soviets persuaded that agreement was impossible and only then did they move "ruthlessly to extend and consolidate . . . control over eastern Europe."[36] It was American policies and responses that led the Soviet Union to expand.

One inconsistency that should be noted in the revisionist view on Eastern Europe is the coupling of a criticism of Roosevelt's not using economic assistance as an instrument with the opposite criticism of President Truman and his advisers, especially Ambassador Harriman, for attempting to exercise economic leverage on the Soviets at a later point in history. What historians such as William A. Williams appear to be saying is that skillful use of economic assistance as a quid pro quo early in the Cold War might have prevented more aggressive Soviet policies. However, the contradiction between their criticisms of Roosevelt and Truman for precisely the opposite reasons remains. Nevertheless, other revisionists appear more aware of the narrow margins within which President Roosevelt worked. His enemies challenged his concessions at Yalta but their criticism originated more from an anti-FDR, anti-New Deal viewpoint than from a realistic consideration of the options open to the U.S. delegation to Yalta—a consideration revisionists such as Theoharis kept in mind as they interpreted his actions.

The Polish Question: Orthodox and Revisionist Views

A more comprehensive judgment concerning the two schools of thought must await our discussion and review of the emerging crises in the Cold War. Two events which occurred before the convening of the Yalta Conference, however, throw some light on the validity of the two approaches as they relate to the Polish question. The first lends credence to the orthodox approach and the second to the revisionist approach. Each deserves attention and study for its own sake before we turn to the conference itself.

On August 1, 1944, the Polish Home Army, made up of anti-Communist forces in Warsaw, launched an attack against German troops. Soviet troops in a powerful drive westward had advanced to the eastern bank of the Vistula River and taken up positions north and south of the

36. Williams, *The Tragedy of American Diplomacy*, 223, 224, 228.

city. The Poles, with food and ammunition to last only a week, faced five of Germany's mightiest divisions. Mikolajczyk, who was in Moscow for meetings with Stalin, and Churchill, recognizing the underground's desperate need of help, appealed to Stalin to aid the Polish revolt. The Soviet leader was evasive, questioning whether a significant uprising was taking place, and would go no further than to say that the Soviets would give some assistance. When the United States asked permission for its Air Force, which was engaged in dropping arms to the Poles, to land behind Russian lines, its request was denied, the Russians making it clear they did not wish to associate themselves with "the adventure in Warsaw." Lacking Russian assistance, the Poles fought on in the streets of Warsaw for sixty-two days, losing 15,000 of their 40,000 troops; German losses were also substantial in the fierce man-to-man struggle. Churchill proposed that American planes be instructed to land without Russian consent but Roosevelt feared a major confrontation with Russia. Churchill, agreeing with the president in words that summed up a classic wartime dilemma, responded that "everyone always has to keep in mind the fortunes of millions of men fighting in a worldwide struggle, and that terrible and even humbling submissions must at times be made to the general aim."[37] After forty-two days of bloody fighting, Russians provided limited artillery and air support and on September 18, after forty-nine days, one flight of American war planes dropping supplies to the underground was allowed to use Russian landing fields. But by then it was too late. Historian William H. McNeill wrote: "It seems clear that Stalin resolved to crush utterly and permanently the organization which the Polish Government in Exile had created within Poland, and he chose to use the situation which had developed in Warsaw as a means toward his end."[38]

To compare, as McNeill does, the events within Poland in August of 1944 and the Athenian attack on Melos as recounted by Thucydides seems not at all inappropriate. All the main elements of tragedy and the march of events with the inevitability of a Greek drama were present in the Warsaw revolt. "Poland's fall, like that of Oedipus, came as a result of the defects of Polish virtues. Courage, pride, stubbornness, and impetuosity became folly and recklessness, and brought dire catastrophe." Stalin demonstrated he was willing to sacrifice Allied unity to his cold-blooded decision to destroy anti-Communist forces in Poland. Roosevelt

37. Churchill, *Triumph and Tragedy*, 141.
38. William H. McNeill, *America, Britain, and Russia: Their Cooperation and Conflict, 1941–1946* (London: Oxford University Press, 1953), 432.

too must bear some responsibility because by obscuring his position in talks with Polish leaders on the boundary question he misled them and may have contributed inadvertently to their folly. Whatever history's judgment of Roosevelt's position may be, it appears indisputable that failure to find a peaceful solution to the Polish question in the first seven months of 1944 was a turning point in East-West relations. The most that the negotiations at Yalta could achieve was a superficial appearance of harmony. "Despite all later efforts to mend the breach . . . the bad blood created in Poland in 1944 proved the beginning of the end. The streets of Warsaw had been sown with dragons' teeth; the world had yet . . . to reap the whole harvest." [39]

The second event which closely followed the first comes under the category of "missed opportunities" as Cold War critics analyze it. As we have seen, Churchill and Eden had sought to persuade Polish leaders to accept the Curzon Line as Poland's postwar boundary. In October, 1944, Churchill traveled to Moscow to review East European problems with Stalin. (Roosevelt was unable to attend because of the 1944 elections.) When the two leaders turned to examine the proposals of the London Poles, Churchill urged that Mikolajczyk be summoned to Moscow. The London Poles were willing to grant one-fifth of the positions in a new Polish government to Communists but refused to accept the Curzon Line. Molotov pointed out that at Teheran Churchill, Stalin, and Roosevelt had accepted that line as the frontier defining Poland's postwar boundaries, an assertion which Ambassador Harriman, who was present, did not immediately deny. Churchill struggled to bring the Polish and Russian views closer together but without success. Mikolajczyk held firm to his view that Poland must emerge from the war undiminished and intact. He warned that the Soviet aim was to take all of Poland and then all of Europe. General Anders, who commanded the Second Polish Corps fighting in Italy, announced that Polish soldiers would not give up "a scrap of Polish territory to the Bolsheviks." As he reported in his own account of the meeting, Mikolajczyk invoked the Atlantic Charter and Poland's sovereign rights as an independent state, provoking Churchill's impassioned response: "How near we got at the beginning of the year! . . . If you had come to an agreement with the Russians at that time, you would not have today those Lublin people. . . . They will build up a rival government and gradually take over authority in Poland." Then he added: "I talked to your General Anders the other day, and he seems to

39. *Ibid.*, 433.

entertain the hope that after the defeat of the Germans the Allies will then beat Russia. This is crazy. You cannot defeat the Russians. I beg of you to settle upon the Curzon Line as a frontier. Suppose you do lose the support of some of the Poles. Think what you will gain in return. You will have a country."[40] It is reported that Churchill then was asked whether he would accept a cession of British territory if Britain were in Poland's situation. He replied: "I certainly would, and be blessed by future generations. There is no other alternative. Poland is threatened with virtual extinction."[41]

If revisionist critics as a group would have difficulty in accepting the harsh and thorough-going realism of Churchill's statement, the group of writers we have called interpreter-critics, such as Lippmann and Kennan, would not. For the principle Churchill was proclaiming was one of national survival and national interest. Would the history of East-West relations after the war have been the same if Churchill's counsel had been heeded? No one can assure that it would not, but it is significant that his dire prophecy was to be realized with utter and devastating tragedy.

All this provides background for a full discussion of negotiations at the Yalta Conference itself and the conflicting interpretations which came into play. At the outset, it is important to ask what the aims and objectives were which the three nations sought to achieve. Stalin had consistently emphasized two overall principles as guides to Soviet policy. First, its army in wartime must be protected and its supply and communications lines maintained as it moved across Poland. Second, Poland must have a government "friendly" to the Soviet Union and one which would assist in safeguarding Soviet security. Stalin had grown impatient with Western urging that such a government must also be democratic, and more than once he stated that he had no direct knowledge as to whether governments within the Western sphere had been democratically elected. A profound difference between Stalin and Churchill on the one hand and Roosevelt on the other arose. Specifically, the former were frank in acknowledging the reality of spheres of influence while the latter was ambivalent, recognizing it for areas such as Latin America and the Far East but opposing it in Eastern Europe, in part because of his "Grand Design" for a universal collective security system.

As corollaries of his two working principles, Stalin opposed first the

40. Stanislaw Mikolajczyk, *The Rape of Poland: Pattern of Soviet Conquest* (New York: Whittlesey House, 1948), 97–98.
41. Jan Ciechanowski, *Defeat in Victory* (Garden City, N.Y.: Doubleday, 1947), 335.

establishment of a non-Communist regime in Poland, which he perceived would be hostile to the Soviet Union; second, the creation of an
East European federation of the type proposed by the London Poles and
by Anthony Eden in October, 1943, at the Moscow Conference. Eden's
proposal, entitled the "Joint Responsibility for Europe," would have
made possible the establishment of a confederation or union of states in
east Central Europe. Molotov's statement on the future of Poland and
the Danubian and Balkan countries and his attack on Eden's proposal
buried all plans for integration in east Central Europe.[42] Stalin feared
such an arrangement might become a new *cordon sanitaire* encircling the
Soviet Union. Third, he resisted any departure from the Curzon Line,
which he recognized as fundamental to the Soviet security system. Looking back, it would be tempting to assume that Stalin's sole aim was the
expansion of Soviet power throughout the world, but Ambassador
Charles E. Bohlen, who served as Roosevelt's interpreter at the Yalta
Conference, later wrote: "The main Bolshevik aim is to protect the Soviet system, above all in Russia and secondarily in satellite countries. The
extension of Communism to other areas is a theoretical and secondary
goal."[43]

The principles underlying Western policy, as Diane Shaver Clemens
has shown in what is perhaps the single most authoritative work on Yalta, were more difficult to formulate. "It was easier to determine what the
Western leaders did *not* want rather than what they did,"[44] a situation
with analogies in the post–World War I period. Neither Churchill nor
Roosevelt could afford, politically, the appearance of unilateral concessions that organized Polish groups within Britain and the United States
could exploit against the Allied governments. Also, as Churchill put it, "a
strong, free, and independent Poland was much more important than
particular territorial boundaries." Churchill's willingness to accept the
Curzon Line as the boundary was an expression of this principle, for
"Poland must be mistress in her own house and captain of her soul. Such
freedom must not cover any hostile design by Poland or any Polish
group, possibly in intrigue with Germany, against Russia." Both Churchill and Roosevelt undertook repeatedly to assure Stalin that the proposed international organization would never tolerate hostile action
against Russia or leave the Soviets to face such a threat alone. This was
the crux of the issue which divided the wartime allies, a clash between

42. *Foreign Relations of the United States*, 1943, Vol. I, pp. 701, 736–37.
43. Bohlen, *Witness to History*, 290.
44. Diane Shaver Clemens, *Yalta* (New York: Oxford University Press, 1970), 176.

two conceptions of security. The Western Allies called on the Soviets to trust an emerging worldwide security system, the embryonic United Nations, for their safety while Stalin continued to place his faith in a security system which in effect constituted a *cordon sanitaire* in reverse. Beyond this, the Western Allies, however impatient they became with the intransigence of the London Poles, remained committed to the liberal nationalists within the London Poles. Early in the Yalta discussions Churchill, having stated that Whitehall recognized the London Poles but in recent months "had not sought their company," also declared that "Mikolajczyk, Romer, and Grabski [three non-Communist Poles favored by the West] were men of good sense and honesty, and with them we had remained in informal but friendly and close relations." Both Churchill and Roosevelt appealed to Stalin for magnanimity in determining the future of these "honest men," magnanimity being a cardinal virtue of politics, as they viewed it. Finally, the Western Allies, however committed to the Poles in exile, recognized that "the three Great Powers would be criticized if they allowed these rival Governments to cause an apparent division between them, when there were such great tasks in hand and they had such hopes in common."[45] Churchill in particular was determined that Allied unity not be destroyed by the dispute over Poland.

Yet Stalin's objectives at Yalta were unequivocal and clear-cut, supported by a favorable distribution of power, while the positions of Churchill and Roosevelt were sometimes in tension, often ill-defined and frequently enigmatic. The immediate military situation was overwhelmingly to Stalin's advantage. The Red Army held most of prewar Poland and "in a series of gigantic offensives in January 1945, it had cut across Poland and into Germany all the way to the Oder River and had spearheads only forty miles from Berlin." Russian troops were eighty miles from Vienna and had penetrated Upper Silesia. "Meanwhile, in the West, the Allies had only just regained the line they had been holding six weeks before when the Rundstedt offensive had begun."[46] Hitler's offensive in the Ardennes (which was premised on the hope of a separate peace with the Western Allies, expressed in his prediction to the German generals that "if we can now deliver a few more heavy blows, then at any moment this artificially-bolstered common front may collapse with a gigantic clap of thunder")[47] had weakened the Western

45. Churchill, *Triumph and Tragedy*, 368.
46. Martin F. Herz, *Beginnings of the Cold War* (New York: McGraw Hill, 1966), 76.
47. Chester Wilmot, *The Struggle for Europe* (New York: Harper & Brothers, 1952), 578.

power position and augmented Stalin's suspicions without in the slightest weakening Western resolve to continue to fight for "unconditional surrender."

On the eve of Yalta the United States, far from facing the Russians from a position of overwhelming power (as some revisionists have maintained was the case), negotiated from a position of weakness. Stalin held almost all the trump cards. "His troops were occupying Poland, his protégés effectively controlled the reins of government in Poland." [48] He had only to wait and, given his Marxist conviction that history was moving irresistably toward the triumph of communism, especially in Eastern Europe, he chose not to raise the issue of Poland at Yalta, leaving Roosevelt or Churchill to make the first move. He sensed that the vital interests of the Western Allies were marginal in Poland as compared with the Soviet Union's and he prepared himself to parry every argument which Roosevelt and Churchill put forward.

On February 6, the second day of the Conference, Roosevelt as chairman raised the question of Poland. "He pleaded rather than argued." [49] He reminded Stalin that at Teheran he had indicated general American support of the Curzon Line as the eastern frontier of Poland, but he noted that it would have a salutary effect in the United States and would ease his position at home if the Soviet Union would make some concession to Poland. He raised the question again as he had at Teheran, of allowing Lwow with its oil deposits to remain in Poland to counterbalance the loss of Königsberg and of ceding East Prussia and part of Germany to Poland as American Poles desired. For Roosevelt, the most important issue was a representative and independent government for Poland. "General opinion in the United States was against recognising the Lublin Government, because it represented only a small section of Poland and of the Polish nation. There was a demand for a Government of national unity, drawn perhaps from the five main political parties." Churchill spoke next and reminded his colleagues that he and the foreign secretary had supported in Parliament the Soviet claim to the establishment of the Curzon Line despite widespread political opposition in Britain. He observed that "after the agonies Russia had suffered in defending herself against the Germans, and her deeds in driving them back and liberating Poland, her claim was founded not on force but on right." He then called on Stalin to make "a gesture of magnanimity to a

48. Clemens, *Yalta*, 177.
49. Herbert Feis, *From Trust to Terror: The Onset of the Cold War, 1945–1950* (New York: W. W. Norton, 1970), 522.

much weaker power, and some territorial concession, such as the President had suggested," but as Stalin himself had proclaimed, the question of a free and independent Poland was a fundamental concern.[50] For this end, Britain had gone to war in 1939 at grave risk to its own survival. (Soviet minutes of the conference questioned whether Britain had in fact sought to implement its promise to help Poland and quoted Churchill's own *Memoirs* in which he acknowleged that Britain and France remained passive while Poland was attacked.)[51] Churchill explained Britain had no material interest in Poland but that "honour was the sole reason why we had drawn the sword to help Poland against Hitler's brutal onslaught."[52]

Stalin responded with great skill and political cunning, acknowledging on behalf of the Soviets the need for Poland to be a strong and independent state. Nevertheless, because of its weakness, it had been the corridor for repeated invasions of Russia. The Soviet Union, moreover, had a right to Lwow, which lay to the east of the Curzon Line. That line had not been invented by the Russians. It had, in fact, been accepted against the will of Russia. It had been framed by Curzon and Clemenceau and by American representatives at a conference in 1919 to which Russia had not been invited. Although Lenin had never accepted this agreement wherein Bialystok had been given to Poland, Stalin had not supported Lenin's position. Now it was proposed that the Russians should accept what Curzon and Clemenceau had already conceded. Stalin appealed to Soviet domestic politics, saying that "when the Ukranians came to Moscow they would say that Stalin and Molotov were less trustworthy defenders of Russia than Curzon and Clemenceau" if he abandoned what the West had earlier conceded to his predecessors.[53] By this argument, Stalin sought to trump Roosevelt's appeal to the views of six million American-Poles.

A more practical political issue which divided the wartime allies came to the fore over the question of establishing a new government in Poland. Roosevelt had urged a presidential council of respected Polish leaders to join in choosing a provisional government and Churchill supported his proposal. Stalin, sensing that negotiations were moving toward the heart of the matter, requested a ten-minute recess. After the

50. Churchill, *Triumph and Tragedy*, 367–68.
51. Soviet Crimea Documents. USSR. "Documents: The Crimea and Potsdam Conference of the Leaders of the Three Great Powers," *International Affairs*, No. 6, p. 107.
52. Churchill, *Triumph and Tragedy*, 368.
53. *Ibid.*, 370.

recess, he put forth the Soviet position in the strongest and most uncompromising terms, directed to the arguments of his colleagues. The question of Poland, he repeated, was not only a matter of honor to the Soviet Union but a matter of life and death. Poland's independence and security required internal stability and order in Poland not only to protect the rear of the advancing Soviet army but to guarantee Poland's security from external threat. He managed to turn the tables on the democratic leaders by admonishing Churchill, whom he addressed as his principal adversary, saying: "Hopefully the Prime Minister has only engaged in a slip of the tongue by proposing the establishment of a Polish government." He as a dictator could not conceive of dictating to the Poles without prior consultation as to what type of government they wished to create. He hammered away at the weakest point in the Western position, saying that the London Poles had forfeited their right to form a government by refusing to consider the Curzon Line and refusing to negotiate with the Lublin Poles. Further, they constituted an intolerable threat to the security of the Red Army, as the London Poles were engaged in forming forces of internal resistance which had already killed 212 Russian army officers. Only the Lublin government had cooperated with the Russians.

Roosevelt responded promptly to Stalin's clever appeal to democratic procedures and proposed in a letter for consideration by the fourth plenary session that a group of Polish leaders, two from the Lublin government and two from a list to be presented to Stalin, be invited to Moscow to undertake the creation of a provisional government. Stalin was once more evasive and told of having tried unsuccessfully to contact the Lublin leaders, though "it seems likely that the Soviet delegation placed no telephone calls and made no effort to reach either the Lublin Poles or . . . any other persons whose presence Roosevelt requested."[54] In the past, the Soviets had always been successful in contacting the Lublin leaders for earlier visits of Western leaders. To sidetrack this issue Stalin offered as a *quid pro quo* his acceptance of the American voting formula for the United Nations, which restricted use of the veto to substantive matters and limited individual membership to two or three separate republics of the Soviet Union rather than all Soviet republics. In exchange, a draft written by Molotov proposed: adoption of the Curzon Line as Poland's eastern frontier with adjustments in some areas of up to five to eight kilometers in favor of Poland; Poland's western frontier to run

54. Clemens, *Yalta*, 188.

from Stettin in the north southward along the Oder and western Neisse Rivers; the addition to the provisional Polish government of some democratic leaders from Polish émigré circles; recognition of the enlarged provisional government by the Allied governments with that enlarged government to conduct elections as soon as possible; and Molotov, Ambassador Harriman, and Sir A. Clark Kerr (British ambassador to Moscow) to have responsibility for discussing formation of the enlarged government. Roosevelt objected to the word *émigré*, suggesting that Polish leaders be sought within Poland as well, and Churchill joined the president in expressing dislike of the term *émigré*, arguing that, as it derived from the French aristocracy driven out by the French Revolution, it properly applied only to those who had been driven from their country by their own people. "Poles abroad" would be a more fitting term. With respect to Poland's western frontier, Churchill observed: "It would be a great pity to stuff the Polish goose so full of German food that it died of indigestion." If Poland absorbed East Prussia and Silesia, it would mean moving six million Germans back to Germany. Stalin responded that most of the Germans had already fled. Churchill concluded, "I was not afraid of . . . transferring populations, so long as it was proportionate to what the Poles could manage and to what could be put into Germany."[55] George Kennan was to argue later that a Poland whose boundaries had moved significantly west would be dependent on Russia. Such a plan required study; it was not merely a matter of principle but of numbers and geopolitics. By implication, Churchill and Kennan were saying that Stalin had undertaken to create a Poland which depended on Russia for its survival.

On February 8 at the fifth plenary session, the British and Americans rejected the Molotov draft and returned to the concept of a *new* Polish government. Roosevelt proposed that the three ambassadors select a three-member presidential council representing the Lublin group as well as democratic forces within Poland and abroad. Once chosen, the council's main task would be the formation of a provisional government which would hold elections for a constituent assembly that in turn would elect a permanent Polish government. The Soviets opposed the proposal, arguing that a national council already existed and the creation of a presidential council would merely establish two competing governments. Churchill warned that Allied unity was jeopardized by the Soviet position, but Roosevelt temporized by saying that the participants were

55. Churchill, *Triumph and Tragedy*, 374.

in accord on the need for elections; their only differences stemmed from differences on the details of an interim government. Stalin challenged Churchill, bluntly asserting the Red Army was in Poland and had revolutionized Polish thinking. A democratic government which had earned the right to represent its people by remaining in Poland throughout the war years already existed and was in power. Roosevelt asked when general elections could be held and Stalin guessed in about a month.

Stalin in a moment of candor asked why more was being demanded of Poland than of France. He observed that the Soviets had recognized de Gaulle even though he had not been elected. Why was one standard applied in the West's sphere of influence and another demanded in the Soviet sphere? The exchange between the three leaders on spheres of influence was particularly revealing, however much they differed in public. When discussing this means of maintaining world order, Roosevelt and Hull had made public speeches in the United States proclaiming that the new world organization would eliminate the need for spheres of influence. In private, however, Roosevelt spoke of the difficulty of the American secretary of state's meeting with the British and Soviet foreign ministers because "my Foreign Secretary has all South America to take care of." The British were also reminded that the Soviets had no thought of intervening in Greece or Yugoslavia, both of which fell within the British sphere. Stalin's question should have left no doubt that the Soviet policy for Poland was based on the premise of spheres of influence.

On February 9, the Americans dropped the idea of a presidential council, exchanging it for the prospect of elections to take place in a month. What Roosevelt appeared to say was that a democratic government was the most important factor—not its being represented by a new government or the present government in Poland. The British objected in part because of pressures on Churchill from his own government but found themselves alone, with the Americans and Soviets united in a desire to drop the question of which Polish government called for elections. Molotov, who alternated with Stalin in speaking for the Soviets, added substitute language for an American proposal drafted by Edward Stettinius. He wanted the words *non-Fascist* and *anti-Fascist* to precede all references to democratic parties in Poland that had the right to participate in elections. He also urged deletion of any reference to the fact that the three ambassadors in Warsaw should observe the Polish elections, saying this was superfluous and would offend the Poles.

The conference recessed to allow the Americans and the British to consult. When discussions resumed, Roosevelt observed they were close to an agreement and what divided them was "only a matter of words." Both Roosevelt and Churchill challenged the Soviet rejection of observers, Roosevelt because of the reactions of American Poles and Churchill because the British without observers would have to obtain their information on Poland from underground and intelligence sources. Stalin quoted the Declaration on Liberated Europe, which had explicitly called on the Allies to eradicate fascism as the basis of democratic regimes.

In subsequent discussions, the British sought unsuccessfully to require that an elected government should be "fully representative" of the Polish people. The final text substituted "anti-Nazi" parties for "anti-Fascist" ones and provided that the Lublin government was to be reorganized rather than a new government created. The principles that Churchill and Roosevelt had pressed so determinedly were largely ignored in the final text. Being unable to agree on a clear-cut statement, the negotiators in effect settled for what diplomatists have historically called a "diplomatic formula"—a statement to which the embattled parties were enabled to give different interpretations to satisfy their own interests. The question of the role of ambassadors' observing the election remained unresolved because the Soviets argued that the conduct of the elections must be left to the Poles, although Molotov in the same breath rejected Stettinius' proposal for a written guarantee that the Poles be given authority to decide their own elections. The Americans finally agreed to a statement that *in effect* the ambassadors should be enabled to observe and report on the elections, but the crafty Stalin argued as soon as the Western Allies recognized the Lublin government, the problem would solve itself. Stalin coupled the use of a vague oral promise on the right of observation with a corollary that this would depend on recognition of the present Polish government.

The British, at the plenary session on February 10, raised the issue of frontiers, saying that whereas there was agreement on Poland's eastern frontier, the parties differed on whether Poland should be given German territory to the Oder River or as far as the Neisse River, as the Soviets had proposed. Roosevelt was alone in opposing the inclusion of a statement on frontiers in the agreements, explaining that he had no authority to agree to a Polish territorial settlement. Under the American Constitution, approval of such an agreement was a matter for the U.S. Senate. Churchill and Stalin joined in urging an immediate settlement but differed on the lines of demarcation. Roosevelt, knowing of the pressures on Churchill, particularly of his war cabinet, which had cabled that the prime minister was conceding too much, then went along with the insertion of a final paragraph in the agreement stating that "the three Heads of Government [as differentiated from the three governments which Roosevelt could not accept] consider that the Eastern frontier of Poland should follow the Curzon Line with digressions from it in some regions of five to eight kilometers in favor of Poland." To meet Churchill's objection to the Soviet demand for a western frontier on the Neisse River, the next sentence read, "It is recognized that Poland must receive substantial accessions of territory in the North and the South." Stalin accepted this wording because through it he gained the objective he had pursued since 1941, a written commitment to the Curzon Line as part of Poland's eastern boundary. No country gained everything it had proposed, but Churchill described the assurances concerning free elections and the agreement as a whole as "the best I could get." The final documents and official communiqués were signed on February 11.

In looking back on the Yalta Conference it is difficult to escape the conclusion that America and Britain undertook to make the best of a bad situation and did so without conspicuous success. Yet the agreements and provisions affecting Poland were heralded by some Western leaders as the dawn of a new day. Roosevelt clearly "shared with Churchill and Stalin, at the close, not only satisfaction over work done but also a kindled sense of common purpose and personal attachment."[56] Other wartime conferences had resulted in official statements and declarations; Yalta went beyond this to hard decisions. "The mood of the American delegates, including Roosevelt and Hopkins, could be described as one of supreme exaltation as they left Yalta."[57] No sooner had the president come aboard the *Quincy* on Great Bitter Lake (so ominously and prophetically named) than he received a flood of cables reflecting the enthusiastic response of Americans to the Yalta communiqués. One quoted former president Herbert Hoover, who said: "It will offer a great hope to the world." William L. Shirer called it "a landmark in human history." Senator Alben Barkley cabled: "I regard it as one of the most important steps ever taken to promote peace and happiness in the world." Harry Hopkins later told Robert Sherwood: "The Russians had proved that they could be reasonable and farseeing and there wasn't any doubt in the minds of the President or any of us that we could live with them and get along with them peacefully for as far into the fu-

56. Feis, *From Trust to Terror*, 557.
57. Sherwood, *Roosevelt and Hopkins*, 869.

ture as any of us could imagine."[58] Roosevelt on his return delivered a speech to the Congress in which he declared that Yalta spelled the end of unilateral action, exclusive alliances, spheres of influence, power blocs, and "all other expedients that had been tried for centuries—and have always failed."

Churchill left the conference more unhappy than either Roosevelt or Stalin. His grasp of the realities of power had made him more cautious about the hoped-for attainment of Anglo-American purposes. He may have looked back to certain vital issues on which he had made concessions not only to Stalin but to Roosevelt, no doubt because of his sense of Britain's declining influence in the world. Yet on February 27, 1945, he asked the House of Commons to approve the results of the Crimea Conference, asserting that it "leaves the Allies more closely united than before, both in the military and in the political sphere." The impression he brought back was that "Marshal Stalin and the Soviet leaders wish to live in honourable friendship and equality with the Western democracies. I feel also that their word is their bond." He testified that he knew of no government "which stands to its obligations, even in its own despite, more solidly than the Russian Soviet Government."[59] A colleague, Sir Alexander Cadogan, went even farther, writing on the last day of the conference: "I have never known the Russians so easy and accommodating. In particular Joe has been extremely good. He *is* a great man, and shows up impressively against the background of the other two aging statesmen."[60]

It is of course possible to explain the prevailing euphoria of early statements by Western leaders as designed primarily to gain popular support for the Yalta agreements. Both Churchill and Roosevelt were determined to win legislative support for proposals that were bound to generate political controversy. However, any responsible historian must acknowledge that the Yalta solutions did not wear well. In retrospect, it is fair to ask whether the defense by one of the prime minister's Conservative party colleagues was not closer to the mark than the political rhetoric of the two great leaders. On February 28, 1945, Captain Peter Thorneycroft in a speech in the House of Commons declared: "I do not regard the Polish settlement as an act of justice. It may be right or wrong, it may be wise or foolish, but at any rate it is not justice as I understand the term. It is not the sort of situation in which you get two

58. Quoted *ibid.*, 870.
59. Churchill, *Triumph and Tragedy*, 400–401.
60. Yergin, *The Shattered Peace*, 65.

parties to a dispute putting their case forward in front of a disinterested body and in which the strength and power of one of the parties is never allowed to weigh in the balance."

Privately, Churchill asked: "What would have happened if we had quarrelled with Russia while the Germans still had three or four hundred divisions on the fighting front?" From this standpoint it was necessity, not justice, that led to the Yalta settlement. Soviet power and the need for unity in the struggle were the determinants. Those who chart the course of states "have to take definite decisions from day to day . . . [and] adopt postures which must be solidly maintained." Germany was the threat at Yalta. Once the mighty German armies had been turned back, it was easy "to condemn those who did their best to hearten the Russian military effort and to keep in harmonious contact." Churchill acknowledged "Our hopeful assumptions were soon to be falsified . . . [but] they were the only ones possible at the time."[61]

Following Yalta, the Soviets soon made clear their intentions. They did nothing about broadening the Lublin government. Not one of the Poles whom the Western Allies had mentioned within or outside Poland was invited to take part in forming the future government of Poland. When Western ambassadors in Moscow asked Molotov about sending observers to Poland, he dismissed the question, arguing that the independence and prestige of the provisional government must be respected. On February 27, 1945, the Soviets called on King Michael of Rumania to dismiss the all-party government which had expelled the Germans and on March 2, a Soviet-designated government was installed in Rumania in the shadow of Soviet troops and tanks.

The spirit of Yalta was disappearing and Britain and America were again divided on the tactics to use in protesting Soviet actions. Churchill wanted to denounce in the strongest terms the Soviet breach of the Yalta agreements. He asked Roosevelt's approval for the sending of a long and carefully detailed statement expressing his concerns. Delay would only assure the liquidation of all Polish groups not acceptable to the Soviets. Roosevelt preferred, however, that the American and British ambassadors in Moscow make these concerns known directly to Molotov and only then, when diplomatic remedies had been exhausted, should a protest be sent to Stalin. Roosevelt considered that a personal message sent prematurely would give Stalin an excuse for repeating his charge that the underground forces of the London Poles were conducting ter-

61. Churchill, *Triumph and Tragedy*, 400–401.

rorist actions against the Red Army and the Lublin Poles. Roosevelt also feared that only the latter were actively engaged in much-needed land reforms. Churchill deferred to the president and did not send his message to Stalin but expressed apprehension that Roosevelt's instructions to the American ambassador calling for a political truce between the Polish parties would merely enable the Soviets to claim that the truce was being broken by anti-Lublin Poles.

In a telegram to the president on March 13, 1945, Churchill declared in one of his strongest appeals: "Poland has lost her frontier. Is she now to lose her freedom?" He warned of an impending political conflict in Britain and feared he might be forced to announce in the Parliament that Britain and the United States disagreed. He also declared: "The moment that Molotov sees that he has beaten us away from the whole process of consultations among Poles to form a new Government, he will know that we will put up with anything." [62] Churchill believed that "dogged persistence and pressure" in defending the Allied views and a personal message to Stalin had the best chance of success.

Because of Roosevelt's declining health, State Department officials apparently had taken over responsibility for communications with Churchill. Roosevelt dispatched a stiff rejection of Churchill's statement about the differences which had arisen and the prime minister in replying agreed that their differences were primarily in the realm of tactics. The impasse in consultations of the ambassadors in Moscow worsened when the Soviets proposed that the Poles should be represented at the San Francisco Conference on the United Nations only by the Lublin government. When the Western Allies opposed this proposal, the Russians refused to send Molotov to San Francisco, thus threatening the effectiveness of the conference. On other matters, Molotov answered "nyet" to every suggestion of the Western Allies advanced in Moscow, insisting that the Soviets had agreed only to add a few other Poles to the Russian-dominated regime and claiming the right to veto any Pole the West suggested and refusing to discuss the list of names of non-Communist Poles for lack of information.

On March 27, 1945, Churchill, in another message to Roosevelt, returned to the question of communicating directly with Stalin. The president replied that he agreed and on March 29, he sent a full statement to Stalin outlining his concern over the discouraging lack of progress on

62. *Ibid.*, 426.

Poland. He mentioned particularly the obstacles placed in the way of the Commission of Ambassadors meeting in Moscow, the Soviet tendency to assume a new Polish government would be little more than a continuation of the Lublin regime, and the unwillingness of the Soviets to invite other Poles to Moscow for consultation with the commission. On all these issues and on the question of visits and observation of the situation in Poland by American and British members of the commission, he maintained that the Soviets had departed from the spirit of the Yalta agreements. Stalin replied after a week's delay, blaming the American and British ambassadors in Moscow for bringing "the Polish affair into a 'blind alley.'" Whereas, the Allies had agreed at Yalta on the reconstruction of the Lublin government, the Western envoys were now seeking to abolish it and establish a totally new government. At Yalta, the agreement had been to consult five Poles from Warsaw and about three from London. The ambassadors were now asking for an unlimited number from both capitals. Only the commission as a whole had the right to choose those it wished to invite and the criteria of choice had to be Poles who accepted the Yalta agreements and the Curzon Line and desired friendly relations with the U.S.S.R. The only trace of a concession in Stalin's reply was in his assurance offered to Churchill that he would use his influence with the provisional Polish government to make it withdraw its opposition to an invitation to Mikolajczyk provided he accepted the decisions of the Crimea Conference. On April 11, Roosevelt cabled Churchill: "We shall have to consider most carefully the implications of Stalin's attitude and what is to be our next step." On April 12, President Roosevelt died suddenly at age sixty-three at Warm Springs, Georgia.

At Roosevelt's death, no tribute to the fallen American statesman matched Churchill's who said of him, "His love of his own country, his respect for its constitution, his power of gauging the tides and currents of its mobile public opinion, were always evident, but added to these were the beatings of that generous heart which was always stirred to anger and to action by spectacles of aggression and oppression by the strong against the weak."[63] However, the peace for which he had given his life faced an uncertain future. A growing concern appeared in his last telegram, sent a few hours before his death on April 12, to Churchill containing two competing thoughts. "I would," he said, "minimize the general Soviet problem as much as possible, because these problems, in

63. *Ibid.*, 474.

one form or another, seem to arise every day, and most of them straighten out." Then he added: "We must be firm, however, and our course thus far is correct."

Without attempting to resolve the cruel dilemmas which surrounded wartime and early postwar discussions of Poland, the observer seeking understanding can find at least four distinct interpretations of Yalta and its aftermath. In bringing our own discussion of the Polish issue to a close, we shall review the main conclusions derived from each interpretation.

The first rested on the weakest intellectual foundations of the four. It was largely political and reflected deep-seated antagonism toward Roosevelt and the New Deal. It sought to build political capital from the reactions of Polish-American congressmen such as Alvin O'Konski and Thaddeus Wasielewski of Wisconsin and the Polish-American Congress, which condemned the Curzon Line as the fifth partition of Poland. In 1945, the only Yalta agreement the Republicans criticized in the National Republican Club Bulletin of March 27 was the boundary decision. On February 26, 1945, Congressman William Barry of New York had introduced House Concurrent Resolution 31, which was referred to the House Foreign Affairs Committee but not reported out of committee to the Congress. The resolution urged congressional disapproval of the Curzon Line decision without demanding repudiation of the agreement or questioning the president's use of his constitutional authority. Other more extreme congressional voices, however, including Lawrence Smith of Wisconsin, Clare Hoffman and Paul Shafer of Michigan, Clare Boothe Luce of Connecticut, William Cole of Missouri, and Daniel Reed of New York, attacked the agreements reached at the Yalta Conference as a sellout to the Soviet Union and proof of Roosevelt's penchant for secrecy and his sinister imperial ambitions. Writers for the *Chicago Tribune* and columnists such as George Sokolsky and David Lawrence joined in the criticism denouncing Roosevelt's abuse of presidential authority and his pro-Soviet leanings, evidenced more strongly as time went on by reports of the role he was allowing Alger Hiss to play at Yalta. Although some of the criticism centered on Roosevelt's concessions to power politics and his abandonment of the Atlantic Charter, it is significant that critics also called for a reappraisal of the commitment he was making to the proposed United Nations. It is difficult to escape the conclusion that the motivating force of this opposition was a smoldering distrust of Roosevelt and the New Deal.

A little group of former American officials, including William C.

Bullitt and General Patrick J. Hurley, also condemned the president's actions, but their criticism was more ideological than political, as evidenced by Bullitt's comment: "The weary President [at Yalta] was on the verge of thrombosis . . . and, in a moment of weakness . . . made the agreement to recognize in the future a government of Poland satisfactory to the Soviet Government."[64] General Hurley charged that "your diplomats and mine surrendered in secret every principle for which we said we were fighting. They talk about Stalin breaking his agreements. . . . He never had one to break. We cowardly surrendered to him everything . . . and we did it in secret. President Roosevelt was already a sick man at Yalta."[65] With the rise of McCarthyism in the 1950s, the political attacks on Yalta were to intensify and criticism of Roosevelt's betrayal of Poland was coupled with condemnation of "the loss of China."

The second view of Yalta was inspired by a largely ideological interpretation of the Cold War. Compared with the political attacks on Roosevelt and the New Deal, the orthodox interpretation of the Yalta agreements constituted a defense of his policies and proceeded from an opposing set of assumptions. According to this view, the president had no illusions about the dangers and difficulties of dealing with the Soviet Union. He understood the nature of Soviet society and the threat it posed to freedom. However, he believed that the Soviets might change and in any event he was convinced that peace must be given a chance. He and some of his closest associates, as well as the so-called official school of historiography which tried to explain their actions, felt that Western leaders had no alternative. They wanted to work with rather than against the Soviet Union, believing that the Soviets must discover it was in their self-interest to seek international cooperation. (The underlying principle of this philosophy was rooted in the premise that Russia should not be pictured as an outsider, beyond the pale of political ethics and world politics, for men and nations often come to act as they perceive others expect them to act.) High-level diplomatic contact (particularly given Stalin's propensity to reserve all important decisions for himself) might serve as one method for dispelling mutual suspicions. When the Russians referred to the atmosphere of Yalta as "Roosevelt weather," they recognized the president's unceasing efforts at personal under-

64. William C. Bullitt, *The Great Globe Itself* (New York: Charles Scribner's Sons, 1946), 24.
65. Hearings before the Committee on Armed Services and the Committee on Foreign Relations, U.S. Senate, to Conduct an Inquiry into the Military Situation in the Far East and the Facts Surrounding the Relief of General of the Army Douglas MacArthur from His Assignment in that Area [June, 1951], 2839.

standing among the Big Three: when historians today write of the "Yalta axioms," they have reference to his unceasing efforts to build a climate of trust and personal relationships. Men who later were to emerge as the principal American spokesmen for resistance to Soviet expansion at the time shared much of Roosevelt's hope and optimism. Thus John Foster Dulles on February 27, 1945, characterized Yalta as "a new era" in Soviet-American relations because "the United States abandoned a form of aloofness which it has been practicing for many years and the Soviet Union permitted joint action on matters that it had the power to settle for itself."

But what if the worst rather than the most desired eventuality came to pass? What if it proved impossible to work with the Russians? What if Bullitt not Roosevelt were to be proven right? On this Roosevelt and his most trusted lieutenants were never in doubt. If the Western nations, war-weary and weighed down by the bitter sacrifices of war, were called on once again to assume the heavy burdens of resisting Soviet expansion and keeping the peace, they would need to know that every effort had been made to determine Soviet intentions and good faith. "Until agreements were made and tested, the world could not clearly know of the difficulties of securing Russian compliance with agreements. The Western nations could not follow their . . . [Cold War] policy toward the Soviet Union unless they had behind them the record of President Roosevelt and Prime Minister Churchill in their joint effort to deal with the Russian leaders in an honest and honorable manner at Yalta."[66] Containing Soviet expansionism presupposed that an honest effort at cooperation had been undertaken and had failed.

Opposed to the orthodox interpretation of the Cold War is that of a third viewpoint, the revisionist school. According to one of revisionism's major tenets, the breach over Yalta between East and West occurred because: "Within a few months after the Conference, the United States attempted to undo those agreements at Yalta which reflected Soviet interests." In effect, following Yalta, the Western allies sought to renegotiate the Polish agreements. "The United States camouflaged its demands by accusing the Soviet Union of breaking the Yalta agreements, while, in fact, attempting to make new agreements superseding Yalta."[67] The British in particular had recognized the limitations of the understandings on Poland. At the end of the conference, Churchill spoke of the

66. Edward R. Stettinius, Jr., in Walter Johnson (ed.), *Roosevelt and the Russians: The Yalta Conference* (Garden City, N.Y.: Doubleday, 1949), 324.
67. Clemens, *Yalta*, 268, 269.

final comuniqué as "this bloody thing" and disposed of the entire conference by saying in a moment of unconcealed depression: "Anyway, that's done with and out of the way."[68]

One revisionist has written: "The 'betrayal of Yalta' . . . was really a deflation of the illusions cultivated, not in the results obtained." Because the Western Allies left important issues subject to future clarification and agreement, they assured themselves "immediate agreement and subsequent dispute." Roosevelt at Yalta did not openly challenge Soviet domination in east Central Europe:

> After interminable haggling . . . the Allies produced an agreement on Poland vague enough to leave the impression of formal unity where in fact there was none. Each Ally read into it what he chose. . . . The Russians unequivocally stated that they would regard the Lublin government as the basis for any modest alterations in the existing administration, the Americans said they would prefer a government *de novo*. It was precisely this point, and not the even vaguer question of free elections or borders, that was to plague the commission authorized to meet in Moscow to consider the implementation of the Yalta decision.[69]

When the commission did meet on February 23, 1945, each side sought to interpret the Yalta agreements to serve its own interests. The Soviets insisted no outside Pole could be invited to Moscow without concurrence of the Warsaw Poles; Ambassadors Harriman and Kerr maintained that the Lublin group was to be a part, but not the core, of the new Polish government. A deadlock occurred within the commission and Molotov, who had at first invited the two allies to send observers to Poland, withdrew the offer. The Soviets, recognizing the need to broaden the provisional government, made an independent but unsuccessful approach, without American or British sanction, to Mikolajczyk and some of his followers in London to join the Warsaw government. The Soviets "tolerated profound factions within the Communist party in Poland . . . and did not challenge the Catholic Church . . . [exempting] its estates from redistribution; land that the government divided it gave to small holders rather than collectives, thereby winning powerful new supporters for the regime."[70]

As Churchill had feared and Stalin had anticipated, time was work-

68. Lord Charles Moran, *Churchill: Taken from the Diaries of Lord Moran* (Boston: Houghton Mifflin, 1966), 248–50.
69. Gabriel Kolko, *The Politics of War: The World and United States Foreign Policy, 1943–1945* (New York: Random House, 1968), 368, 390.
70. *Ibid.*, 391.

ing to the advantage of the Soviets and the Warsaw government. British and American intelligence reports did not exclude the possibility of radical changes given impetus by the liquidation or exiling of the prewar officer class and the elimination of the Jewish commercial class by the Nazis. As respected a figure in the American leadership elite as John J. McCloy was to declare at the end of April: "There is complete economic, social and political collapse going on in Central Europe, the extent of which is unparalleled in history unless one goes back to the collapse of the Roman Empire. . . . In this atmosphere of disturbance and collapse, atrocities and disarrangement, we are going to have to work out a practical relation with the Russians." The presence of the Red Army gave powerful incentives to opportunists to join with the more radical groups, and "in the bitter, hard environment of deprivation, wartime membership in the Communist party was a considerable asset in obtaining jobs, housing, and food." Revisionists contend that prewar militant socialists sought a united front with the Communist party, itself split between "a genuinely nationalist wing" under Wladyslaw Gomulka and a "slavishly pro-Moscow wing" under Boleslaw Bierut. The Polish people did not consider the Communist party a Russian puppet and all parties favored long-overdue social and economic change. "Even the bitterly anti-Russian underground advocated far-reaching nationalization of industry, land reform, and social welfare. It seems unlikely . . . that many Poles would have welcomed the success of the Anglo-American aims for Poland."[71]

Stalin, seen from the revisionist perspective, had been willing to make concessions to the Western Allies. He sensed that Poland had become the single most important cause of tension between himself and the West. He therefore agreed to invite five Polish leaders from Poland and three from London to meet with the commission in Moscow. He informed Churchill of his willingness to urge Mikolajczyk's participation on the Warsaw Poles provided he accepted the Curzon Line. When Eden and Churchill once more pressed the Polish leader on the boundary question, he first ignored their specific request for taking a stand but later issued a circuitous acceptance of the Curzon Line as the fiat of the Great Powers but added that he would have preferred that the Lwow Province be retained as part of Poland.

Revisionists, while recognizing that the deterioration in East-West

71. Harry S Truman, *Memoirs: Years of Decision* (Garden City, N.Y.: Doubleday, 1955), I, 101, 392.

relations after Yalta began while Roosevelt was still alive, have held his successor and President Truman's immediate advisers primarily responsible for the Cold War. "Roosevelt's successor was less sympathetic to Russian aspirations and more responsive to those of Roosevelt's advisers . . . who had urged that he resist Soviet efforts in Eastern Europe." Harry Truman on entering the White House "did not seek to follow Roosevelt's tactics of adjustment and accommodation."[72] Eleven days after coming to office, he moved toward a showdown with Russia over Poland. He ignored the counsel of Marshall and Stimson, who were very doubtful about the wisdom of too "strong" a policy. Stimson wrote: "I said that in my opinion we ought to be very careful and see whether we couldn't get ironed out on the situation without getting into a head-on-collision.[73]

On April 22, Molotov and Eden were in Washington en route to the San Francisco Conference. "Harriman returned on his own initiative to sound the tocsin on the menace of Russia." He warned of the need to stand firm on "the barbarian invasion of Europe." On April 23, Truman met with his cabinet and advisers, including Harriman, Leahy, and Forrestal, and urged a more decisive stand on Poland, even at the risk of a break with the USSR. "By the time the Cabinet adjourned Truman was in something of a rage." He had warned Eden he would speak to Molotov "in words of one syllable." On the United Nations, he announced he would tell Molotov the Russians must "join us [or] they could go to hell." Yet Truman's sharp confrontation with Molotov accomplished nothing, although he argued strongly that the Yalta decision committed Russia to the creation of a "new government" and said the United States would proceed only on this basis. As the revisionists saw it, "there was nothing in this approach likely to succeed because Truman not only conveniently misinterpreted the Yalta agreement . . . but . . . asked Stalin to agree to a procedure for a new government that not merely violated Yalta but required a fundamental revision of Soviet policy."[74]

On April 24, Stalin responded with equal vigor, challenging the Anglo-American interpretation of requirements for the formulation of Poland's future government and defending, as the heart of the matter, Russia's need for a friendly Poland on its borders. He maintained that

72. Barton J. Bernstein, in Thomas G. Patterson (ed.), *The Origins of the Cold War* (Lexington, Mass.: D. C. Heath and Company, 1974), 93.

73. Henry L. Stimson and McGeorge Bundy, *On Active Service in Peace and War* (New York: Harper & Brothers, 1947), 609.

74. Kolko, *The Politics of War*, 394, 395, 396.

the Greek and Belgian position in the West's sphere of influence was a precedent for what Russia wanted in the case of Poland. He added that the Soviet government was not consulted when the Greek and Belgian governments were being formed, nor had it claimed the right to interfere because it realized how important the two countries were to the security of Great Britain. The issues over Poland were now reduced to the bare essentials—security and spheres of influence—and on both the two sides held incompatible views. The conflict by the end of April had reached a total impasse.

A fourth interpretation opposed both to orthodoxy and revisionism has been advanced by the small group of writers who have been called "interpreters-critics." According to Walter Lippmann: "The Yalta military boundary was the datum line from which the diplomatic settlement of the war had necessarily to begin." But precisely at this point "American diplomacy became confused and lost sight of the primary and essential objective." Yalta registered an agreed estimate by the Allies of what the military balance would be at the close of hostilities. After Yalta, the Western Allies for the best of reasons, including their debt to countless patriots in Eastern Europe, "came to the conclusion that they must wage a diplomatic campaign to prevent Russia from expanding her sphere . . . [and] consolidating it, and to compel her to contract it. But they failed to see clearly that until the Red Army evacuated eastern Europe and withdrew to the frontiers of the Soviet Union, none of these objectives could be achieved." [75]

Another interpreter-critic, the political scientist Hans J. Morgenthau, was even more outspoken: "The Yalta agreements . . . were an attempt, doomed to failure from the outset, to maintain a modicum of Western influence in the nations of Eastern Europe which the Red Army had conquered. That influence was to be maintained through the instrument of free democratic elections. Yet in view of the fear and hatred with which most of Eastern Europe had traditionally reacted to the colossus from the East, free elections in Eastern Europe could be considered by the Soviet Union only as a weapon with which first to limit, and then to destroy, Soviet control." [76]

A third interpreter-critic, Ambassador George F. Kennan, went beyond Lippmann and Morgenthau, saying: "The Yalta Declaration, with

75. Walter Lippmann, *The Cold War: A Study in U.S. Foreign Policy* (New York: Harper and Brothers Publishers, 1947), 37, 38.
76. Hans J. Morgenthau, *Politics in the Twentieth Century: The Restoration of American Politics* (Chicago: University of Chicago Press, 1962), 329.

its references to the reorganization of the existing Polish-Communist regime 'on a broader democratic basis' and to the holding 'of free and un-
fettered elections' . . . struck me as the shabbiest sort of equivocation,
certainly not calculated to pull the wool over the eyes of the Western
public, but bound to have this effect." Kennan noted with what "bore-
dom and disgust" he served as Ambassador Harriman's aide and interpreter through long hours of wrangling with Molotov and Vishinsky
concerning the formation of a coalition Polish government. Later he
learned that Soviet authorities during these negotiations had arrested
some of the very non-Lublin Poles being considered for that government and put pressure on them to become Soviet agents. Looking back,
he summed up his feelings at the time, saying: "I never doubted that it
was all a lost cause."[77]

Kennan more than the others also felt deep concern about the question of Poland's western boundary. On December 18, 1944, *Pravda* devoted almost half of its foreign affairs page to an article by Dr. Stefan
Jedrichowski, propaganda chief of the Lublin Committee in Moscow,
recommending that Poland's border should extend from Stettin to the
Oder and Lower Neisse Rivers. Not knowing that Churchill and Roosevelt had already agreed to substantially this arrangement at Teheran
(although it had not been clear whether the boundary lay along the eastern or western portion of the two Neisse Rivers), Kennan expressed
concern that the result would be an increase of Poland's dependence on
the Soviet Union. The Soviets knew, he wrote, "that to fix the line of the
Oder as the western-most limit of Germany must inevitably bring this
dependence to a point where no Polish regime in the territory east of
that line can be anything more, in effect, than a local authority." It was
bound to become a protectorate of the Soviet Union. As Kennan saw it, a
border so unnatural as the Oder-Neisse one could be maintained and
defended, in the long run, only by armed force—and Poland alone
could not expect to muster such a force. Poland could not rely either
on its own manpower or on that of the Western powers to defend its
borders. The experiences of 1938 and 1939 had confirmed this fact.
Therefore: "A Poland carved out of a good portion of Germany would
be simply obliged . . . to assure itself at all times of Russian support, and
to accept it . . . on Russian terms." For Kennan the evidence was clear
that "it made little sense to go on arguing with Stalin and Molotov about
the composition of a future Polish government, as though there was a

77. Kennan, *Memoirs, 1925–1950*, p. 212.

real chance of genuine Polish independence. This was simply an attempt, and an unpromising one at that, to lock the stable door after the horse was stolen."[78]

Underlying the concern of the interpreter-critic group was another concern not always openly stated. Every foreign policy decision has its own momentous and far-reaching consequences. The decision to enter into endless negotiations and debate with the Soviet Union over a future Polish government flew in the face of military strategy. Because the Soviets based such strategy on their political objectives and the Americans did not, the datum line for diplomacy left Poland within the Soviet sphere of influence. Kennan saw wartime strategy as one arena in which American political objectives for Poland might have been pressed. The other missed opportunity occurred with the Warsaw uprisings when the Red Army remained passive on the other side of the river as Poland's independence heroes were slaughtered by the Germans. The heinous crime was compounded when Stalin and Molotov cruelly denied permission to the American airforce to use the shuttle base in the Ukraine to aid in the dropping of supplies to the beleaguered Poles. In Kennan's opinion "this was the moment when, if ever, there should have been a full-fledged and realistic political showdown with the Soviet leaders." Five months before Yalta and seven or eight months before the gravest crises over Polish affairs, the Soviet Union "should have been confronted with the choice between changing their policy completely and agreeing to collaborate in the establishment of truly independent countries in Eastern Europe or forfeiting Western-Allied support and sponsorship for the remaining phases of their war effort." By then the West had opened a second front and Allied troops were on the continent in force. Soviet territory had been totally liberated. What lay ahead was the future of non-Soviet troops overrun by the Germans. America might have withheld help to any further Soviet military operations so long as they were conducted in the spirit of the Warsaw uprising. Even here, Kennan was not wholly optimistic that resistance would have had a chance, for he harbored the fear that the Soviets, beyond all their demands for friendly East European governments for security reasons, were influenced by another acutely embarrassing consideration. Soviet police authorities had almost certainly perpetrated the worst possible excesses and crimes against the Polish people in 1939 and 1940. The Soviets by 1944 were determined that no postwar Polish government should have

78. *Ibid.*, 214.

either the inclination or the ability to investigate these acts and make public disclosure. "What was bothering Stalin was not . . . just the desire to have a 'friendly government' on the other side of the Polish frontier. What was bothering him was the need for the collaboration of any future Polish political authority in repressing evidences and memories of actions by Soviet police authorities in the period 1939–1941, for which no adequate and respectable excuse could ever be found."[79] Only a Communist regime under tight Soviet control could assure such collaboration.

What then were the alternative policies available to Western leaders in the face of such unfavorable circumstances? What might Roosevelt and Churchill have done or not done as the interpreter-critics saw it? Their first proposal was negative, calling for the divesting of themselves of any responsibility for Soviet actions. In Lippmann's words: "Had they seen clearly the significance of the military situation, they would not have committed the United States to anything in eastern Europe while the Soviet government had the power to oppose it, while the United States had no power to enforce it." The Western Powers could have noted the pledges and promises Stalin offered at Yalta respecting the independence of Poland without guaranteeing to the United States that Stalin would keep his promises. "For since the United States could not make good this guarantee, the onus of the violation of the pledges was divided between the Russians who broke them, and the Americans who had promised to enforce them and did not."[80] A far wiser course would have been to base our policy on the realities of the balance of power, leaving Stalin with the full responsibility for breaking those promises he alone could fulfill. It would have been better to concentrate all our efforts on the making of peace settlements which might end the occupation of Europe.

Ambassador Kennan makes a similar argument in recounting his interview with presidential envoy Harry Hopkins, who came to Moscow at President Truman's request to discuss with Stalin the deteriorating relations between America and the Soviet Union. Hopkins outlined his discussions with Stalin and Stalin's terms for the settlement of the Polish question and asked Kennan if he thought the United States could do any better. Kennan replied negatively and Hopkins then asked if he thought the United States should come to an agreement on this basis. Again Ken-

79. *Ibid.*, 210, 211, 203.
80. Lippmann, *The Cold War*, 38.

nan replied negatively, maintaining "we should accept no share of the responsibility for what the Russians proposed to do in Poland." Hopkins responded, "Then you think it's just sin and we should be agin it." "That's just about right," Kennan answered. "I respect your opinion," Hopkins said sadly. "But I am not at liberty to accept it."[81]

But there was a more positive side to the arguments of the interpreter-critics, foreshadowed in Lippmann's brief comment about peace treaties to end the European occupation. The core of the problem was to force or persuade the Soviets to withdraw their armies to Russian territory. "For if, and only if, we can bring about the withdrawal of the Red Army from the Yalta line to the new frontier of the Soviet Union—and simultaneously, of course, the withdrawal of the British and American armies from continental Europe—can a balance of power be established which can then be maintained. For after the withdrawal, an attempt to return would be an invasion—an open, unmistakable act of military aggression." Against such aggression the main deterrent would be what it had always been—the American capacity to strike at the vital centers of the Soviet Union. "And until treaties are agreed to which bring about the withdrawal of the Red Army, the power of the United States to strike these vital centers would be built up for the express purpose of giving weight to our policy of ending the military occupation of Europe."[82] That the American strategic deterrent has not been used for this purpose testifies to the distance remaining between Lippmann's and official thinking. Yet it is reasonable to ask whether his conviction and that of other interpreter-critics that the specter of two mighty armies facing one another in the center of Europe was not then and does not remain today the basic issue and gravest threat to peace in the struggle. Would Poland's crisis in 1980/81 have been as threatening? In any event, the perspectives of this group of critics, so different from the other schools, offer help in various significant ways in illuminating certain essential and neglected questions concerning the beginnings of the Cold War.

81. Kennan, *Memoirs, 1925–1950*, p. 213.
82. Lippmann, *The Cold War*, 39.

Chapter Three

America's Response

Containment Revisited

Two difficulties confront the investigator who wishes to analyze America's response to the onset of the Cold War. One is the problem of historical materials; the other is conceptual and theoretical. While some of the basic documentation has appeared for the period under discussion (in 1973, the Department of State in accordance with the twenty-five year rule published the volumes for 1947 and 1948 in the series *Foreign Relations of the United States*), the question persists whether this material tells the full story. In 1862, when the Department of State initiated these publications, the series, which included departmental memoranda, correspondence, cables, and records of conferences, was seen as providing substantially all the material required for diplomatic history writing. By the time of the Cold War, the responsibility for actions ramifying across the ever-widening spectrum of events in foreign relations had spread to a host of other agencies including Defense, Treasury, Agriculture, and Commerce. Moreover, America's relations no longer were confined to its traditional European allies and rivals but extended to Communist and non-European states whose policy-making processes were shrouded in secrecy and oftentimes deception. If the debates and discussions within American and European governments were open to scrutiny only decades after the event, who could claim knowledge of what went on within the Politburo?

The other problem for analysis and interpretation is conceptual in character. As we have seen, the historical and political consensus regarding American foreign policy began to dissolve in the mid and late 1960s. Americans who had responsibility for the conduct of foreign policy had been schooled in what Gaddis Smith has called "the Great Cycle Theory."[1] According to Smith this theory rested essentially on a residual be-

1. Gaddis Smith, "The United States in World Affairs Since 1945," in William H. Cart-

lief in the unique moral character of America and its policies. Only America among the Great Powers had been conceived in liberty and was dedicated to equality and justice. It had not tarnished its good name by imposing its will on others. Moreover, American power was an outward expression of inner virtue. Twice the world had teetered on the brink of moral and political destruction and at the eleventh hour the United States had intervened. America's fault was not lack of resolve. Delaying entry into the struggle because of a prevailing isolationism reflected downturns in "the Great Cycle." Following World War I, the Senate rejected Woodrow Wilson's vision of a new world order, abandoned his crusade for a world made safe for democracy, and lapsed into isolationism with repudiation of the League of Nations. Totalitarianism and aggression went unchecked in Europe and Asia and World War II resulted. Then the cycle turned sometime in the years 1939 to 1941 and the United States became the leader of a Grand Alliance which turned back German and Japanese aggression and preserved Western civilization.

The lesson that postwar policy makers derived from these experiences was that the most powerful nation in world politics could no longer afford sharp upward and downward trends in the cycle of American foreign policy. When the Soviet Union replaced Hitler's Germany as the major threat to the stability of Europe after World War II, the American answer, resolutely proclaimed, was that we would resist aggression at its source. Not only was it essential that declaratory policies make clear American intentions, but the response had to be organized politically, militarily, and economically. With its atomic superiority unchallenged, America assumed responsibility for organizing the postwar world order. Politically, international order required that the United States redeem itself for having repudiated the League by fashioning a global collective security system within the United Nations and, when that proved ineffectual because of Soviet obstructionism, through regional security pacts such as the North Atlantic Treaty Organization. Economically, the task was the rebuilding of postwar Europe through the Marshall Plan, designed to eliminate the power vacuum which was being penetrated by Communist forces. Militarily, America, which after victory had supposed its military power could be drastically curtailed, had to refashion its military might to give it the capacity to deter aggression. For most interpreters and especially the orthodox historians, the years from

wright and Richard L. Watson, Jr. (eds.), *The Reinterpretation of American History and Culture* (Washington, D.C.: National Council for Social Studies, 1973), 546.

1945–1953 were the heroic era in postwar American foreign.
They witnessed the evolving of a worldwide strategy which was based on
historical lessons and was internally coherent, logically consistent, and
free of contradictions. The Truman Doctrine, the Marshall Plan,
NATO, European rearmament, the alliance with Japan, and the Korean
War were all of a piece. They were designed to resist Communist expansionism at its source, not waiting until the eleventh hour.

Americans congratulated themselves that at last we had a consistent
foreign policy, which such critics as Walter Lippmann had found lacking
since the time of the Monroe Doctrine. Although Lippmann and a handful of scholars and diplomatic correspondents persisted in their criticism, a foreign policy consensus emerged in the executive and legislative branches of government and generally in the public at large. Given
the climate of opinion, it is hardly surprising that few responsible officials foresaw either the eight years of retrenchment and consolidation
that characterized Dwight D. Eisenhower's presidency or the crisis which
reached its height in the debate over the Vietnam War. The early triumphs of an all too brief Kennedy presidency, particularly the resolution of the last vestiges of the Berlin blockade, the firm and masterful
handling of the Cuban missile crisis, and the conclusion of the Test Ban
Treaty in the summer of 1963 heralded the success of containment.

Looking back, we can see the portents of future problems present in
the inconclusive war in Korea, the continuing strength of the Italian and
French Communist parties, debates with Europeans over the nature of
the Soviet threat, the Communist victory in China, the rise of the non-
aligned nations, the decline of French influence in Indochina, the intensification of divisions and strife in the Middle East, and the impending
Sino-Soviet split. However, the euphoria of a nation which at long last
had learned the lessons of history obscured the warning signs. The architects of early postwar American foreign policy were "the children of
Munich" who had learned not only from American mistakes but from
Chamberlain's illusion that Hitler could be appeased. *Appeasement*,
which in the language of traditional diplomacy had meant necessary accommodation with forces of change and territorial adjustments with
nations whose goals were not worldwide or unlimited, had acquired a
wholly negative meaning. To appease an aggressor meant preparing the
way for future conflicts far more devastating in their political and military consequences.

The theoretical problem for interpreters of the Cold War, therefore,
is whether to judge postwar American foreign policy by the prevailing

assumptions of 1947–1953 or by the assumptions of 1969–1978 or by the assumptions of the present day, by what men knew then or what is known today. This dilemma is of course a perennial problem of historical interpretation. Is the historian to evaluate the decisions which were made in one historical period by what was known or believed at the time or from a broader perspective of history? Are good and decent men to be judged by the dominant perceptions of their time or by the evidence of subsequent events? And who is to say with any assurance whether the failures or tragedies which came to pass, for example the Vietnam War, might have been avoided if the prevailing views of policy makers had been modified in time?

What is beyond dispute is that by 1969 the theoretical basis of American foreign policy had begun to change. Detente replaced confrontation. Accommodation with the Soviet Union and China was given dramatic form in President Nixon's visit to China in 1972 and his subsequent Moscow summit meeting—both firsts for an American president. Strategic Arms Limitation Talks were initiated. The Helsinki Accords which followed included recognition of territorial divisions between the rivals. President Nixon announced at Guam that the United States henceforth would help those nations willing and able to defend themselves. As rapprochement continued into the 1970s with both the Soviet Union and China, American policy makers spoke less and less in the language of the late 1940s and 1950s: containing communism throughout the world, basing policy on the domino theory, or eliminating communism in other countries through economic assistance programs. Official silences concerning these goals provoked critics who denounced faithless Americans for having abandoned the anti-Communist crusade of the early Cold War. The consensus on which the most dramatic responses to the Soviet Union and international communism were based crumbled as deep divisions within the major political parties appeared.

The children of the 1940s and their intellectual and political heirs confronted the children of the 1970s in what gave signs of becoming an irreconcilable political debate. The differences were manifest not only in conflicts between the major parties; the schism could be traced within the same administration. Among President Carter's foreign policy advisers, the friends of Senator Henry Jackson (James Schlesinger, Zbigniew Brzezinski, and Samuel Huntington) opposed the supporters of the Nixon-Kissinger detente (Cyrus Vance, Marshal Shulman, and Harold Brown). In the public at large, the Nitze-Rostow viewpoint expressed in declarations of the Clear and Present Danger Committee vied with the Kennan-Fulbright approach reflected in the goals of the Committee on East-West Accords. These differences among men of good will ran deep and were not easily reconciled; they were the dominant influences underlying specific policy debates.

Then, as the 1970s came to an end, the great cycle turned once again. The debate over SALT II became a debate over rearmament or of shoring up American defenses that critics charged had been weakened and diminished. A president who had announced his aim of reducing military budgets by $5 to $7 billion promised to increase military spending by $5 billion. The students in revolutionary Iran seized the American Embassy in Teheran and refused to release some fifty American hostages until the Shah was returned. The Soviet Union, for the first time since their occupation of Eastern Europe, sent troops across national boundaries and overthrew one puppet regime in Afghanistan and installed another. Kremlinologists in the West sought to penetrate Soviet intentions, asking whether concern over the restlessness of fifty million Moslems on Soviet territory, the need for oil by 1985, or the drive for warm-water ports had motivated the invasion. Was the move defensive to preserve Afghanistan as a buffer or did it herald a Soviet design for conquest throughout the Near and Middle East? Had the great powers returned to the strident clashes of the 1940s and 1950s? Were the lessons of the 1940s once more relevant to American foreign policy? Was the world on the threshold of a new era of dangerous confrontations and bitter Cold War rhetoric with little chance of accommodation or negotiation? By 1981 President Reagan appeared bent on completing the cycle.

Charting the Cold War: 1945–1951

In understanding the current debate, it is vital that we return to the beginnings of the American response to Soviet expansionism to understand the intellectual and political foundations on which postwar policies rested. It is vital as a first step in such a review to rehearse the events which surrounded and shaped the American response. As we have seen, the first sparks in the Cold War were ignited in 1945 by the clash over Poland and by the Yalta Conference. The Soviet Union had recognized the Lublin government on January 5 and in April the two announced a treaty of mutual assistance. That same month President Roosevelt died and Harry S Truman became the thirty-third president of the United States. The Allies celebrated "Victory in Europe" on May

6, and on May 8 lend-lease was cancelled (later reinstated by President Truman). On June 29, the Soviet Union, Britain, and the United States recognized the Polish provisional government. The Potsdam Conference convened July 15 and President Truman met for the first time with Premier Stalin and Prime Minister Churchill and his successor, Clement Attlee. In August the Soviet Union entered the war against Japan, occupying North Korea. Japan surrendered following the August 6–9 atomic bombing of Hiroshima and Nagasaki. On August 20, America again cancelled lend-lease. Negotiations in London of the Council of Foreign Ministers collapsed on October 2, but by the end of 1945 the British and the Americans had recognized the government in Hungary and apparently reached agreements on broadening the governments in Rumania and Bulgaria (early in 1946, they would recognize a reconstituted government in Rumania but not Bulgaria), and on an approach to peace treaties in Europe. (The United States was ready to recognize Enver Hoxha in Albania in November, 1945, but recognition was held up and the small American mission was withdrawn from Albania in November, 1946. Thus formal recognition of Albania never took place.)[2]

In 1946, the Iran dispute erupted over continued Soviet occupation of Azerbaidjan in northern Iran. The dispute was brought before the Security Council of the United Nations with the United States and Britain supporting Iran. The Soviet Union responded by charging that British and French troops were still in Syria and Lebanon and British troops remained in Greece and Indonesia. On March 5, Churchill declared in a speech at Fulton, Missouri: "From Stettin, in the Baltic, to Trieste, in the Adriatic, an Iron Curtain has descended across the continent." (It is often forgotten that Churchill also called in the same speech for negotiations between East and West). On March 24, the Soviet Union promised to leave Azerbaidjan by May 6. In April, Secretary of State James Byrnes proposed a four-power treaty providing for the demilitarization of Germany and its exclusion from all alliances. The Soviet Union turned down the proposal. In the fall of 1946, Greece brought a complaint to the Security Council that Yugoslavia, Albania, and Bulgaria were supporting guerrilla warfare in northern Greece. In late autumn, America and Britain protested the conduct of elections in Bulgaria and Rumania, but Communists joined Social Democrats in a National Front to take over the government of Rumania. As the year ended, a more hopeful development was the substantial agreement

2. See John C. Campbell, *The United States in World Affairs, 1945–1947* (New York: Harper & Row, 1948), 155.

reached in the Council of Foreign Ministers on the European peace treaties and on preparation for a treaty with Germany.

In early 1947, as cleavages deepened, the British and Americans established a bizonal economic union in Germany, and on January 19 they protested Communist-organized elections in Poland, the defeat of the Peasant party and Mikolajczyk's flight from Poland. On March 12, 1947, President Truman, in an address to the Congress on aid to Greece and Turkey, proclaimed: "It must be the policy of the United States to support free peoples who are resisting attempted subjugation by armed minorities or by outside pressures." Friends and critics agreed that the Truman Doctrine universalized America's defense of freedom around the globe but disagreed on whether this was a realistic strategy. In March and April, the Foreign Ministers announced that discussions of reparations and of a united government for Germany had failed. On June 5, 1947, Secretary of State Marshall set forth a plan for European recovery which was rejected by the Soviet Union, though first accepted by Czechoslovakia only to be turned down in response to Soviet pressure. In July, George F. Kennan published his famous "Mr. X" article on "The Sources of Soviet Conduct" in the influential journal *Foreign Affairs*, setting forth what came to be known as the "containment doctrine," a capsule characterization of postwar American foreign policy toward the Soviet Union. Despite Kennan's insistence he had not intended his proposal to constitute a global foreign policy approach, it was interpreted this way. In late autumn, the Cominform (Communist Information Bureau) was established, curiously enough in Belgrade. The United Nations condemned Communist guerrilla activity on the northern boundaries of Greece.

In February, 1948, a full-fledged Communist government came to power in Czechoslovakia and the leader of the former coalition government, Jan Masaryk, died under circumstances which aroused deep suspicions in the West. In March the Brussels Treaty was signed between Britain, France, Luxembourg, Belgium, and the Netherlands, and on March 20 the Soviet Union withdrew from the Allied Control Council. The Western Powers announced at the London Conference (June 7—20) a common policy for their zones in Germany. Three days later on June 23, the foreign ministers of the Soviet Union and the East European governments denounced Western policy as a violation of the Potsdam Agreement and imposed a blockade of all rail traffic between Berlin and the western zones of Germany. In June, Yugoslavia was expelled from the Cominform. On July 1, the Soviet representative withdrew from the Berlin Kommandatura. Near the end of July, the West imposed a counter-blockade of the Soviet zone, and with all highway and water routes blockaded into Berlin, initiated an airlift to fly in supplies. In August, the United Nations Military Staff Committee announced that efforts to form a Security Council military force under Chapter VII of the charter had failed.

The next year, 1949, was the year of the North Atlantic Treaty (April 4), of Comecom, a new system for integrating the economies of the Soviet Union and the East European countries (April 28), of agreement on ending the Berlin blockade (May 5), of the first Soviet atomic bomb, of the establishment of separate German governments in West Germany and East Germany and of purges of political and religious leaders in Eastern Europe. (Indeed large-scale purges of political and religious leaders in Eastern Europe began in 1948 and in Bulgaria and Rumania even earlier.) On October 1, the People's Republic of China was created, and in January of 1950 the Soviet Union left the Security Council protesting the U.N.'s denial of China's seat to the People's Republic. On June 24–25, North Korea invaded South Korea and the Security Council called on members to aid South Korea, to repel armed attack and to restore peace and security in the area. By the end of September, U.N. troops had reached the 38th parallel in Korea, with China warning she would not "stand idly by" if they crossed the parallel. By November 8, China had entered the conflict and had called for American withdrawal from Korea, Formosa, and the Far East. Under the Uniting for Peace Resolution which had been approved on October 5, 1950, the General Assembly condemned China as an aggressor on January 31, 1951. In June of 1951, Ambassador Malik of the Soviet Union, in a broadcast in New York, proposed a cease-fire in Korea. In September, the Japanese Peace Treaty was signed in San Francisco without agreement on China's participation.

The Iron Curtain Speech

If the American response to the Soviet threat can be described as the containment of Soviet expansion, the two official formulations of greatest weight were Winston Churchill's "Iron Curtain Speech" and Harry Truman's address to Congress that came to be known as the Truman Doctrine. The two public statements carried great weight because Churchill, although no longer prime minister, was the only living wartime leader of the Western Allies and spoke presumably with the blessings of the Truman administration. For his part, the president delivered his message at a turning point in American history. (Two Soviet historians, Nikolai V. Sivachev and Nikolai N. Yakovlev, confirmed in 1979 that the Fulton speech and the Truman Doctrine were the two most decisive western actions in launching the Cold War.[3]) Stalin spoke of Churchill's speech as a call for war and the beginnings of a new crusade against Eastern Europe. In language more threatening than Churchill's, the Soviet premier warned that "Mr. Churchill and his friends . . . will be beaten back just as they were beaten back twenty-six years ago."[4] While there is no doubt that high American officials including the president had read Churchill's speech before it was delivered and the president told him the speech was admirable and would do nothing but good, the administration was determined to ride out the popular criticism by remaining in the background of public debate.

President Truman had predicted the Fulton speech would create a stir in the United States and Britain. Yet Truman underestimated the intensity of the first reactions. Churchill, while praised for his wartime leadership, was viewed by liberals in the two countries as a bold but impetuous buccaneer, a soldier of fortune, a political adventurer and politically unreliable. British opinion was consistently unwilling to accept him unreservedly except in the supreme climactic moments of its history. His critics charged he was possessed of a tragic-heroic conception of war and politics. He was pictured as the happy warrior, brave in periods of crisis and stress but reckless and unpredictable in time of tranquillity. Not surprisingly, therefore, he was denounced as one of the great anachronisms of his time and a leader with an old-fashioned and outmoded conception of world affairs. Norman Cousins, writing in the *Saturday Review of Literature*, described him as the spokesman of retrogression and counter-direction clinging to practices which had never succeeded. Editorialists in the *New Republic* explained that his idolatry of Tory capitalism, royalty, and authoritarianism betrayed him into uttering bitter words of hatred of the Soviet Union. They proclaimed the world stood at a crossroads. Mr. Churchill's path led to power politics, imperialism, spheres of influence, and unending war; the liberal path led to democracy, freedom, and peace. Men of good will had no choice but to rally all mankind to support the second course. For former vice

3. Nikolai V. Sivachev and Nikolai N. Yakovlev, *Russia and the United States*, translated by Olga Adler Titlebaum (Chicago: University of Chicago Press, 1979).

4. Herbert Feis, *From Trust to Terror: The Onset of the Cold War, 1945–1950* (New York: W. W. Norton and Company, 1970), 79.

president Henry Wallace, Churchill was the Mephistopheles of alliances and the balance of power. A reversion to the ancient practice of nations combining against other nations was a fatal counter-force to the progress of the Atlantic Charter and the newly created United Nations. The American people were shocked by the implications of an irrepressible conflict. On September 12, 1946, Mr. Wallace delivered a major speech intended to dispel "the fog" Churchill had created. Because of the Wallace speech, Secretary Byrnes, who was heading the American Peace Delegation in Paris, threatened to resign immediately unless Wallace resigned.[5] Churchill to his critics was a war-monger refusing to uncouple foreign policy from power and the instruments of violence. For those who confidently assumed that the nature of international politics had been transformed overnight, Churchill was indeed the high priest of conflict.

The intense reaction to Churchill's speech resulted from another prevailing viewpoint among contemporary Americans. Liberal writers set forth two notions that were frequently used to judge Western statesmen, the categories of optimism and pessimism. Policies were shaped by the statesman's temperament and his tendencies regarding foreign policy. According to this distinction, some statesmen are by nature optimistic and sanguine in viewing the future. Such leaders have faith in man's perfectibility; history for them is a straightforward account of mankind's capacity for infinite progress and unending growth and development. Man through reason is capable of controlling nature and human destiny, and the main business of statesmen and educators is to inculcate and inspire faith in the limitless horizons of the future. The pessimist, on the contrary, sees trouble ahead, accepts the status quo and is content with the management of difficulties, not their abolition. The optimist condemns surrender to the blind rush of events; the pessimist charges that a fatuous devotion to the mystique of progress can destroy more than it saves. The optimist is hopeful; the pessimist resigns himself to caution. He suspends judgment on the future.

The optimist-pessimist dichotomy presents the student of international politics with at least three practical difficulties. To call someone an optimist or a pessimist refers to his expectations. What anyone expects or prophesies for the future is never verifiable at the time. The basic weakness of the two distinctions is the lack of objective criteria against

5. James F. Byrnes, *Speaking Frankly* (Connecticut: Greenwood Press, 1974), 239–43.

which they can be measured. Secondly, optimism and pessimism are so weighted down with emotional content as to seriously limit their usefulness. In popular usage, optimism suggests a positive and dynamic approach while pessimism is characterized as mere negativism. Yet one man's affirmations are often hostile denials of another man's judgments, leaving open the question of who is positive or negative. Optimism and pessimism refer to two sets of opinions and leave unresolved whose opinions are more reliable. Thirdly, the central problem with optimism and pessimism is their shifting and changeable application. In 1947, Churchill to his critics was the supreme pessimist in warning of the Soviet threat. By 1951, Churchill spoke out more strongly than other Western statesmen in offering hope of negotiations with the Russians and rejecting the inevitability of war. Even in his somber warning at Fulton he declared that the Russians wanted not war but the fruits of war and the indefinite expansion of their power and doctrines. By the 1950s, his liberal critics were defending war in Korea as a necessary path to resisting Soviet expansion while he favored a peaceful settlement. Optimism and pessimism are poor ways of describing international politics; the statesman and the historian who would describe the international scene must focus on the changing political situation, not the temperamental habits of a few leaders.

Churchill was both an optimist and a pessimist as demonstrated in a letter he sent during World War II, on March 4, 1942, to the dominion secretary regarding the military situation in the Far East: "I do not see much use in pumping all this pessimism throughout the Empire. It is the fashion here; but it will do great harm wherever else it goes." A division of the world's statesmen into optimists and pessimists is likely to prove defective and becomes almost meaningless when it is applied concretely.

In calling at Fulton for a defense against Soviet expansionism, Churchill argued that prevention was better than cure. He openly acknowledged no one could foretell what Soviet Russia intended in the immediate future or what limits if any would emerge in their expansive and proselytising tendencies. The one fact which to him was clear was the situation in the heart of Europe, the Soviet influence and control of the ancient states of Central and Eastern Europe and the disturbances in Turkey and Iran. This precarious situation had come about because American and British armies had withdrawn at some points 150 miles westward to allow their Russian allies to occupy vast territory which the Western Allies had conquered. Churchill had vigorously pressed Truman to delay the withdrawal of American forces from this area, but Truman refused.[6]

Churchill's plea in the Fulton speech was for a deeper awareness of the importance of strength: "I am convinced that there is nothing they [the Russians] admire so much as strength, and there is nothing for which they have less respect than for weakness." Once the military, economic, and moral strength of America had been added to that of the English-speaking Commonwealth, he believed security was possible and with it progress toward understanding between East and West. The present situation in Europe, as he saw it, was one not of strength but weakness and until an equilibrium if not a preponderance of power had been established, the situation offered temptations to "ambition and adventure." Knowing what we know today of the persistent rivalry and the testing and probing of the Great Powers in the Cold War, we cannot but view with surprise the sharp reactions to Churchill's historic speech at Westminster College in Fulton, Missouri.

The Truman Doctrine

Exactly a year and seven days after the Fulton speech, President Truman delivered his message on aid to Greece and Turkey. On March 12, 1947, he spoke to the Congress on the defense of freedom and the need to contain Soviet expansion. America's response was historic in at least four respects. First, its action marked the ending of a long tradition of isolationism in American foreign policy. Second, undergirding the succession of policies beginning with the Truman Doctrine was an objective reality of postwar international politics: the New World had been called on to redress the balance of power in the Old. Third, with respect to the internal workings of the American government, rarely if ever has the government acted so decisively on the basis of a broad political consensus in response to bold leadership. Fourth, the momentous shift in American foreign policy occurred in a period of twelve historic weeks from March 12 to June 5, 1947. At the end of the twelve weeks, in a commencement address at Harvard University, Secretary of State George C. Marshall unveiled his plan for the economic recovery of Europe.

The events leading up to the Truman Doctrine led to a revolution in American policy. On February 21, 1947, the British ambassador in Washington, Lord Inverchapel, urgently requested an appointment with Sec-

6. Winston S. Churchill, *Triumph and Tragedy* (Boston: Houghton Mifflin Company, 1953), 603–606, Vol. VI of *The Second World War*.

retary of State George C. Marshall. In Marshall's absence, Dean Acheson, undersecretary of state, arranged for Loy Henderson, director of the Office of Near Eastern and African Affairs, to receive H. M. Sichel, first secretary of the British Embassy. The British envoy delivered two notes, the first calling on America to give substantial economic assistance to Greece, assistance which a war-devastated Britain had once given but was unable to continue after March 31. The second note outlined the crisis in Turkey, whose government lacked the resources necessary for both economic development and military preparedness. Britain was appealing to America to fill the vacuum created by Britain's withdrawal from key world areas such as Egypt and India and the decline of British power from the Mediterranean to the South China Sea. The United States in fact had already provided postwar aid to Greece on an emergency basis through the United Nations Relief and Rehabilitation Administration, but for a more comprehensive program new authorizations by the Congress were needed. Greece's plight was desperate. Its collapse would greatly enhance the prospects of Soviet domination in a region of vital strategic importance to the West. Without external help, the near inevitable triumph of communism in a country threatened by Communist guerrillas in the north and with less than $14 million of available foreign exchange in its treasury was threatened. Turkey's continued decline made it vulnerable to communism. Not since the Monroe Doctrine had America been called on to take so dramatic a step in foreign policy leadership.

Critics of American foreign policy from Alexis de Tocqueville through Alexander Hamilton to Walter Lippmann and Hans J. Morgenthau had warned that democracies were weak in their capacity for prompt and decisive action. History tended to confirm their judgment in the periods surrounding World Wars I and II. Against such criticism, the response to the Greek and Turkish crisis offers a partial refutation. Partisanship in the Congress yielded to a national imperative merging with the political conversion to internationalism on the part of powerful leaders such as Senator Arthur Vandenberg. Vandenberg and Secretary Marshall joined hands in a bipartisan effort with few parallels in American history. On both sides of the aisle, congressional leaders united behind bold new policies. Yet the political scene in Washington was anything but auspicious for change. Actually the preconditions for stalemate were present, for the Democrats, who controlled the White House, were in a minority in Congress. (The Republicans in the 80th Congress had a 51 to 45 advantage in the Senate and a 245 to 118 majority in the House.) President Truman in his first year and a half in office had not proven to himself, to say nothing of a war-weary public, that he was capable of taking control of his new office for which he appeared ill-prepared, especially in foreign policy. When President Roosevelt chose him as a running mate he had been a compromise candidate and the four-term president had seen fit to keep the former senator from Missouri largely in the dark about the details of foreign policy. Truman inherited the resentments and frustrations against his party that were inevitable given Democratic control of the White House for some fourteen years. It was widely assumed that he was the head of a caretaker administration that would remain in power only until the next election.

All signs pointed to a rollback of America's world leadership, not a continuation of Roosevelt's wartime leadership. Republicans called for a 20 percent reduction in income taxes and a joint congressional committee on the legislative budget cut the president's proposed budget of $37.5 billion to $31.5 billion and implemented a 50 percent reduction in the $1 billion requested by the War Department for fighting disease and starvation in Germany and Japan.

To prevent the economic misery that bred economic crises and recession and deep political unrest after World War I, State Department planners had sought to build a new international economic structure after World War II with convertible currencies and freer trade essential to the revival of production and trade. Loans for reconstruction and development were floated and new financial institutions such as the International Bank for Reconstruction and Development and the International Monetary Fund were created. However, few planners imagined the impact of the destruction and demoralization of Europe or the effects of two successive years of unprecedented natural disasters and crop failures brought about by drought and floods, blizzards and protracted cold, leading to breakdown in will and organization. Financial reserves within and loans however liberal from newly established international institutions were insufficient to turn the tide especially in Greece, France, and Italy, where Communists stood to gain from persisting disorder. Republicans in the Congress who had voted overwhelmingly against the Reciprocal Trade Agreements Act in 1934, 1937, 1940, and 1946, threatened to dismantle the entire program or to curtail it sharply. The behavior of some Republican congressmen was characterized as that of men wielding a meat axe in a dark room threatening to cut off their own heads.

In such an atmosphere, the best hope lay with the influential Republican senator and president *pro tempore* of the Senate, Arthur H. Vandenberg, who as chairman of the Senate Foreign Relations Committee wielded a decisive influence. As early as January 11, 1946, Senator Vandenberg joined Secretary of State Byrnes in proclaiming before the Cleveland Council of World Affairs the need for a bipartisan foreign policy. He called not only for support of the United Nations but for "reasonable rehabilitation credits" and the continuation of reciprocal trade agreements subject only to protection of the nation's economy. He assumed responsibility for tactical leadership within the Congress to hold back the nullification of the trade agreements system, subject to escape clauses to protect the American economy. With his colleague Senator Eugene Millikin, he persuaded key Republican leaders, not including Senator Robert Taft, to accept a limited internationalist position. More than any other Republican senator, he helped lay the basis for the turn in American foreign policy.

Within the administration, three leaders—the president, the secretary of state, and the undersecretary of state—were the chief actors. On April 16, Secretary of State Byrnes had privately submitted his resignation to President Truman, citing reasons of health. Through General Dwight D. Eisenhower, who was touring American military bases in the Far East, the president learned on May 9, 1946, that General George C. Marshall would accept the responsibilities of secretary of state. Truman and Byrnes had enjoyed at best an uneasy relationship, resulting in part from the secretary's belief that Roosevelt should have chosen him as his vice president. They differed over Byrnes's independence of the president, his horse-trading with Soviet Foreign Minister Molotov and British Foreign Secretary Ernest Bevin, and his handling of the peace treaties and the German question. The president felt that the secretary was making commitments which exceeded his authority. Moreover, the president and his associates were concerned over Byrnes's management of the State Department, made worse by his having to spend 350 days out of the 562 days of his tenure traveling or negotiating.

The secretary accompanied President Truman to the Potsdam Conference (July 17 to August 2, 1945). In the absence of agreed peace aims, Western leaders at Potsdam established a Council of Foreign Ministers, representing the five principal victors in World War II, to draw up peace treaties with Italy, Rumania, Bulgaria, Hungary, and Finland. Secretary Byrnes headed the American delegation which met in London (September 11 to October 2, 1945), in Paris (April 25 to May 16 and June 15 to July 12, 1946), and in New York (November–December, 1946). Not only was Byrnes present at these conferences but also at the Paris Conference of twenty-one nations from July 29 to October 15, 1946, and the tripartite Moscow Conference of Foreign Ministers from December 16 to 26 following up the Yalta Conference.

Throughout 1946, a period historians have described as "the unraveling of the old order," General Marshall had served as the president's special representative and mediator in China. His task proved impossible from the beginning. As Soviet troops withdrew from occupied areas in Manchuria in the winter of 1946, the Chinese Communists moved in to take their place, violating a truce arranged January 10, 1946. The Nationalists, unwilling to accept Communists in a government and fearing Soviet influence, advanced north toward Harbin, confident of victory in Manchuria. Marshall, convinced that Generalissimo Chiang Kai-shek's troops were overextended and that only massive intervention by America in a costly land war on the mainland could save them, warned of an uncontrollable civil war in the north. In August, the Chinese Communist party ordered general mobilization. In October, Marshall warned both Chiang and Chou En-Lai that unless they were prepared to negotiate he would terminate his mission. By the end of 1946, both sides having demonstrated an unwillingness to accept a coalition government, Marshall returned to Washington to become secretary of state.

The quiet and respected general soon imposed his design on the organization of policy making and paved the way for the Truman Doctrine. He brought order to the State Department sorely lacking since before FDR, who preferred to improvise and functioned as his own secretary of state. Marshall straightened out lines of authority in the department, identified Undersecretary of State Dean Acheson as his chief of staff, and instituted workable staff procedures including the requirement of a one-page covering statement for each staff memorandum recommending concisely and specifically what it was the official wanted the secretary to do. He shunned staff conferences, which he believed tended to deteriorate into bull sessions. He prepared colleagues for action by saying, "Gentlemen, don't fight the problem, solve it." Without pretending he himself was an intellectual, he knew how to use intellectuals as in his appointment of the brilliant George F. Kennan as the first head of the Policy Planning Staff. He was able to distinguish the essential from the less important issues. He helped educate Americans to the relation between power and order in international politics both by his speeches and his actions. Despite the failure of his China mission, Marshall's reputation as a leader, comparable in stature to George Washington in American history, lent credibility to the policies the Truman administration inaugurated. Indeed, Truman was to justify the Marshall Plan as essential to the viability of his regime, drawing on Marshall's superior standing with the American people.

Marshall's success as secretary depended, however, on the skills and experience of his principal lieutenant, Undersecretary Acheson, who understood the inner workings of the department so fully that he earned the reputation of being the last administrator to exercise control of the department. Despite his aristocratic demeanor and agile mind, Acheson was able to subordinate himself to the wartime hero he served. Nevertheless, it was Acheson characteristically who was called on to make the case for administration policy with congressional leaders who found Marshall's rhetoric dry, understated, and uninspiring. It was Acheson who excelled in drawing out the staff, working effectively with a multitude of task forces, and marshaling their professional competence to give substance to policy directions. In Marshall's absence, Acheson was responsible for the conduct of policy meetings with the president four or five times a week. To outsiders, the relation between the tall, elegantly dressed Groton man with the mustache of a guardsman and the Missouri politician who had worked as a haberdasher appeared incongruous. Insiders knew that the president and the undersecretary had established a relationship of deep trust. Acheson never forgot that Truman was president; the chief executive never failed to seek the undersecretary's counsel and concurrence or, whenever he consulted others within or outside the State Department, he kept Acheson fully informed. No one who knew the two men and their relationship was surprised when on Truman's reelection in 1948 and Marshall's resignation, the president chose Acheson as his secretary of state.

The president's strengths uniquely qualified him to lead the nation at a turning point in history. His love of history, unquestioned fortitude, capacity for growth, practical common sense, and extraordinary decisiveness were qualities attuned to the times. Some historians speculate that he might have been a lesser president in another era where the issues of right and wrong were more ambiguous and measures for resisting communism more subject to debate. His courage in pursuing what he conceived to be the right course of action without counting the political costs equipped him for responding to the challenge of the Cold War. He asked of his foreign policy associates that they recommend the right policies and leave judgments about politics to him, the professional politician.

Consensus was not confined to the top leaders in the executive branch. It pervaded the government; not one voice was raised in the cabinet in opposition to the Truman Doctrine. Influential figures such as James Forrestal, Robert P. Patterson, W. Averell Harriman, and William L. Clayton gave active support in the formulation of containment. The State Department bureaucracy was revitalized and fell in line. Its best energies and most creative efforts were unleashed and "it was the State Department staff that swept through the breach made by the Truman Doctrine and was to a very important degree responsible for the advance to the Marshall Plan."[7] Two prevalent weaknesses of democratic foreign policy in ordinary times—bureaucratic inertia and the isolation of the president—were overcome by the extraordinary nature of the crisis and by a remarkable foreign policy consensus.

By itself, efforts by the executive branch would not have produced the legislation necessary to bring about a dramatic shift in American foreign policy. Leadership in Congress, as we have seen, came from the chairman of the Senate Foreign Relations Committee, Arthur H. Vandenberg. The son of a harness maker, he had been editor of the Grand Rapids *Herald* and a staunch isolationist before World War II. On January 10, 1945, he delivered a well-timed speech in the Senate renouncing isolationism and announcing his conversion to internationalism. As Senator Robert A. Taft of Ohio was the Republican leader in domestic affairs, Vandenberg became the Republican spokesman for bipartisanship in foreign policy. Without Vandenberg's initiative, Republican support for Truman's policies in Europe might never have materialized.

At first, Vandenberg spoke mainly of the need for postwar international cooperation and the maintenance of peace. He elicited a surge of popular support by declaring in his Senate speech: "If World War III ever unhappily arrives, it will open new laboratories of death too horrible to contemplate." He had called in August of 1944, in the Mackinac Charter of Republican leaders, for "responsible participation by the United States in postwar cooperative organization among sovereign nations," and he helped write the United Nations Charter at San Francisco. By 1947, he had grown less hopeful of cooperation with the Soviets and, off the floor of Congress, had criticized the administration for not opposing Soviet expansionism. He was fully prepared, therefore, to join in support of the Truman Doctrine and, after initial hesitation, the Marshall Plan as well. The strength of the Republicans in the Congress made

7. Joseph M. Jones, *The Fifteen Weeks* (New York: Viking, 1955), 117.

Vandenberg's role as leader of the loyal opposition a precondition of success. Marshall and Acheson were able to turn repeatedly to him; his era in Congress was a high-water mark in bipartisanship. Particularly for America's European policies, this period in executive-legislative relations was an example of "politics stopping at the water's edge." The magnitude of his effort is measured by the fact that Truman could speak of the eightieth Congress in every other policy area as a do-nothing Congress. Weeks before Truman's declaration that a crisis threatened Europe, the House had pushed through a resolution recommending a $6 billion cut in the president's budget (the Senate proposed a $4.5 billion cut). It required a continuous and single-minded effort in Congress led by Vandenberg to turn the tide.

The initial push in the Congress began with the meeting of congressional leaders at the White House on February 27, 1947. President Truman made it clear that he was seeking not advice but tangible support expressed in legislation to aid Greece and Turkey. It was at this meeting that Acheson followed Marshall in outlining the full gravity of the crisis. He warned that if Soviet expansion was not resisted, it threatened domination of two-thirds of the globe and three-quarters of the world's population. Senator Vandenberg, stirred by Acheson's persuasive appeal, promised his support, provided the president made clear to the Congress and the people the nature of the threat. Marshall's more prosaic explanation of the nature of the threat which defined the issue in the language of power and human needs in Europe was not by itself sufficient to forge a new American foreign policy consensus. The president in order to rally the nation would have to formulate the issues in dramatic, unequivocal, and worldwide terms.

In the brief span of a single week beginning February 21, 1947, the extensively documented statement of position and recommendations on which the Truman Doctrine was based was hammered out by the staff of the Department of State. The facts of the situation were clear. Greece was on the point of economic and military collapse, tempting the advance of Communist elements and a possible takeover. Britain was no longer able to play its historic role; its strategic economic support would soon be terminated. Secretary Marshall recommended that legislation be drafted for congressional approval calling for a direct loan to Greece and the transfer of military equipment by the executive to Greece. George F. Kennan presided for the first and last time at the staff meeting the evening of February 21. (He returned on March 6 and took exception to the universalistic character of the draft of the president's message, which had been prepared under Acheson's supervision by public affairs officer Joseph Jones. Kennan favored economic aid to Greece with limited military support but not aid to Turkey. More important, he objected to the ideological content of the draft with its open-ended commitment to help free peoples everywhere.) On February 22, discussions continued with heavy involvement by such high-ranking military officers as Admiral Sherman and General Norstad. On February 24, the Secretaries of War and Navy (Patterson and Forrestal) met with Undersecretary Acheson and his associates. Agreement was reached that the defense of Greece and Turkey was essential to the national interest. On February 25, Acheson met with his political, economic, legal, and information officers and consensus was achieved on the points to be covered in the final version of statement on "Position and Recommendations." On February 26, Marshall and Acheson met with Forrestal and Patterson and the issue of aid to countries other than Greece and Turkey was reviewed, including China and South Korea. A joint Defense and State Department working group concluded that the administration should proceed with legislation for aid to Greece and Turkey and that possible assistance to other countries should await future study.

February 27 was the day when the president, Secretary Marshall, and Undersecretary Acheson made their initial presentation to congressional leaders. This was the famous meeting at which Acheson took over from Secretary Marshall, who had based his argument for aid to Greece and Turkey largely on grounds of humanitarianism and loyalty to an ally in shoring up Britain's role in the Middle East. Acheson spoke in broader, more forceful terms, describing the Soviet intention as being domination of the eastern Mediterranean and the Middle East, opening the way to its penetration of South Asia and Africa. The Soviet aim was to encircle Turkey and Germany and establish Soviet hegemony on three continents. The Soviets sought military and naval bases in the Turkish Straits. If Turkey and the West made concessions, Turkey's independence would be destroyed. The fate of Greece, Turkey, and Iran were inseparably linked. If one or the other were to fall within the Soviet sphere or if Italy were to go Communist, the fate of all would be sealed. The struggle was not only one between two superpowers more polarized than any two rivals since Rome and Carthage but also between the protagonists of two irreconcilable ideologies.

It was the reported clash between "Eastern communism and Western democracy" that stirred the congressional leaders. They were given an issue they could take to their constituents. One witness records: "At the meeting with congressional leaders Acheson discovered that he had to pull out all the stops and speak in the . . . boldest, widest terms to attract their support for a matter which in parliamentary democracies without a tradition of isolationism would have been undertaken without fanfare."[8] Vandenberg, in giving provisional support, set one "condition": that the president in bringing the crisis before the American people must define the issue in its ideological not merely its strategic or humanitarian dimensions. In effect, the decision to universalize the Truman Doctrine was reached at the February 27 meeting. The president accepted, indeed welcomed, Vandenberg's "condition" and that same evening Acheson invited twenty prominent newspaper columnists to meet with him and reviewed the history of the situation in Greece and the broader context of the problem. On the morning of February 28, Acheson called departmental officers to a meeting in the State Department and made assignments for drafting legislation, preparing the president's message to Congress and the nation, and launching a public information program.

The legislative history of the Truman Doctrine is instructive for understanding the foreign policy consensus which emerged. Republican gains in the mid-term election of 1946 confirmed that economy was uppermost in the minds of the electorate. The only issue that loomed larger was halting the spread of communism. A subcommittee of the State-War-Navy Coordinating Committee was established to handle public information or, as one observer wrote, "propaganda, in short." A paper was prepared called "Public Information Program on United States Aid to Greece." It referred to support to free people everywhere and language from the paper, at Acheson's instruction, was inserted word for word into the first draft of the president's speech. The defenders of the approach, including Clark Clifford, justified its rhetoric as "the opening gun in a campaign to bring people up to [the] realization that the war isn't over by any means."[9] Others dissented, and Robert Donovan has written: "Marshall's feelings about the final State Department draft are in some question. Acheson said it was sent to him in Paris while he was on the way to Moscow, and he approved it. Charles E. Bohlen, who was with Marshall, recalled that the two of them thought the rhetoric too flamboyantly anti-communist."[10]

8. *Ibid.*, 143.
9. Notation, March 9, 1947, in Papers of George M. Elsey, Truman Doctrine Speech folder, Harry S. Truman Library, Independence, Missouri,
10. Robert J. Donovan, *Conflict and Crisis: The Presidency of Harry S. Truman, 1945–1948* (New York: W. W. Norton & Company, 1977), 282.

According to Bohlen, Marshall informed Washington of his reservations but was told that the president and his advisers saw congressional action as being dependent on the boldest possible statement delineating the worldwide threat of communism.[11] Men like Paul H. Nitze and C. B. Marshall have confirmed that those leaders who testified on the Truman Doctrine, the Marshall Plan, and NATO were convinced that congressional support required a stirring and unqualified statement of the global threat of communism. Kennan, Bohlen, and General Marshall were not alone in questioning this approach, and George M. Elsey, who reviewed the draft of the Truman message with Clifford in the White House, wrote in a memorandum to Clifford dated March 7: "There has been no overt action in the immediate past by the U.S.S.R. which serves as an adequate pretext for 'all-out' speech. The situation in Greece is relatively 'abstract'; there have been other instances—Iran, for example—where the occasion more adequately justified such a speech and there will be other occasions—I fear—in the future."[12] Yet for reasons of domestic politics if nothing else, the Kennan-Bohlen-Marshall-Elsey viewpoint was overruled.

On March 12, 1947, Truman addressed the Congress. His biographer wrote of the speech: "The collectively written speech . . . was certainly the most controversial of his presidency and probably remains the most enduringly controversial speech that has been made by a president in the twentieth century."[13] The debate over its scope and framework continued in the 1960s and 1970s, particularly on the issue of Vietnam. Not only had Greece requested assistance from the United States but, it was reported, had asked for American technicians, including a military mission. to administer economic and military aid. In response to liberal critics, Truman acknowledged the deficiencies of the Greek government and the grievances of those Greeks who had fled to join the guerrillas. However, the civil war had been intensified and expanded by military aid to the Communist-dominated Popular Army of Liberation (ELAS) provided by Albania, Bulgaria, and Yugoslavia under directions from Moscow. The decision was made that the United States would not stand idly by and allow outside forces to impose a new order on a free people particularly when its own vital interests were threatened. It had fought

11. See Dean Acheson, *Present at the Creation: My Years in the State Department* (New York: W. W. Norton & Company, 1969), 221; Charles Bohlen, *Witness to History, 1929–1969* (New York: W. W. Norton & Company, 1973), 261.

12. Elsey memorandum to Clifford, March 7, 1947, in Papers of Clark Clifford, Greek speech folder, HSTL.

13. Donovan, *Conflict and Crisis*, 283.

World War II to prevent the destruction of free institutions and it would not see freedom destroyed in the postwar world. The line must be clearly drawn and forthright distinctions made between democracy and totalitarianism and between regimes which safeguarded and those that suppressed personal freedoms.

The root principle of the Truman Doctrine was its definition of the threats to freedom that the United States would resist. The threats as defined were specifically subjugation by "armed minorities" or by "outside pressures." Containment, which Kennan had urged in his long telegram and in his Mr. X article in the July, 1947, issue of *Foreign Affairs*, would come into play whenever freedom was threatened either by "armed minorities" or "outside pressures." Kennan had counseled a "patient but firm and vigilant containment of Russian expansive tendencies." He had favored political, not military containment because of the inherent nature of the Soviet threat, which was not primarily military as was Hitler's challenge to the West. The Truman Doctrine recognized the urgent need of bringing America's vast economic resources to bear to forestall economic chaos in Greece. It called for $300 million for Greece and $100 million for Turkey and an important segment of the aid was for economic and political purposes. (It is worth noting that three decades later, the leader of Pakistan was to call proposed military aid of this magnitude "peanuts".) There were important reasons, however, why the program took on a strong military emphasis. One was the decline of American military strength with profound effects on America's influence and power in the world. As we have seen (page 59), the armed forces had declined from 12 million to 1.5 million troops with military spending declining from $90.9 billion annually early in 1945 to $10.3 billion in early 1947. A second reason was continued fighting in Greece, with weakened government forces fighting ELAS troops supplied by Communist countries. A third reason was the linkage between ideological warfare and military conflict. The senior senator from New York, Daniel Patrick Moynihan, has argued that as military conflict declines ideological warfare intensifies, suggesting an inverse relationship between the two. Moynihan notwithstanding, the Cold War would indicate precisely the opposite relationship. In peak periods of open conflict, the threat of military conflict has almost always been accompanied by more extreme Cold War rhetoric. Conversely, the so-called era of detente of Nixon and Kissinger witnessed a decline in ideological crusading. It was inevitable, therefore, that the Truman Doctrine, which signaled the full recognition by America of the harsh reality of the Cold War, also heralded a sharp increase of both military and ideological competition between East and West. If the doctrine was a turning point in history, it led also to a rigidity in American foreign policy which, in the opinion of leaders like Senator Walter George, made any relaxation of tension difficult to achieve for more than a generation.

By late spring, the Congress passed the Greek-Turkish aid bill and on May 22 President Truman put his signature to the act. Congressmen who had been isolationists or had led the fight for reduced military and economic spending yielded to the momentum of the administration's campaign. Skeptics found themselves between the rock and the hard place and were forced to suspend their own crusade for economy in the face of the president's anti-Communist crusade. Senators like Vandenberg and Tom Connally of Texas paid lip-service to the United Nations by introducing harmless amendments that reconciled American unilateral actions with the Charter of the United Nations, which almost everyone agreed was powerless to act in any great power conflict. The president disarmed critics like Eleanor Roosevelt, who proposed that the administration would defend democracy best by strengthening American society at home, by agreeing that social progress was vital. When others proposed that American strength be used to bring the Russians to the conference table, Acheson responded that negotiations were useless. Only if the Soviets over a long period of time came to recognize that America possessed the strength and the will to defend its interests would they be prepared to negotiate.

Therefore, the Truman Doctrine ushered in the most intense years of the Cold War, a period of protracted and unremitting struggle which was to last for more than a decade. It was a time of unrestrained political, ideological, and economic warfare verging on military conflict, which threatened to erupt around the globe. Unanswered was the question whether the Soviets wanted war or, as Churchill had prophesied, the fruits of war. It was a period, however, in which the foundations for another great policy initiative were laid, one with even more far-reaching consequences, namely, the Marshall Plan, to which attention must now be directed.

The Marshall Plan

The beginnings of the Marshall Plan are linked with discussions concerning the broader context of the Truman Doctrine. A special ad hoc committee representing the State, War, and Navy Departments was appointed to review the European and international setting and assess economic and military needs. Questions to be explored for each country included the extent and nature of the threat, internal resources available, the possibility of effective aid, forms of assistance, the nature of American interests, conditions for assistance, and the consequences of giving or withholding aid. The Committee on Extension of Aid to Foreign Governments was created within the State Department and its economic, social, and political studies prepared the way for the Marshall Plan. At first, the State Department group was composed of middle-level officers; key figures such as Acheson and Marshall were preoccupied with defending the Truman Doctrine or in negotiations with Moscow. Upon returning from Moscow on April 28, 1947, Secretary Marshall summoned George Kennan to his office and told him to return from the War College to the State Department and set up a policy-planning staff without delay. Kennan was ordered to assemble a staff and address the problem of Europe immediately. The staff was formally created on May 5 and it submitted its recommendations to Marshall on May 23. In discussions leading to the recommendations, priorities and the prospects for mutual assistance especially within Europe were considered. The recovery of larger countries like Germany and Japan was studied as it related to recovery needs within their regions. The role of East European countries was reexamined. In important economic sectors, the strength of an interdependent Europe cut across the Iron Curtain, with France needing Polish coal and Germany grain from the Balkans. The single most important factor in promoting concern for economic stability in Europe was the growth of a widespread reaction in America and Europe that the Truman Doctrine placed too great an emphasis on military and ideological issues.

In part, the popular reactions especially in Europe were understandable. Half the aid proposed for Greece and all the aid for Turkey was military in character. Europeans from the beginning of the East-West struggle tended to view the threat more as economic and political than military, if we can judge public sentiment by the statements of Europe's more articulate spokesmen. War's devastation had deprived European societies of the sinews of economic health. A succession of severe winters intensified the crisis as shortages of fuel, food, and raw materials took a heavy toll. Europeans, and in particular liberals and socialists, saw the threat of communism in weakened economies and political unrest more than in military conflict.

The administration set about fashioning a response to its critics.

Acheson undertook to turn back the growing tide of opinion in a major foreign policy speech. The president had accepted an invitation to speak on May 8 in Cleveland, Mississippi, at the annual meeting of the Delta Council. Faced with a bitter intraparty fight that swirled around the question of who should be appointed to succeed Senator Bilbo, Truman chose not to go but invited Acheson to replace him. The speech outlined the major dimensions of Europe's economic problems and estimated that Europe would require some $5 billion in external assistance over a period of several years.

Meanwhile, at the Moscow Conference of the Council of Foreign Ministers meeting from March 10 to April 24, 1947, Secretary Marshall had sought to negotiate a peace settlement and determine Germany's position within a European settlement. As the negotiations proceeded, the economic condition of Germany and Europe loomed ever larger in Marshall's mind. In a radio address on April 28 on his return from Europe, the secretary defined the problems facing Europe, saying: "We were faced with immediate issues which vitally concerned the impoverished and suffering people of Europe who are crying for help, for coal, for food, and for most of the necessities of life." The future of Germany was a vital issue, but Germany's recovery would be acceptable to the rest of Europe only within the wider European community. The Soviets had shown little willingness to accept a settlement that provided for the demilitarization of Germany nor were they any more responsive than they had been with Secretary Byrnes on the question of a Four Power Pact that would have guaranteed German disarmament for twenty-five to fifty years.

As Marshall prepared to leave the conference, he warned that Soviet opposition to Germany's demilitarization or its economic unification had thrown a grim shadow over East-West understanding. Stalin responded saying that he was more optimistic, that the talks thus far had been only first skirmishes and that with patience the problem of Germany could be resolved. Marshall and the Americans returning to the United States concluded that the Russians saw continued economic stagnation in Germany and Europe to be in their interest and were playing for time to improve the prospects of Communist successes in these countries. In his radio address, Marshall dealt directly with Stalin's tactics in a frank and terse appraisal, observing: "But we cannot ignore the factor of time involved here. The recovery of Europe has been far slower than had been expected. . . . The patient is sinking while the doctors deliberate."

The secretary called for action and summoned the policy planning staff under Kennan's leadership to come forward with a plan for European reconstruction. Soon the informed public would be clamoring for a greater sense of proportion in America's aid to the world with a better distribution of military and economic assistance and a clearer definition of priorities. Indeed, the day after Truman's message, Walter Lippmann wrote: "Never was it so necessary to budget our means and our commitments. Never was it so necessary to define our commitments by a unified strategical conception as to where our available power, prestige, money, and expertness, which are not unlimited, can be invested with the best prospect of achieving the best that is judged to be possible."

By May 5, Kennan had recruited personnel for the policy planning staff, selected more for their professional competence and early availability than for their public image. General Marshall's only advice as the staff began its work was "avoid trivia." On May 23, Kennan submitted recommendations to Marshall, drafted largely by himself but drawn not only from the thinking of his immediate colleagues (such as Joseph E. Johnson, who was later to become President of the Carnegie Endowment for International Peace, Colonel Charles H. Bonesteel III, and Jacques Reinstein, the economist) but also from reports, studies, and expert testimony from the Department of State and other branches of government. The report recommended a crash program to solve Europe's glaring shortage of industrial fuel by rebuilding its coal production capacity. For the long term, it proposed a large-scale effort "directed not to the combatting of communism as such but to the restoration of the economic health and vigor of European society." It was Europe's economic maladjustment which made it vulnerable to exploitation by Russian communism or by any other totalitarian movement. The staff paper drew a sharp line between what America might do and the responsibilities Europe itself must assume. No one formulated this with greater wisdom and clarity than General Marshall, who on June 5, 1947, unveiled the broad outlines of the European Recovery Program at the 296th Harvard University Commencement.

At the commencement exercises, General Marshall joined General Omar N. Bradley, J. Robert Oppenheimer, T. S. Eliot, Hodding Carter, Jr., and William F. Gibbs as recipients of honorary degrees. His simple dress of gray sack suit, white shirt, and blue necktie was less conspicuous than the resplendent gowns and military decorations of others in the ceremony, yet the eight thousand people assembled in the outdoor theater under the elms facing the Memorial Church singled him out in the procession. President James Conant spoke of Marshall as "a soldier and statesman whose ability and character brook only one comparison in the history of this nation." The reference was unmistakably to President Washington.

In his address toward the end of the ceremony, Marshall began by observing that the problems of Europe took on enormous complexity and "the facts presented to the public by the press and the radio make it exceedingly difficult for the man in the street to reach a clear appraisement of the situation." He spoke of the breakdown of Europe's economy, with industry producing too few goods to supply people in the towns and countryside and farmers drawing back and producing only for their own consumption. Governments were using up scarce foreign exchange to buy food and fuel abroad and Europe faced the grim prospect of lacking the resources and confidence to reverse its economic decline over the next three or four years. "The remedy lies," declared Marshall, "in breaking the vicious circle . . . in the economic future of their own countries and of Europe as a whole. The manufacturer and the farmer . . . must be able and willing to exchange their products for currencies the continuing value of which is not open to question."

In looking back and comparing Marshall's response to that of other Cold War policies, four characteristic elements in his approach stand out. First, the Marshall Plan was addressed to an urgent problem, the recovery of Europe, which the secretary graphically described both in its particulars and its broader manifestations. Secondly, it was, in Marshall's words "not directed against any country or doctrine but against hunger, poverty, desperation and chaos. . . . Any government that is willing to assist in the task of recovery will find full cooperation . . . on the part of the United States government." If this was the idealistic dimension of the plan, Marshall, who was no innocent in world politics, added, "Governments, political parties, or groups which seek to perpetuate human misery in order to profit therefrom politically will encounter the opposition of the United States." Third, the secretary's plan was not "made in Washington" but in its details awaited the formulation of an agreed design by the countries of Europe and commitments by them as to the part they would play. In language that anyone experienced in foreign assistance could take as a model, Marshall explained: "It would be neither fitting nor efficacious for this government to undertake to draw up unilaterally a program designed to place Europe on its feet economically." This was the business of Europeans. The initiative had to come from Europe. Moreover, the proposal should be a joint European appeal. It should be addressed "as a joint request from a group of friendly nations, not as a series of isolated and individual appeals." In Kennan's view, the emphasis on Europe as a whole rather than a series of uncoordinated national programs rested on sound economic and political logic. One of the long-term weaknesses of the European economy was its fragmentation, the rigidity of commercial exchange and the absence of a large economic market. In Kennan's words: "By insisting on a joint approach, we hoped to force the Europeans to begin to think like Europeans, and not like nationalists in their approach to the economic problems of the continent."[14] Finally the Marshall Plan was to have a beginning, a middle, and an end, a watchword for rational foreign assistance programs. Marshall saw economic assistance to Europe as a cure, not a palliative.

Marshall took pains to point out that no foreign observer could read the future. At the end of his Harvard speech, the secretary removed his glasses and spoke extemporaneously: "We are too remote from all these countries to grasp at all the real significance of the situation." He warned against merely reacting to the passions and prejudices of the moment. Yet mindful of the Congress and wise to the tendencies of external aid becoming a dole rather than the catalyst that helps a self-reliant people recover economic health, Marshall was equally clear that: "The program must contain reasonable assurance that if we support it, this will be the last such program we shall be asked to support in the foreseeable future."

The Marshall Plan captured overnight the imagination of European leaders. Ernest Bevin, Britain's foreign minister, had the full text as the secretary finished speaking at 9:00 P.M. London time. He read and reread the text and, in his words, resolved to "seize the offer with both hands." He arranged to go to Paris to meet the French foreign minister, Georges Bidault. The idea of European recovery served to counteract two dangerous misimpressions that the Truman Doctrine had left with Europeans. These were that the American approach was exclusively a defensive approach to Communist pressure and that the doctrine gave a blank check of military and economic aid to any country in the world where the Communists gave evidence of being successful.

On the day following his Harvard speech, Marshall raised the question at a regular staff meeting whether the Soviet Union would join the plan. The secretary understood that an offer must be made if the world

14. George F. Kennan, *Memoirs, 1925–1950* (Boston: Little, Brown & Company, 1967), 337.

was to accept his declaration that the plan was "not directed against any country or doctrine." Yet he also knew, as Charles E. Bohlen warned, "that Soviet acceptance might easily kill the plan in Congress." Marshall turned to his Soviet experts, Bohlen and Kennan, and both gave much the same answer. They were convinced that the Soviet Union "would not accept American verification of the use of the goods and funds." They "did not think the Soviet Union would be able to maintain its control over Eastern Europe if those countries were able to participate."[15] They prophesied that the Soviet Union would withdraw from cooperation with the West.

Bohlen's and Kennan's prediction was borne out in the weeks that followed. In July, Molotov and a staff of eighty came to Paris for exploratory talks with the British and French on the plan. Although Molotov expressed interest, the Soviet delegation left the meeting, presumably at Stalin's direction, when its proposals were turned down. Molotov's proposals called for each country to draw up its own shopping list, which the United States was to accept and fund. It was clear the Soviets would reject on-site inspection of the use that was made of any assistance. As for the Soviet satellites, the Soviets from the outset recognized "that the Marshall Plan imperilled Soviet control of Eastern Europe." In Bohlen's account: "The Czechs made a move toward joining the plan by accepting an invitation to a second meeting. According to a member of the Czech government who subsequently defected, Stalin called the Czechs to Moscow and forbade them to accept the Marshall Plan. . . . Prague had no choice; it had to withdraw."[16]

The manner in which the Marshall Plan was put forward had considerable political impact throughout Europe. Bohlen, who had prepared the original draft of the secretary's speech, was responsible for the wording affirming that the policy was directed against hunger, poverty, and chaos, not against any country or ideology and specifically not against communism. Marshall deleted the reference to communism but added *desperation* to *hunger* and *poverty*. Once the Communists rejected the plan, they became "partisans of hunger, poverty, desperation, and chaos." The West by its approach won a propaganda victory of substantial proportions, especially in European countries which had large Communist parties. It was claiming too much to promise that the Marshall Plan would eradicate communism in Western Europe. More to the point, the tactics of the Communists in a country like France where political strikes

15. Bohlen, *Witness to History*, 264–65.
16. *Ibid.*, 265.

were organized soon demonstrated that Communists understood that if European recovery were achieved, their prospects of coming to power would be sharply curtailed. Marshall had turned the tables against the adversary. The Communists were put on the defensive.

By November, Congress began hearings on the legislation proposed by the administration, but months were to pass before a full plan was adopted. Failure of the Congress to act promptly led to interim measures that added some $587 million to the funds required for the plan itself. The interim aid for winter relief in Austria, China, France, and Italy, much like an earlier emergency appropriation passed by the Senate in May for Austria, Hungary, Poland, Italy, Trieste, China, and Greece, represented a piecemeal approach. Sentiment was growing in the Congress that the United States, which earlier had channeled billions to Europe through UNRRA, the British loan and Greek-Turkish aid, required a more comprehensive approach. It was not enough to patch a badly leaking roof; a new one had to be built.

Despite the buildup of this sentiment, Congress resisted action, for the idea fell on a Republican Congress dedicated to reducing taxes and cutting government spending. As Senator Vandenberg saw it: "There was deep concern, not only in Congress but throughout the country, that scarce American goods would be drained off the domestic market for foreign consumption. There was similar concern lest the United States strain its financial and material resources only to 'pour its money down a rat hole.'" Businessmen questioned whether the plan's success would simply increase competition for American business.

Vandenberg's response to such opposition was to urge the president to appoint a bipartisan advisory council of America's "ablest and most experienced citizenship drawn from industry, labor, manufacturing and agriculture." It was necessary to determine what the nation could "safely and wisely" undertake in its own self-interest. Truman established a nonpartisan advisory council under the chairmanship of W. Averell Harriman, the secretary of commerce, to inventory Europe's needs and America's resources. A parallel group came into being in Europe (the Committee of European Economic Cooperation) at the initiative of Bevin and Robert Schuman. The Soviets soon withdrew from the committee, as did other East European states, forming their own Cominform. The remaining sixteen European nations met throughout the summer to determine agricultural and industrial targets and work out the basis for economic cooperation.

Out of the stocktaking, estimates emerged of the amount of American assistance required, originally set at $29 billion over four and a quarter years, reduced to $22 billion, and then to $17 billion. The price tag in the end came down to something around $13 billion based on a strategy of self-help by the Europeans and outside aid. In Bohlen's opinion, "One of the reasons the Marshall Plan worked so well was that the sixteen European countries that joined it contained the necessary qualified personal skills, and institutions. All the United States was doing was injecting a little economic blood into a system that had stopped functioning."[17] Bohlen concluded, as did almost every student of foreign assistance who compared Marshall aid with later assistance to the developing countries, that Europe's needs were for rebuilding economic systems whereas less developed countries required the wholesale creation of the necessary institutions and skills.

On the domestic political front, Vandenberg was troubled by the lack of agreement within his own party. He wrote his wife on November 13, 1947: "Evidently I am to have some degree of trouble with Bob Taft. . . . The world is full of tragedy; but there is no tragedy greater than we have to have a presidential election next year. . . . That must be what's biting Robert." Vandenberg had differences with his predecessor as chairman of the Senate Foreign Relations Committee, Senator Tom Connally, and he wrote of politics being heavy in the air. By the end of November, Vandenberg grew more optimistic, partly because of the magnificent preparatory work by the State Department and the report of the Harriman Commission—"three inches thick." By month's end, he was able to write his wife: "I think we shall finish [interim aid] Monday afternoon; and I shall be greatly surprised if more than a dozen Senators dare vote against the bill. Even Taft announced in a speech today that he would vote for it."[18]

Vandenberg's success in the political arena resulted from his energetic defense on myriad fronts of a plan which he understood had to be acceptable to diverse political constituencies. He answered those who saw impossible conundrums in balancing Europe's needs with America's necessities by acknowledging that "anyone who says 'I know the right answer' is way off base. We are dealing with a world in unpredictable flux. . . . So we have no alternative but . . . to balance one 'calculated risk' against another." He wrote to Clark M. Eichelberger, who asked re-

17. *Ibid.*, 266.
18. Arthur H. Vandenberg, Jr. (ed.), *The Private Papers of Senator Vandenberg* (Boston: Houghton Mifflin, 1952), 379.

assurance that the plan would not weaken the United Nations: "I do not think it is any reflection on the United Nations to admit that . . . there are some basic questions with which it cannot be expected to cope." Considerations beyond "charity" or "communism" had entered the picture, including the fact that some European countries would soon be totally without foreign exchange to buy American commodities. He urged Robert A. Lovett, undersecretary of state, who became an indispensable ally, that it was vital to enlist "four or five top level business executives" who would appear as "aggressive witnesses" in committee hearings on the plan. In an address at the University of Michigan, he counseled that America had to balance the calculated risk of undertaking too much—"we cannot indefinitely underwrite the world"—with an opposite risk of not responding, which was, in Secretary Marshall's words: "the danger of the actual disappearance of the characteristics of Western civilization on which our government and our manner of living are based."[19]

In 1948, the political task of steering the Marshall Plan through Congress began for Vandenberg. The study committees had reported that the effort fell within America's capacities. Vandenberg's prestige mounted as he called on Michigan Republicans to withdraw his name from a "Vandenberg-for-President" campaign. In the days from January 8 to February 5, the Senate Foreign Relations Committee called on more than ninety witnesses representing every major segment of American life. As the hearings came to an end, a group of twenty Republican senators sought revisions to the legislation. Working with Lewis W. Douglas, ambassador to Britain who became a link between the Senate committee and Marshall and Lovett, Vandenberg cut the initial request from $17 billion over four-and-a-quarter years to an estimated $5.3 billion over twelve months, because no Congress could bind another on spending. The initial funds would come from the common treasury, not from new taxes. Vandenberg reported to one of his constituents anxious about increased taxes that Secretary of Defense Forrestal and Secretary of the Army Royall had testified "that without legislation of this character they would find it necessary immediately to ask for heavily increased appropriations for defense. Why? Because it is infinitely cheaper to defend ourselves by economic means."[20]

At Vandenberg's insistence, provisions were added to the bill emphasizing Europe's responsibilities and a continuous audit of their perfor-

19. *Ibid.*, 379, 380–83.
20. *Ibid.*, 387.

mance. A debate ensued regarding the administration of the program. At first, the State Department draft placed the administrator under State Department control. Buttressed by a Brookings Institution study, the senator proposed to Marshall and the president that an administrator of cabinet rank be appointed to head an independent economic coopera-tion administration, who would keep the secretary of state informed. In the event of a dispute between him and the secretary, the president was to settle the differences.

Thanks to Vandenberg's willingness and that of the administration to accept compromises and changes, the Foreign Relations Committee approved the bill by a vote of 13 to 0. On March 1, Vandenberg spoke for an hour and twenty minutes to senators and House members who crowded the Senate galleries. He stressed America's self-interest, the re-gional nature of Europe's problems, the threat of expansive Soviet com-munism, the issue of economic survival of 270 million people, the need for a comprehensive approach, the intellectual and political foundations of the plan, the eight months of study by "more devoted minds than I have ever known to concentrate upon any one objective in all my 20 years in Congress," and the turning point in history for American lead-ership represented in the plan. His speech, which had gone through seven drafts, brought him to "the climactic role" in his political career.

The Senate debated the bill in all its details for two long weeks. The isolationist chairman of the Appropriations Committee in the House, Congressman John Taber, delayed procedures by holding continuous hearings for several weeks concerning questions which had already been clarified by other committees. People in Europe, not familiar with con-gressional procedures, could not understand that a single representative was able to cause substantial delay when the president and a large major-ity in Congress approved the legislation. However, by March 14, 1948, the Senate had voted its approval 69 to 17. The House promptly ac-cepted the major provisions of the bill, differences were ironed out in conference, and soon thereafter the president signed the bill and it be-came law.

The Marshall Plan having been enacted, Vandenberg fought to gain administrative support for one remaining element in the plan. He insis-ted on a "business administrator' who would be recruited from outside government. The administration sent up several trial balloons of men being considered for the post, including William L. Clayton, undersecre-tary of state for economic affairs, Ambassador Lewis W. Douglas, and, finally, Dean Acheson, who at the time was outside government in the practice of law. Vandenberg, while expressing admiration for all three, insisted on a business executive and himself canvassed some one hundred business leaders, at least half of whom recommended Paul G. Hoffman, president of the Studebaker Corporation and chairman of the board of the Committee for Economic Development. Hoffman was reluctant, but Vandenberg prevailed and Hoffman later explained, "He knocked all my defenses down and by the time I spoke to the President I couldn't say 'no.'" Throughout Hoffman's tenure as ECA administrator, Vandenberg defended him as having put together the best nonpolitical organization of any government project, never yielding to White House pressures on such issues as the selection of personnel.

The political struggle was not over, however, and in June, 1948, the House moved to gut the program. Its most determined advocate of economy, John Taber, ordered a cut of 26 percent, or $2,160,000,000 in the first year's appropriation for the plan. Alarms were sounded throughout Europe that America's credibility was at stake. Vandenberg appeared before the Senate Appropriations Committee lashing out at the House action. Despite the politically charged atmosphere with the Republican national convention only a few days off, his appeal was successful and most of the cuts were restored. Vandenberg's successful appeal was based on the national interest and the necessity of giving the plan a fair chance.

The lessons of the Marshall Plan in its intellectual and legislative history are self-evident. First, it demonstrated that the United States could respond to economic and political crises as well as military threats. The long history of isolationism as described by writers like Lippmann and Morgenthau had been the story of continued passivity and indifference followed by abrupt military intervention at the eleventh hour. The plan gave a signal to Europe and the world that the United States could allocate its resources to achieve economic purposes over a sustained period as needed. It was a positive and constructive program possessing its own dynamics, not a merely defensive measure.

Second, if the Truman Doctrine was a universalistic and indiscriminate response to the threat of communism everywhere, offering a blank check to the foes of communism wherever they might be, the Marshall Plan at its core was a well-crafted and discriminate response to an urgent problem the dimensions of which were explicitly defined by the recipient states at the outset. For anyone schooled in foreign assistance, it is curious how often indiscriminate responses survive legislative scrutiny. Even small private foreign assistance agencies working abroad require a plan that defines local needs in considerable detail and promises in effect "If you do this, we will do that." By contrast, it happens primarily in the military sphere, as the threat to national survival seizes the public, that popular hysteria and military necessity may converge to cancel out the need for such discriminating planning. (I write this as a former soldier, not as a chronic critic of the military.) If one thinks back to late 1979 to the proposed $5 billion supplementary military appropriation—or in 1981 for larger sums—and asks "how fully were the precise allocations of such funds spelled out and set forth publicly before the Congress and the president decided to act," the truth of this proposition is evident. Especially at election time, legislators display a penchant for throwing money at a problem before its magnitude is defined.

Third, both political parties came to see that they had a political stake in the plan. In Vandenberg's words; "The ECA was an example of bipartisan foreign policy at its best." The parties joined hands in seeing the program through Congress and gave it their continuing support, in Vandenberg's case long after he retired as chairman of the Senate Foreign Relations Committee. "It was this continuing support . . . that enabled the agency [ECA] to make such a successful record of accomplishment."[21] Individual groups in the United States supported the plan for their own reasons—churchmen because of its humanitarianism, military men because of its strategic implications, and businessmen and economists because of the economic prospects for Europe.

Finally, the plan at its core was founded on the convergence of the national interests of Europe and America. It did not rest alone on a universal ideological doctrine nor on fragmentary interests of sub-national groups, although some revisionist historians have argued the point. In this regard, it had both a realistic and idealistic basis—which historically has been a vital component for almost every successful American foreign policy.

21. *Ibid.*, 394, 398.

Chapter Four

Collective Security and
the Balance of Power

NATO as the Model

In the same way the Marshall Plan was put forward because of concerns and anxieties in Europe and America over the Truman Doctrine, the formation of a North Atlantic alliance resulted in part at least from France's fears of a resurgent German economy within the Marshall Plan. As before World Wars I and II, France sought security guarantees particularly in the military and political field as a precondition of their full participation in the European Recovery Program. The North Atlantic Treaty Organization provided the instrument for guaranteeing the nations of Europe that their independence would be preserved. It came to be viewed uncritically as a model for the rest of the world.

Ideas and Architects of NATO

The idea of collective security was in the air in the 1940s, and while proposals for a North Atlantic security system fell short of the universal concept of the peace planners in the early postwar period, regional and universal ideas were linked at almost every point in the discussion. Provision had been made in the United Nations Charter for collective self-defense arrangements; Articles 51, 52, and 53 required the Security Council to accord them priority in the settlement of regional disputes. Principles of collective security were invoked at successive stages in NATO planning. Dean Acheson took the lead among those who saw the need for regional security arrangements consistent with the charter but filling the gap that the breakdown of Great Power unanimity had created for security arrangements by the United Nations. In Acheson's view, there was need for restoring a balance of power in Europe, but this was dependent upon a regional collective security system. He wrote:

"The idea of an attack on one considered as an attack on all came from the Treaty of Rio de Janeiro and the idea of allies jointly and severally taking measures to restore peace and security came from Article 51 of the United Nations Treaty."[1] Acheson perhaps more than any of his colleagues recognized that the United Nations was incapable of providing the security guarantees that Europe and especially France required, and he undertook to construct a system comparable to that of the inter-American system established by the Treaty of Rio.

Collective security was a vaulting idea which came to rest for Acheson and others at a regional level. Universal collective security, which Acheson and a majority of writers on international relations had embraced before and after World War II, rested on the proposition of one for all and all for one. It assumed that no nation could be secure if any nation were insecure. No nation was an island unto itself. True collective security presupposed that overwhelming strength could be brought to bear against an aggressor, that agreement was possible on the status quo to be defended, and that states would subordinate conflicting interests to the common good. Before and after World War II, practice consistently fell short of the ideal. As Churchill observed: "With the invasion of Ethiopia by Italy, England knew that sanctions meant war. Englishmen determined there would not be war. England chose sanctions." In 1950, the Korean War was defended as collective security action authorized by the United Nations, yet only the United States, Britain, Canada, and Turkey sent substantial numbers of troops. Once China entered the Korean War, the war became a conflict of two alliances. Something more than collective security was at stake. The Asian balance of power came into play, as neither China nor the United States could afford to accept the other's hegemony over the whole of Korea. The national interest of the United States required that Japan's security be preserved and with it the overall political stability of Northeast Asia. The clash of national interests determined the extent and the limits of American and Chinese actions in Korea, not some abstract notion of collective security. A war that gained its legitimacy at the outset from the idea of collective security became a war the contours of which were determined essentially by the balance of power.

Alongside Dean Acheson, another strong personality who played a role in the formation of NATO was John Foster Dulles, who served first

---

1. Dean Acheson, *Present at the Creation: My Years in the State Department* (New York: W. W. Norton & Company, 1969), 280–81.

as an adviser to Secretary Marshall and then to Acheson. Dulles' philosophy of international relations was a product of internationalism in the interwar and wartime periods. He like others who evolved a world viewpoint was convinced that America's failure to support the League of Nations had brought on World War II. He espoused collective security, but when Soviet intransigence made collective enforcement by the United Nations impossible, Dulles turned to regional collective security arrangements first in Europe and later in Southeast Asia and the Near East. It would be difficult to imagine the widespread appeal of the idea of regional security systems following World War II without the dominant influence of Acheson and Dulles. By contrast, Kennan was to describe NATO as "the first of the major undertakings in General Marshall's time with relation to which I failed to exert any effective influence, and which took from the start, a course adverse in important respects to my own concept of what we ought to be attempting." [2]

It would be wrong to say that the initiative for a regional security system was wholly, even largely American. Following the London Conference of Foreign Ministers, which ended December 15, 1947, a little over nine months after the announcement of the Truman Doctrine and six months after the proclamation of the Marshall Plan, Britain took the initiative. In mid-January, 1948, Ernest Bevin with American encouragement opened discussion with France and the Benelux countries on plans for the common defense of Europe. France was responsive both because of its domestic situation imperilled by Communist-inspired strikes and its fear of the external threat of a resurgent Germany in the absence of a European security system. These early discussions on defense, moreover, preceded the interim aid to Europe or first phase of the Marshall Plan. The French were not alone. The Labor government in Britain also feared a revival of German militarism. Dulles warned that France felt "naked" and their cooperation in the Marshall Plan required an American military commitment. Thus the Marshall Plan was linked more closely to a commitment to NATO than to the carrying forward of the Truman Doctrine.

As important as the American guarantee to France and Britain was Europe's resolve to defend itself. On January 22, 1948, Bevin, in a major foreign policy speech before the House of Commons, called for a Western union among Britain, France, and the Benelux countries with strong mili-

2. George F. Kennan, *Memoirs, 1925–1950* (Boston: Little, Brown & Company, 1967), 397.

tary connotations. His initiative was welcomed by the Europeans and on March 16, following a conference in Brussels, a treaty was signed creating the Brussels Union.

Leadership in the American government had shifted during this period from Dean Acheson, who returned to private law practice, to the new undersecretary of state, Robert A. Lovett, who had been assistant secretary of war for air during World War II. The personalities of the two leaders profoundly influenced policy making. They were the human equation of NATO; Lovett had all the proper credentials. Like Acheson, he was a graduate of Yale. He was a senior partner in the New York investment banking firm of Brown Brothers Harriman. He had been a naval aviator in World War I and organized the Army Air Corps in the period 1940–1945. He had close ties with the prewar and postwar economies of Europe. He had the confidence of General Marshall and the respect of Senator Vandenberg. During his eighteen months of service from the summer of 1947, he, like Acheson before him, often served as acting secretary of state in Marshall's absences. His close working relations with Congress and especially with Senators Vandenberg and Connally led not only to legislation for the Marshall Plan but to the Vandenberg Resolution, which was the forerunner of NATO. Lovett was tough-minded but less razor-tongued than Acheson, whose disdain for those who rivaled him as a speaker but had less mastery of foreign policy is illustrated in his comments on a joint speaking assignment in Duluth, Minnesota, with the young mayor of Minneapolis, Hubert Humphrey: "I spoke on the Marshall Plan, Humphrey on Humphrey. . . . In time, we reversed the order of speaking, since the Mayor seemed to have more ideas than I, or less terminal capacity, or both."[3] Lovett's "put-downs" were more subtle if no less devastating, but his adversaries remained his friends, whereas only the hardiest egos survived Acheson's barbs.

I recall a Lovett response in the late 1950s that illustrates his style. At a meeting of the trustees of the Rockefeller Foundation, Lovett listened patiently to both the presentation by the director of humanities of a project on electronic music and a tape of this form of music making, then responded: "I have lived a long life enjoying Bach and Beethoven without suffering electronic music. However, out of deference to the Director, I move the item." Kennan described Lovett as "personally, one of the most charming of men, a seasoned financier and a very smooth, capable

---

3. Acheson, *Present at the Creation*, 240–41.

operator," noting, however, that Lovett was prone to "catering to senatorial opinion in instances where one might better have attempted to educate its protagonists to a more enlightened and effective view."[4] While Kennan could write of his abiding respect for Acheson, that relationship was colored by the latter's tendency to dispose of opposing viewpoints with a cutting edge that was rapier-like in measuring and shattering its target. Of the Brussels talks, Kennan was to write: "I regarded the anxieties of the Europeans as a little silly; this was not, it seemed to me, the time to start talking about military defenses and preparations. I agreed that they needed some sort of reassurance; but I saw dangers in any form of such reassurances that would encourage them in their military preoccupations."[5] He and Acheson could not have been further apart.

History was to pass Kennan by, however, when on March 11, 1948, news was received of the mysterious death, by murder or suicide, of Jan Masaryk, the Czech foreign minister, son of the former president and a staunch friend of the West. Events such as this prompted General Lucius Clay, who had earlier prophesied war with the Soviet Union was unlikely for at least ten years, to cable Washington: "Within the last few weeks, I have felt a subtle change in Soviet attitude which I cannot define but which now gives me a feeling that it [war] may come with dramatic suddenness."[6] It mattered little that men like Bohlen and Kennan warned of overreacting to Soviet actions. Shortly after the end of the European war when Clay had been appointed second in command to General Eisenhower responsible for German affairs and had urged that getting along with the Soviets involved giving trust to gain trust, Bohlen had cautioned him that within a few months, or certainly within a year, he would become one of the officials in the American government most opposed to the Soviets, because "anyone who started with too many illusions about the Soviets came out disillusioned."[7] Writing of Clay's telegram Kennan observed: "I cannot help but believe that a deeper backgound in Russian affairs would have saved him from the error of interpretation that this message reflected and that the State Department, together with the rest of official Washington, would have done better in evaluating his message

4. Kennan, *Memoirs, 1925–1950*, pp. 404, 405.
5. *Ibid.*, 399.
6. Walter Millis (ed.), *The Forrestal Doctrine* (New York: Viking Press, 1951), 387.
7. Charles E. Bohlen, *Witness to History* (New York: W. W. Norton & Company, 1973), 222.

to rely on the judgement of some of us who knew something about Russia."[8]

The events of March, 1948—the tightening of Soviet control in Czechoslovakia and the first signs of Soviet efforts to force the Western powers to abandon Berlin—were to some Russian experts "defensive reactions on the Soviet side to the initial successes of the Marshall Plan initiative and to the preparations now being undertaken on the Western side to set up a separate German government in Western Germany." The reaction of official Washington was quite different. For the military establishment and the intelligence community, largely dominated by the military, war was seen as imminent. On March 16, the Central Intelligence Agency advised the president that war was "not probable within sixty days." On the day the Brussels Treaty was signed, March 17, the president addressed a joint session of Congress saying, "The grave events in Europe were moving so swiftly . . . that the United States will, by appropriate means, extend to the free nations the support which the situation requires." The die was cast; the political and intellectual foundations for NATO had been laid. Forgotten were warnings like Kennan's as early as 1947 that Western successes in restoring Europe's strength would predictably lead to the Soviets playing their last remaining cards to preserve the disorder of Europe, to strikes in France and Italy, a coup in Czechoslovakia, and the Berlin blockade, or to what he described as "baring of the fangs." "Washington's reactions," Kennan wrote, "were deeply subjective, influenced more by domestic-political moods and institutional interests than by any theoretical considerations of our international position."[9]

On June 11, 1948, the Senate passed Resolution 329, the Vandenberg Resolution, which reflected discussions between Lovett and Vandenberg. The resolution, which supported the Brussels Pact, spelled out two conditions introduced by the Michigan senator as essential to congressional approval of American participation in a North Atlantic security system. They were that America must not make an automatic commitment to go to war under certain conditions without congressional action and that benefits from a security treaty should be mutual, not unilateral, with a specific European country. The United States was to pledge itself to defend Europe, and the Europeans in turn to defend the United States. Critics argued that a formal legal commitment was unnecessary,

8. Kennan, *Memoirs, 1925–1950*, 400.
9. *Ibid.*, 401, 400, 403.

for the facts of the situation and America's defense of Europe in World
War II, let alone the Marshall Plan, made it patently clear that the
United States would come to the aid of Europe. Kennan wrote: "The
Vandenberg Resolution struck me then, as did nine-tenths of the 1,263
pages of testimony later taken by the Foreign Relations Committee of
the Senate in connection with the NATO pact, as typical of that mixture
of arid legalism and semantic pretentiousness that so often pass, in the
halls of our domestic-political life, for statesmanship."[10] Kennan argued
that what was needed was action, not promises to act, not legal undertakings or attempts to generalize future action. The Europeans should
draw up their own defense policies and take responsibility for carrying
them out. The real threat was the spread of communism by political
means throughout Europe. Intensive rearmament would be a diversion
from the greater danger of political instability and economic malaise in
Europe. Moreover, to expand membership in NATO to countries like
Greece and Turkey and to link European defense to the defense by Europeans of the United States would feed Russian fears of aggressive en-
circlement of the Soviet Union. It would obscure the purely defensive
nature of the Brussels Pact and complicate negotiations over the future
of Germany. Inclusion of countries like Italy, which was not a member of
the Brussels Pact, would affect the delicate balance of the political struggle in that country.

The actual negotiation of the Atlantic pact was postponed until after
the American elections in 1948. The original idea had been that the Congress would authorize the sending of military supplies to Europe on a
lend-lease or grant basis. The Vandenberg Resolution, which reflected
the views of the Congress, was a far broader concept. It provided the
basis for the United States joining a regional collective security organization. Kennan's ally in other matters, Bohlen, wrote: "NATO was simply a
necessity. The developing situation with the Soviet Union demanded the
participation of the United States in the defense of Europe. Any other
solution would have opened the area to Soviet domination."[11] When the
NATO pact was signed on April 4, 1949, it was seen as essentially a traditional military alliance of like-minded countries. Few if any of the participants envisioned the type of military setup into which NATO evolved
(and from which de Gaulle was to withdraw French forces in 1966). None
of the original framers anticipated the idea that John Foster Dulles was

10. *Ibid.*, 409.
11. Bohlen, *Witness to History*, 267.

to introduce in the presidential campaign of 1952 of rolling back Soviet power from Eastern Europe by military force or other means.

The mood of the late 1940s is difficult to recapture as the Soviet Union appeared on the move. Bohlen summarized the thinking that led to NATO and ended a long era of American isolationism by concluding: "Had the United States not inaugurated the Marshall Plan or something similar and had the United States not departed from its historical tradition and agreed to join NATO, the Communists might easily have assumed power in most of Western Europe."[12] With the apparent success of NATO, a pattern was set. In successive world crises, the American response characteristically became one of seeking security for itself and its allies in military collective security arrangements, the Southeast Asia Treaty Organization, Central Treaty Organization, and a variety of more limited security treaties. Containment increasingly became military containment and at least to a limited extent, the prophecy of its critics was fulfilled. Military measures took precedence over economic and political arrangements. That this approach reflected the views of a majority of the American people would be difficult to dispute.

Building a System of Regional Security

The American experience with NATO constitutes an important chapter in the Cold War both in itself and in setting a pattern for regional cooperation around the world. In the same way that the Truman Doctrine, as a historic statement of American intentions and commitments, was a forerunner of the Eisenhower Doctrine, the Nixon Doctrine, and the Carter Doctrine, NATO prepared the way for SEATO, CENTO, and other regional security arrangements. It was the model for organizing the power and capacities of non-Communist states to resist Soviet expansionism through limited collective security systems. Indeed it can be said that American foreign policy as it has evolved since 1947 manifests a three-pronged approach to peace and order in the postwar world. The historic doctrines beginning with the Truman Doctrine have provided allies and adversaries with a statement of America's objectives and commitments. The goal has been to minimize the risk of miscalculation of U.S. intentions by rival states. By building a global network of regional security arrangements modelled on NATO, the United States attempted to match commitments with power in its worldwide struggle with the So-

12. *Ibid.*, 268.

viet Union. Finally, America through the Marshall Plan and Point Four and other wide-ranging foreign assistance programs has undertaken to further economic, political, and social development in the industrial and nonindustrial world.

The debates over NATO and its growth as an international collective security organization throw light on the broader issue of an international security network in the Cold War. Its stages of growth warrant a more careful review than they have been accorded by most students of collective security. First, NATO was a response to a clear and present danger perceived by the majority of Western policy makers. In February, 1948, ten years after Munich, the Soviet Union brought Czechoslovakia totally within its sphere by initiating a *coup d'etat*. In June, they imposed a blockade on Berlin with the undisguised purpose of driving the Western powers from the city. However far-reaching the Truman Doctrine may have been as a commitment to the defense of freedom around the world, it was clearly not collective security. Neither it nor the Marshall Plan were formulated with the military security of Europe in mind. Second, NATO was the completion not the beginning of the formation of a European security system. It was preceded by the Treaty of Dunkirk, a mutual defense pact between France and England ratified in March, 1947, and by the Brussels Pact. The European states most directly concerned recognized the need for common defense before the United States entered the picture. In other regions of the world, the United States felt called on to press for the creation of security systems without the same solid foundations of well-recognized common interests. Third, the American commitment to NATO was followed by certain decisive actions which added up to a significant American military presence and an unequivocal commitment to Europe as a first line of defense against the Soviet Union. After two world wars fought to preserve the independence of Europe, few could doubt that Europe's security was a vital interest for the United States. What had changed was American willingness to commit itself in peacetime instead of awaiting the outbreak of a conflict. If the Truman Doctrine heralded a revolution in American foreign policy, NATO represented a yet more decisive turn in history. The United States committed itself not only in its declaratory policies but by throwing the full weight of its military strength into the maintenance of a European balance of power.

Having committed itself in the summer of 1949, the United States faced the momentous task of giving form and substance to its commitment. The framers of NATO both in Europe and the United States had been confronted with difficult constitutional problems. The interests of Europeans and of Americans from a constitutional standpoint were not identical. The Europeans sought "automatic involvement" by the United States if war broke out, while Congress jealously guarded its constitutional power to declare war. The debate had centered upon Article 5 of the treaty, which was based on the idea that an attack on one should be considered an attack on all as embodied in the Treaty of Rio and in the Vandenberg Resolution. A compromise was struck in which the Senate took satisfaction from wording which called for "such action as each deems necessary" by the parties, while the Europeans were reassured by the addition of the phrase "including the use of armed force."

The full-scale development of NATO, paradoxically enough, awaited the outbreak of conflict in Asia. The Korean War which broke out in June of 1950 reinforced the viewpoint that war was possible with the Soviet Union. Throughout the history of the Cold War, Western policy makers have more or less consistently sounded an alarm whenever signs of the threat of Soviet military action have been combined with a measurable increase in Soviet capabilities. The explosion by the Soviets of the first atomic bomb late in 1949 signaled the end of the American atomic monopoly and the possibility of deterring Soviet aggression through American strategic air power and the atomic striking power of the Strategic Air Command (SAC). The North Korean invasion of South Korea put an end to the belief that the Soviets or their satellites would never again use military force and led to the first major rearmament effort by the United States since World War II. Even staunch defenders of NATO in the Senate, including Senator Tom Connally, had insisted NATO did not commit the United States to an arms program. Secretary of State Dean Acheson in Senate hearings had answered Senator Bourke Hickenlooper of Iowa, who asked whether the United States would send a substantial number of American troops to Europe as a more or less permanent contribution to their capacity to resist aggression, with an unequivocal "no."

The defense budget, drastically reduced after World War II, approached $11 billion months before the Korean War. However, within the administration and the Congress, strong pressures were being exerted to slash that figure. Secretary of Defense Louis Johnson, who had presidential aspirations, had from his influential post brandished a meat axe over the defense budget, and within the Senate not only Robert A. Taft but confirmed internationalists like Arthur Vandenberg, Richard Russell, and Walter A. George had opposed increased defense spending. The proposed defense appropriation for fiscal 1950/51 had been $14,600,000,000, but the administration added supplementary requests of $1,200,000 in July, $4 billion in early September, and $12,600,000,000 in late September. In August, 1950, it took steps to double the size of the armed forces and during the Korean War the defense budget rose to $50 billion. Implementing NATO was linked with increases in defense spending but until the outbreak of war in Korea, Americans were deeply divided on the issue.

The document on which a dramatic arms buildup was based was the famous National Security Council Policy Paper No. 68 (NSC 68). On January 31, 1950, President Truman had instructed the State and Defense Departments to initiate a major review of U.S. objectives in peace and war. Paul Nitze had by then succeeded George F. Kennan as head of the policy planning staff and he established a working group made up of representatives of the Atomic Energy Commission and the Joint Strategic Survey Committee at the Pentagon. On March 22, 1950, planners from the State and Defense Departments met in Nitze's office with the secretaries of State and Defense and other top officials. When the purpose of the meeting was stated, Secretary Johnson and his top aides, including General Omar Bradley, stalked from the room with Johnson protesting against State's initiative and claiming he had never seen the document they were being asked to discuss. President Truman supported Acheson and the review continued with a joint report being sent to the president in April, surprisingly bearing Johnson's signature.

NSC 68 set forth in general terms the threat to the United States and proposals for an American response without providing any estimate of costs. Its purpose, in Secretary Acheson's words, "was so to bludgeon the mass mind of 'top government' that not only could the President make a decision but that the decision could be carried out." [13] It offered its own definition of the aims of the two superpowers, the Soviets' being world domination and the Americans' an international environment made safe for free societies. Its authors undertook to simplify the nature of the world crisis. They drafted the statement for the mythical American citizen who might spend at most ten minutes a day concerning himself with international affairs. Nitze and Acheson resented the appeals of critics that the report put too much stress on the military and ideological threat of the Soviet Union, too little on the weaknesses of Europe's political and economic circumstances. Acheson, whose relations with Nitze were as in-

13. Acheson, *Present at the Creation*, 374.

timate as his association with Kennan had been distant, saw the Soviet threat as similar to Islam, which had combined ideological zeal with fighting power. Only military power and social organization could turn back the Soviets and because of the greater costs of maintaining and supporting American troops, substantially larger military expenditures were needed. The report assumed that an expanded military budget rising to $50 billion were entirely within the nation's economic capacity. On April 25, NSC 68 was discussed with the president in the National Security Council, and, following that discussion, became national policy. Its implementation was problematical and in retrospect Acheson was to write: "It's doubtful whether anything like what happened in the next few years could have been done had not the Russians been stupid enough to have instigated the attack against South Korea."[14]

In part, the opposition to increased defense spending resulted from cracks in the bipartisan foreign policy. President Truman had won a stunning election victory in 1948. When the Eighty-first Congress convened after the election, the Republicans had lost control of the Senate and Vandenberg had retired from his chairmanship of the Foreign Relations Committee and the Senate presidency pro tem. Marshall had departed as secretary of state and Lovett had announced his retirement. Vandenberg sensed that the president, now chief executive in his own right and not merely Roosevelt's successor, resolved to take charge. Understandably, Truman saw his victory as a mandate to lead. Vandenberg, who was not lacking in self-esteem, resented Truman's failure to consult as freely as when Marshall and Lovett were his aides. The president did not seek congressional advice on Acheson's appointment as secretary of state, an action Vandenberg interpreted as justifiable presidential prerogative in having close personal advisers. However, with legislation pending on NATO and the military assistance program, Vandenberg questioned the wisdom of the action, as he had an earlier press announcement that Truman was considering inviting Acheson to head the cabinet as secretary of state. The Michigan senator wrote to Senator Clyde M. Reed of Kansas, saying: "I am frank to say that Mr. Acheson would *not* have been my choice for Secretary of State. But the President is not choosing an official family for me."[15]

What upset Vandenberg most was the action of the Democrats in

14. *Ibid.*
15. Arthur H. Vandenberg, Jr. (ed.), *The Private Papers of Senator Vandenberg* (Boston: Houghton Mifflin Company, 1952), 469.

claiming eight seats to five for the Republicans in the Foreign Relations Committee (Vandenberg had insisted in maintaining a ratio of seven Republicans to six Democrats in the Republican-controlled Eightieth Congress). Packing the committee with Democrats was in Vandenberg's eyes a partisan move and a serious blow at a nonpartisan approach. At the same time, Robert A. Taft and Kenneth Wherry, who had voted against legislation for European recovery, gained the top Republican leadership positions. Neither was known for his internationalism. Whereas Vandenberg supported Acheson's nomination, although without much enthusiasm, he was responsible for the release to the press of an excerpt of Acheson's secret testimony before the Foreign Relations Committee, which satisfied those senators who feared he was "soft" on communism. The secretary designate had testified: "It is my view that communism as a doctrine is economically fatal to a free society. . . . Communism as an aggressive factor in world conquest is fatal to independent governments and to free peoples."[16] Acheson thanked Vandenberg for his support but made no particular effort to pursue the close collaboration that had existed between the administration and the senator in the Eightieth Congress (Acheson and several of his successors have noted on this point that too often congressmen see consultation as a one-way street and make little effort themselves to initiate consultation with the secretary). The columnist Stewart Alsop, despite two great issues pending in the Congress, NATO and European rearmament, wrote that bipartisanship had been gravely weakened. "One reason is simply the . . . departure of Marshall and Lovett. . . . By contrast . . . Vandenberg and Acheson . . . have had serious policy differences in the past." Senator H. Alexander Smith of New Jersey, a close ally of Vandenberg, disclosed: "I think he [Vandenberg] felt there was a real difference in the attitude of the State Department toward him after Secretary Acheson took over."[17]

Vandenberg and Connally had been cautious supporters of the NATO Treaty. They had insisted that Article 5 of the treaty be modified so that each signatory pledged itself to take such action "as it deems necessary, including the use of armed force." Vandenberg sought to emphasize that steps short of the use of armed force would be considered, including "effective self-help and mutual aid" (Article 3). On April 15, 1949, he wrote: "When it comes to the supplemental arms program . . . I must confess that I have mixed emotions." Europe must rely on itself

16. Quoted *ibid*, 470.
17. *Ibid*., 472.

in the first instance; American military aid ought to be Europe's "last reliance." He added: "I would have preferred to have the Pact stand by
itself as an all-out warning sustained by our general pledge but since the
State Department has taken this other route [supplementary arms aid] I
am not disposed to enter into any *public* argument lest it be miscon-
strued." Vandenberg's feelings toward Acheson and that of other Republican senators improved, and on May 19, 1949, he wrote: "One thing
is sure—if there ever was any suspicion about his [Acheson's] being pro-
Russian it is all different now. As a matter of fact he is so *totally* anti-
Soviet and is going to be so *completely* tough that I really doubt whether
there is any chance at all for a Paris agreement."[18] Nevertheless, the two
never shared the degree of mutual respect Vandenberg and Marshall
felt for one another.

In the debate over NATO, Vandenberg on July 6, 1949, had defended the treaty in a two-hour speech, his last full dress speech before the
Senate. Having described the treaty as "the best available implement to
discourage armed aggression," he denied that it required the shipment
of arms to Europe. "It is not the military forces-in-being which measure
the impact of this 'knock-out' admonition. . . . It is the potential which
counts." On July 20, 1949, he wrote regarding implementation of the
treaty: "Here I am in sharp *disagreement* with the President and the State
Department. They have gone much too fast too soon [in urging arms
shipments to Europe immediately]."[19]

Other forces were at work that made large-scale rearmament and
arms shipments doubtful. In February, 1950, following the president's
decision to develop the hydrogen bomb, two Democratic senators, Brien
McMahon and Millard Tydings, launched a "moral crusade for peace"
calling for a $50 billion global Marshall Plan largely financed by the
United States but with nations called on to devote two-thirds of their
expenditures for armaments to more "constructive ends." At the same
time, the secretary general of the United Nations announced a twenty-
year program for peace to be pursued through negotiations with the
Russians, coupled with the seating of the Chinese Communists in the
United Nations. Peace plans were in the air and Secretary Acheson felt
constrained to counter them in a long press conference on February 8,
1950, and a succession of speeches delivered in locations from Massachusetts to Texas and at the University of California at Berkeley where

18. *Ibid.*, 479, 485.
19. *Ibid.*, 495–96, 498.

he warned that important settlements through negotiations would be impossible for long years to come and declared: "I see no evidence that the Soviet leaders will change their conduct until the progress of the free world convinces them that they cannot profit from a continuation of these tensions."[20]

The issue between the administration and the Congress and the U.N. secretary general was resolved not through persuasion but by the Korean War. Once America had entered the war, congressional support for large-scale rearmament shaped by the objectives of NSC 68 was inevitable. No less vital was American leadership in the organization of NATO. With the entry of Communist China into the Korean War, President Truman appointed General Eisenhower as supreme allied commander in Europe. The NATO command resolved to defend Europe at the Elbe, but such a "forward strategy" required an expansion of the twelve divisions then in Europe, none at full strength and lacking both training and reserves. Expanded forces would provide both a trip wire assuring American retaliation and a shield to hold the Red Army at the Elbe until SAC bombers could attack the Soviet Union. Crucial to this strategy was Germany. Only it had the manpower and resources to provide the needed forces. The process which began in January, 1947, with the creation of an embryonic West German state necessitated by the breakdown of Four Power control, reached its culmination in West German rearmament which occurred much later than the first crisis over Berlin. The blockade had its origins in the efforts of the Western Allies to unify their zones in Germany. Four days after the introduction of new soundly controlled German currency on June 20, 1948, all rail traffic between Berlin and the West was halted. Military action by the West was not taken because of determined opposition by the Joint Chiefs of Staff. In opposition to their view, one of America's most experienced diplomats, Robert Murphy, advocated military action and noted that "the Berlin Blockade is the one occasion in my long career when I feel I should have resigned in public protest against Washington's policy."[21]

To thwart the forward strategy, the Soviet Union responded by blockading Berlin. There followed a severe test of nerves and strength. To maintain its position in Europe, the United States called up extraordinary resolve. It flew in food and supplies for Berlin's 2,500,000 citizens, with planes taking off and landing at three-minute intervals. To avoid

20. Acheson, *Present at the Creation*, 380.
21. Robert Murphy, *Diplomat Among Warriors* (New York: Pyramid Books, 1965), 354.

war with the Russians, the Western Powers ruled out sending troops and tanks to reopen the corridor into Berlin, a proposal of the colorful wartime head of the O.S.S., General "Wild Bill" Donovan. The Russians chose not to challenge the airlift, recognizing on their side that doing so would inescapably lead to total war. Allied planes succeeded in delivering more food daily than had reached Berlin before the blockade by surface transportation. A strategy of will and strength by the allies coupled with restraint on both sides forced the Russians to call off the blockade by May, 1949. America's commitment to Europe had been demonstrated. Its rearmament program in the second half of 1950 gave further evidence of firm intent to implement commitments to NATO.

Yet Europe and France in particular needed reassurance of another type if NATO was to become a viable collective security organization. Only West Germany had the resources to implement a "forward strategy" in the defense of Europe, yet France feared a resurgent Germany. For the same reason, Russia feared Germany, having fought two wars in thirty years; France had memories of 1870, 1914, and 1940. Europe had been ravaged in two world wars because of failure to solve the German problem, a problem which in essence rested on the fact that while Germany had the power to dominate Western Europe, Europe chose war rather than German domination. Before both World Wars, France looked east for allies against Germany, turning to Russia and certain countries in Eastern Europe. Now France faced west, seeking its security within Western Europe.

After World War II, its alliances having twice failed to prevent war, France saw in European integration an alternative design for controlling German power. In May, 1950, Foreign Minister Robert Schuman put forward a plan for a European Coal and Steel Community linking German and French heavy industry. France possessed Europe's largest iron ore deposits, while the largest coal deposits were located in the Ruhr and the Saar. In exchange for receiving German coal at the same price paid by German manufacturers, France in cooperation with Britain and the United States agreed to eliminate controls on German heavy industry within a united Europe.

The Schuman Plan and the European Coal and Steel Community (ECSC) offered the one acceptable model for German participation in Europe's military defense. The French were determined that a separate German army would never again threaten Europe. However, as the European Coal and Steel Community had enabled France to merge its economic strength with Germany, a European army made up of army corps limited to but two divisions from Germany or any other nationality provided not only for Europe's defense but the control of the threat of German militarism. In May, 1952, the European Defense Community Treaty was signed. Because all EDC states but Germany were members of NATO, a linkage was established between the two with mutual defense obligations. Germany promised to contribute 500,000 men to the EDC organized in twelve divisions. In return, it recovered certain sovereign rights balanced by continued Allied rights to protect their forces in Germany, to govern Berlin, and to negotiate with the Soviet Union the question of German reunification. NATO's strength depended on the revival of German military strength but within the framework of a united Europe.

Collective Security in Asia

The NATO Treaty of April 4, 1949, was the first military alliance treaty signed by the United States since the termination of the French alliance in 1800. After NATO, the United States committed itself to the defense of over forty countries. The principle of individual and collective self-defense had taken its legitimacy from Article 51 of the United Nations Charter. It went back to a philosophy that had captured the imagination of the world's peoples when Woodrow Wilson proclaimed that national interests were receding and international purposes were taking their place. The common purposes of mankind for Wilson would be embodied in a "League to Enforce Peace." The Congress and apparently the American people repudiated Wilson and World War II followed. For American students of international relations in the interwar and postwar period, the lesson to be drawn from the rejection of Wilson's vision of a universal collective security system was that only through collective security could peace be assured. For a century and a half, Americans in times of crisis have had recourse to the lessons of the past. "We cannot escape history," Lincoln had proclaimed in a message to Congress in December, 1862. Dean Acheson, in appearing as the first witness before the Senate Committee on Foreign Relations on the NATO Treaty, had declared: "We have learned our history lesson from two world wars in less than half a century." If the free nations were to disregard threats to the security of any one of their number, they would fall one by one, as had the victims of the Nazi aggression. Alone, any one of the free nations would be overrun by expansive Soviet power. The reason was that: "The stratagem of the aggressor is to keep his intended victims divided, or better still, set them to quarreling among themselves."[22] To prevent history's repeating itself, Acheson maintained that the nations of the North Atlantic area must unite, pledging themselves to self-help and mutual aid.

In his conception of collective security, Acheson laid down certain prerequisites not always made explicit by other proponents. First, in invoking collective security, policy makers are obligated to define the nature of the threat. He observed that "experience has taught us that the control of Europe by a single aggressive power would constitute an intolerable threat to the national security of the United States."[23] In other words, the threat to America was the creation of a vast imbalance of power in the heart of Europe, strategically the single most vital area in the Cold War. In Acheson's mind, the maintenance of a balance of power was linked with collective security.

Second, military power was essential to a balance of power. The nations of Western Europe who, with the exception of Great Britain, had during the years of occupation been virtually disarmed, had barely made a beginning in rebuilding their defenses. It was no longer possible to foresee the day when they could by themselves withstand an enemy until the United States could rearm and come to their aid. By strengthening their collective defense, however, they could help deter an aggressor who had to recognize that attacking one European state entailed substantial risk and cost from the NATO community as a whole.

Third, the NATO states, Acheson insisted, "are anxious to join with us." They are resolved to defend themselves. Their will to fight depends on their having the means to fight and therefore a military assistance program is required to meet both external and internal threats. "Whatever the Communists may claim for the supposedly superior appeal of their ideology . . . the record shows that no Communist government has come to power in any country by the free choice of the people. . . . The pressure of large military forces maintained in readiness at all times behind the Iron Curtain is the club of every Communist government in Europe, and there is little effort made to keep the weapon concealed."[24]

Fourth, some critics of European rearmament had argued that, given the military predominance of the Red Army and the impossibility of Europe's defending itself once an invasion had been launched, any de-

---

22. Dean Acheson, *The Pattern of Responsibility*, edited by McGeorge Bundy from the Record of the Secretary of State (Boston: Houghton Mifflin Company, 1952), 61–62.
23. *Ibid.*, 62.
24. *Ibid.*, 70, 71.

fense program was futile. That was "like arguing that because burglars can break into houses we should not put locks on our doors."[25] The goal of Western defense was not victory but the prevention of an adversary's self-deception. Sufficient strength would disabuse an aggressor of the expectation of a quick and easy victory.

Fifth, America would ensure its own defense by transferring arms abroad, because Europe was America's first line of defense. It was only prudent to send arms to the place where they might be needed first and used with greatest effectiveness.

Sixth, a rational defense structure required a collective organization of defense ministers, finance ministers, professional military people, a supply group, and a standing committee of chiefs of staff with a design for "balanced collective forces" integrating the contributions each nation was best able to make to the common defense. Prior to the Korean War, economic recovery in Europe took precedence; following the outbreak of conflict economic strength became primarily important as part of a pattern of defense.

The six requirements for collective security for Europe were from the outset difficult to apply in Asia. The debate was colored by the triumph of the Communists in China, an event which both General Marshall and Secretary Acheson were called on to explain to the American people. Acheson's argument in support of military assistance in Europe had rested on the proposition that nations there were determined to defend themselves. In discussing the defeat of Chiang Kai-shek, Acheson turned this proposition on its head, saying that American aid could not in itself ensure the survival of a recipient government. China was more divided than Western Europe. The Chinese government (Chiang's government) controlled southwest China. The Soviet Union occupied Manchuria. The Communists and Japanese held north central and southeast China. The Communists controlled one-fourth of China's population, including key industrial centers and railway communications. In China, Communist elements were not scattered throughout the country as in Western Europe. Instead they occupied a defined area and had under their control a population of 116 million people. Communist China with its own government and army was a separate country within China. In formulating policy, the United States had three choices: pulling out of China; supplying massive military aid and American troops to enable the Nationalists to defeat the Communists and drive out the Japanese and

25. *Ibid.*, 72.

the Russians; or aiding Chiang while encouraging the Nationalists to work out agreements where necessary and possible. Chiang himself had stated that the Chinese Communist problem was a purely political problem and should be solved by political means.

American assistance was substantial, a fact often forgotten in the debate over "who lost China." A contingent of fifty thousand Marines organized the return of some three million Japanese troops and civilians from central, southeast, and east China by rail and sea to Japan. America airlifted whole armies from South China to the evacuated areas, a colossal effort to strengthen Chiang Kai-shek. General Marshall undertook his fateful mission to bring Chiang's government and the Chinese Communists together. To supervise a cease-fire, Marshall established an executive headquarters under an American chairman with Nationalist and Communist representation. A plan for reorganization called for a constitutional government within an interim state council in which the Kuomintang had twenty of forty seats. Chiang as president was to fill the remaining twenty seats from the other parties, including the Communists. The Generalissimo had a veto power which could be overridden only by a three-fifths vote of the council. The military forces were to be amalgamated with fifty of the sixty divisions to be Nationalist divisions and ten Communist divisions. In Manchuria, fourteen of fifteen divisions were to be Nationalist divisions. Despite these arrangements favorable to the Nationalists, reorganization failed as the situation deteriorated. Both Nationalist and Communist troops broke their agreements in 1946, each seeking to add key cities or territories to strengthen its position in the negotiations. The Kuomintang, with a numerical advantage in troops of 3 to 1, was increasingly dominated by the extreme right wing of the party; it became overextended militarily and politically. It was unable to maintain its supply lines; it lacked the administrators to manage the cities and countryside that its forces had conquered. Most damaging of all, it failed to bring about the political and economic reforms that would have given people something to fight for and defend against the Communists. The civil war which Marshall had sought to avert broke out and he left China early in 1947, ending the American effort to mediate the struggle between the Kuomintang and the Communists.

Notwithstanding the failure of his mission, Secretary Marshall on his return recommended economic assistance of $570 million to China, warning, however, against a commitment to assume direct responsibility for the civil war in China. The Eightieth Congress slashed the request, appropriating $275 million for economic and $125 mil'ion for military aid. It reasoned that military aid, as with Greece and Turkey, was needed to make economic aid effective. Late 1948, however, witnessed the further military collapse of the Nationalists and by February, 1949, Communist forces outnumbered the Nationalists three to two. In late 1948, the head of the U.S. military mission to China, General Barr, reported: "The military mission has deteriorated to the point where only the active participation of United States troops would effect a remedy. No battle has been lost since my arrival due to lack of ammunition or equipment. Their military debacles . . . can all be attributed to the world's worst leadership and many other morale-destroying factors that led to a complete loss of the will to fight."[26]

In the wake of the defeat of Chiang Kai-shek, American foreign policy in Asia followed a course that was shaped ineluctably by geopolitical realities. While recognizing the importance of preventing a single hostile power from achieving domination in Asia, America's primary interest was the maintenance of stability in Western Europe. Europe came first in American foreign policy because Soviet domination in Europe would signal its victory in the Cold War and greatly increase the threat of war. Whatever the differences within the government, the vast majority of American policy makers were determined to avoid the commitment of American troops to a land war on the mainland of Asia. State Department planners in particular warned against a dangerous overextension of American power and urged that distinctions be made between vital and peripheral American interests. They argued that for the United States a security system in the Pacific would have to be anchored in the island bastions of Japan and the Philippines. The strategic boundaries of the United States lay along the eastern shores of Asia, and to prevent the launching of an enemy amphibious force from the Asian mainland, the United States would require air and naval bases in Okinawa, the Philippines, the Aleutians, and Midway. As early as 1948, General Douglas MacArthur had linked American defense to these strategic points and on January 12, 1950, Secretary Acheson explained that the "defense perimeter runs along the Aleutians to Japan and then goes to the Ryukyus . . . [and] runs from the Ryukyus to the Philippines Islands." Acheson added: "So far as the military security of other areas in the Pacific is concerned, it must be clear that no person can guarantee these areas against military attack." His priorities assumed American involvement in a general conflict. Almost a quarter century before President Richard Nixon

26. Quoted *ibid.*, 172.

was to enunciate the famed Nixon or Guam Doctrine, Acheson warned: "Should such an attack occur . . . the initial reliance must be on the people attacked to resist it." Outside the defense perimeter of the United States, the Pacific nations would have to defend themselves; their security would depend upon self-help. However, Acheson added that such nations having defended themselves might look to "the commitments of the entire civilized world under the Charter of the United Nations which so far has not proved a weak reed to lean on by any people who are determined to protect their independence against outside aggression."[27] In a word, the Pacific nations were counselled to rely on collective security.

In practice, collective security in Asia was weakened by the failure of nations to meet the six requirements laid down by Acheson for Europe's defense. First, American foreign policy in Asia suffered for three decades from a lack of a clear and unequivocal definition of the threat. In Europe, statesmen such as Truman, Marshall, and Acheson helped mobilize Europeans to prepare collective defenses against the Soviet threat. In Asia, policy makers were divided in their estimates of the threat to an Asian balance of power, alternately seeing it as the Soviet Union, mainland China, or Asian nationalism bent on overthrowing the status quo.

Second, the buildup of Asia's military defenses compared with Europe's was complex, uncertain, and problematical, with little consensus on political and military priorities among the nations of Asia. The region was the birthplace of neutralism and nonalignment, symbolized thereafter by the Bandung Conference. The poorer nations lacked the margin of resources necessary to assure strong national defense. With the threat of social revolution hanging over them, they were ill-disposed to place large-scale military expenditures above economic and social development. Moreover, a sufficient number of Asian leaders, including opposition leaders, were inspired by the philosophy of Nehru and Gandhi, so that military threats were underestimated or formulated in essentially political terms. By contrast, the thinking of European leaders had been formed by the lessons of two World Wars and by the casualties and destruction wrought by militarily more powerful states like Germany and the Soviet Union.

Third, Western Europe constituted a community in a broad sense and an emergent defense system. Acheson, who could say that the nations of Europe were anxious to join with us in mutual defense, could

27. Quoted *ibid.*, 199, 200.

hardly make this claim for the nations of Asia. The Red Army on the borders of Europe was an ever-present reminder that military defense was not merely a duty; collective defense was a necessity. The military threat as viewed by a majority of European leaders was a clear and present danger. For Asians, the threat appeared less imminent and its source was more dispersed and many-sided. The nations of Southeast Asia who had fallen within Japan's co-prosperity sphere remained anxious about a resurgent Japan. Particularly the states with a large overseas Chinese population feared cultural and political penetration by China. To the north, China and Japan looked out on expanding Soviet power. Northeast Asia had its own set of interests and concerns which differed from those of Southeast Asia and both saw the world in a different light than South Asia. Even within the separate regions, the withering away in the years which followed of collective defense arrangements like the Southeast Asia Treaty Organization testified to the fragile character of common interests within a single region.

Fourth, deterrence as the primary end of collective defense in Europe was ambiguous and unpredictable in Asia. For one thing, the United States lacked a presence in certain areas threatened by military intrusion. It was difficult to prevent self-deception by an enemy when American policy makers failed to make clear their intentions. Soviet leaders complained following America's intervention in the Korean War that the Soviet Union had been misled by the statements of Acheson and MacArthur that Korea fell outside America's defense perimeter. At the same time, critics looking back on the conflict ignore the widespread concern among Americans that the South Korean leader Syngman Rhee threatened as the one true Korean nationalist to invade North Korea and reunite Korea by force. The basis for firm guarantees in Asia and for building a system of credible deterrence was missing because mutual trust between partners was limited at best.

Fifth, the political conditions in Northeast and Southeast Asia for large-scale arms transfers in peacetime were absent. To speak of Europe-firsters and Asia-firsters among congressional leaders begged the question and obscured the real issue. When the United States finally committed itself to European rearmament, it did so because a consensus had grown up that Europe was its first line of defense. No such consensus developed regarding Asia and what was true of the United States was true *a fortiori* of the European states and the states of the British Commonwealth. The great debate over America's interests, which was evident in Korea, was to divide the republic far more profoundly in the 1960s and 1970s in the irreconcilable differences over whether South Vietnam was a vital American interest.

Sixth, an overall defense and resource structure was essential to a collective defense system. The collective organization of defense and finance ministers which came into being in Europe was only partially realized in Asia. One factor was the absence of key countries like Japan which by common agreement eschewed military rearmament. Another factor resulted from the intraregional conflicts that prevented certain Asian countries from accepting military cooperation with others. Sub-regional security systems such as Maphilindo (Malaysia, the Philippines, and Indonesia) took the place of a general regional security system. Countries like Australia and New Zealand were viewed and viewed themselves as part of Asia but also part of the British Commonwealth defense system. Economic recovery and organization which preceded the formation of a defense system in Europe was a missing ingredient for creating "balanced collective forces" in Asia. More serious still, the political agreements that were reached among the nations of Europe were never realized in Asia.

Thus the European model of collective security for Asia was flawed from the start and the resulting crises in Korea and Vietnam occurred before a viable collective security system was possible. The concept was invoked and the principle applied by the architects of policy seemingly with little awareness of the limitations. The tragedy of American foreign policy in Asia especially in the 1950s and 1960s was that collective se- curity proved unworkable and policy makers had nothing to put in its place. The Cold War, which had been contained in Europe, shifted to Asia. Partly by design and partly by accident, the struggle deteriorated into open warfare in Asia. The Cold War was militarized in a region of the world where a military resolution of the conflict was impossible. The final chapter of the first phase of the Cold War extending from 1943– 1953 took place in Korea, a country which the United States had ex- cluded for various reasons from its defense planning and where col- lective security was least likely to be effective. A decade of conflict for Americans was to end in a faraway corner of the globe where novel prin- ciples of international relations were difficult if not impossible to apply.

Chapter Five
Korea
The Limits of Containment

If the fifteen weeks in 1947 that witnessed the birth of the Truman Doctrine and the Marshall Plan were a turning point in history and in Soviet-American relations, the Korean War in 1950 was an all-important watershed in the Cold War. The anti-Communist consensus which made possible the Truman Doctrine was strengthened and solidified in a new chapter in the Cold War ushered in by the invasion of South Korea. Measured by military expenditures alone, Korea found America undertaking commitments that the nation had found unacceptable in peacetime. A military budget which was $11 billion before the war rose to $22.3 billion in fiscal 1951, $44 billion in fiscal 1952, and $50.4 billion in 1953. The doubts and uncertainties about Soviet intentions which led George Kennan to write of groping "in the unfirm substance of the imponderables" were resolved in the military strike by North Korea. Secretary Acheson, in a meeting with congressional leaders on December 13, 1950, explained: "Since the end of June, it had been clear that the Soviet Union has begun an all-out attack against the power position of the United States. It was clear that the Soviet leaders recognized that their policy might bring on a general war, and it was equally clear that they were prepared to run this risk."[1] The Korean War confirmed for most Americans the worldwide objectives of communism and the Soviet role in orchestrating these objectives.

When President Truman met with his advisers Sunday evening, June 25, 1950, to formulate a response on Korea, the discussion focused on a few basic themes. Their premise determined the action that all agreed must be taken. For the participants, the decision to intervene was to be

1. Box 164, President's secretary's file, Truman Papers, 3, 8, Harry S Truman Library, Independence, Mo.

"the greatest story" of 1949–1953. The president asked Secretary Acheson to report on the situation and make recommendations. The secretary recommended evacuation of all American dependents from Korea, holding the American air force south of the 38th parallel, supplying the Korean army, and sending the Seventh Fleet north to Formosa. In the discussion that followed, two issues were dominant. On the first issue of resistance to aggression, there was complete agreement, with "no suggestion . . . that either the United Nations or the United States" should back away from meeting the attack. In Acheson's words: "This was the test of all the talk of the last five years of collective security."[2] The other issue found differences of opinion being expressed by General Hoyt Vandenberg and Admiral Forrest Sherman, who both believed that air and naval assistance would be sufficient, and General J. Lawton Collins, who foresaw the need for American ground forces if the Korean army faltered. (Collins' view proved to be prophetic, for by June 29, General MacArthur asked permission to move in a regimental combat team as the first step toward committing a force of two divisions, as the Korean army had dissolved.)

On June 27, the Security Council, in the absence of the Soviet Union who had walked out in protest over failure to admit Communist China to the U.N., adopted a resolution calling on members to assist South Korea. "The attack upon the Republic of Korea," the president warned, "makes it plain beyond all doubt that the international Communist movement is prepared to use armed invasion to conquer independent nations." If aggression succeeded in Korea, it would spread throughout Asia and Europe and make world war inevitable. The government of the Republic of Korea had been accepted by the United Nations in December, 1948, following U.N. monitored free elections the previous August. (The Soviet Union had refused to allow the United Nations to enter its zone to supervise free elections.) The United States recognized the new government on January 1, 1949, and other U.N. members followed its lead. Thus the invasion was seen as a direct challenge not only to South Korea and the United States but to the United Nations.

The U.N.'s response to North Korea's aggression viewed by the architects of the policy struck a blow for the concept of collective security. The "entire world was electrified" by the action. Yet collective security demanded more than one dramatic gesture. Speaking to a group of

2. David S. McLelland and David C. Acheson (eds.), *Among Friends: Personal Letters of Dean Acheson* (New York: Dodd, Mead & Company, 1980), 100.

publishers on June 29, 1951, Acheson observed: Collective security is "like a bank account . . . kept alive by the resources which are put into it. In Korea the Russians presented a check which was drawn on the bank account of collective security. The Russians thought the check would bounce. They thought it was a bad check. But to their great surprise, the teller paid it. The important thing was that the check was paid, [but] the importance will be nothing if the next check is not paid and if the bank account is not kept strong and sufficient to cover all checks which are drawn upon it."[3] To cover future checks, Acheson proposed and the assembly passed a "Uniting for Peace Resolution" whereby the General Assembly could consider the maintenance of peace and security when the Security Council was prevented from acting and recommend to members collective measures including the use of force. The resolution, which provided the means for circumventing the Soviet veto, also weakened a possible veto by the United States and, while initiated with bipartisan support, was never subjected to public debate in the United States as were other provisions in the United Nations Charter adopted at San Francisco.

There is a note of irony in the fact that Secretary Acheson should have assumed responsibility for so far-reaching a transformation of the United Nations. In 1947, he had opposed those who urged that Greek-Turkish aid be channeled through the United Nations, and in 1949 he supported NATO as a more hopeful approach to collective security for Europe. By 1950, he found in the United Nations not only a framework for collective security but a place of contact with the Soviet Union. In an address to the General Assembly on September 20, 1950, he argued: "As our efforts to strengthen the collective security system become more and more effective, and as tensions begin to ease, we believe that the United Nations will be increasingly important as a means of facilitating and encouraging productive negotiation."[4] One other step which contributed to Acheson's hope for collective security was the signing of the Japanese Peace Treaty on September 8, 1951, and again he noted that in rejecting militarism, Japan would be enabled to contribute to peace "through collective security and the cooperative activity of the United Nations."

The invoking of collective security in June, 1950, against North Korea and the passage of the Uniting for Peace Resolution in November, 1950, were heralded as the fulfillment at last of the dreams of the

3. Department of State Bulletin, XXV, 125.
4. Department of State Bulletin, XIII, 525–26.

peace planners. The resolution appeared on the surface to have created a new United Nations. If the United Nations should be immobilized by a Great Power veto in the Security Council, and prevented from exercising its responsibility for international peace and security, the General Assembly would be convened in twenty-four hours to deal with threats to the peace. The resolution empowered the General Assembly to recommend to its members collective measures including the use of armed forces. It further could recommend that each member state maintain within its national armed forces elements available for prompt deployment as United Nations units. Two additional international bodies were created, the Peace Observation Commission to observe and report on international tensions and the Collective Measures Committee to study and report on ways to strengthen international peace and security.

The early enthusiasm that surrounded the United Nations action in Korea and the euphoria which accompanied the Uniting for Peace Resolution dwindled and declined in 1950/51. The resolution left the United Nations system where it found it, essentially decentralized with member states free to comply or not with the assembly's recommendations. Of the sixty members of the United Nations only sixteen provided armed forces of any kind in Korea. South Korea and the United States made available about 90 percent of the fighting forces and only a handful of countries—Canada, Great Britain, and Turkey—committed more than token forces. Countries with proven military capabilities like Argentina, Brazil, India, and Mexico chose not to participate on either side.

The primary motivation for states who joined in the United Nations action was not one of legal obligations under the charter but of vital interests and power. Korea's existence for two thousand years had depended on the protection of a major power, traditionally China, or on a balance of power between China and Japan or Russia and Japan. Following World War II, the United States, awaiting the completion of a Japanese Peace Treaty, assumed primary responsibility for the security of Japan. Because Korea was a dagger pointed at Japan, the United States took over Japan's historic function of preventing all Korea from falling into the hands of a hostile power. The Soviet Union and China, once it entered the war, saw their role in similar terms. Neither side could allow Korea to fall under the control of the other; nor was either prepared to risk a general war.

Once China entered the war the conflict became less a war of collective security directed to the putting down of an aggressor by preponderant military force representing the community of nations and mo: a traditional war between two more or less equal coalitions. Despite the less than ideal conditions under which collective security was organized in the first months of the war with South Korea, with the United States providing most of the forces, collective enforcement might have succeeded if the war had been limited to Korea. Once General MacArthur reached the Yalu River and the Chinese intervened, claiming China's security was endangered, the war passed from being a venture in collective security and took on all the characteristics of a traditional war. Once a Great Power had joined with the aggressor, collective security could have succeeded only through an all-out war against a Great Power. The Charter of the United Nations had ruled out this possibility from a legal standpoint by according the veto to each of the Great Powers within the Security Council. From a military and political standpoint, neither Communist China, which was not a member of the United Nations, nor the United States was willing to assume the burdens and the risks of all-out victory in a Great Power war.

Thus the Korean War, which began as an endeavor at collective security, ended as a struggle to determine the possibility and limitations of containment. The division at the center of Korea represented the balance of power in Northeast Asia. The continued division of the country into North and South reflected the persistence of the Soviet-Chinese and the American-Japanese spheres of influence, however unstable and precarious they might be. The United Nations theoretically at least might have succeeded in ending the aggression and restoring peace if the struggle had been confined to the Korean Peninsula. Once Great Powers in the Cold War became engaged, containment supplanted collective security. Neither side, and in particular neither China nor the United States, could accept domination of all Korea by the other. That left each with the sole alternative of containment. As each side was to learn—the United States in Korea and Vietnam, China with Korea and a unified Vietnam, and the Soviet Union with Korea, Laos, and Cambodia—even policies of containment have their limitations. If containment is defined as preservation of the status quo without changes of any kind, containment is more an ideal than a possibility, for containment can never be an absolute. It must leave room for change and accommodation. In Asia particularly, a foreign policy of containment is subject to the limits of American power, the vicissitudes of Asian nationalism, and the inner workings of traditional political and cultural systems. These limitations have led opposing schools of thought to view from different vantage points the crises in Asia beginning with the Korean War.

The Orthodox Version of Korea

At the Cairo Conference in November, 1943, Roosevelt, Chiang Kai-shek, and Churchill agreed that the goal should be a free and independent Korea, not one dominated by any outside power, whether China or Japan. At Teheran, Stalin agreed with Roosevelt that Korea should be independent but might require a period of apprenticeship of up to forty years. At Yalta in February, 1945, Roosevelt in private talks with Stalin suggested a three-power trusteeship involving Russia, China, and the United States, and Stalin added Great Britain. At Potsdam, the military chiefs agreed that following Russia's entry into the Pacific War, a line of demarcation should be drawn in the area of Korea between American and Russian sea and air operations. President Truman wrote: "The 38th parallel as a dividing line in Korea was never the subject of international discussions. It was proposed by us as a practicable solution when the sudden collapse of the Japanese war machine created a vacuum in Korea."[5] The State Department urged that the Americans accept the surrender of Japanese troops throughout Korea, but the military declared there was no way of sending American troops into North Korea without weakening the security of American forces in Japan. Because Stalin had concurred in the idea of a joint trusteeship, American officials expected that the division of the country would serve the purpose of carrying out the Japanese surrender but thereafter joint control would be established throughout the country.

However, the Soviets from the beginning treated the 38th parallel as a permanent line of demarcation. They rejected the idea of free traffic between the industrial north and the rural south. The South Koreans held the Americans responsible for the division; political unrest and economic misery mounted. The issue of Korea's future was discussed by Secretary James F. Byrnes with Foreign Minister Molotov at the Moscow meeting of Foreign Ministers in December, 1945. After some delay, Molotov proposed a joint commission of representatives of the Soviet and American commands in Korea to work out a provisional government. When the American and Russian commanders met in Korea on January

5. Harry S Truman, *Memoirs, Vol. II: Years of Trial and Hope* (Garden City, N.Y.: Doubleday, 1956), 317.

16, 1946, the Russians maintained the conference had no authority to go beyond minor adjustments between the two zones. The joint commission provided for in the Moscow agreement met in Seoul on March 20, 1946, and was soon hopelessly deadlocked on what Koreans could appear before the commission, the Russians seeking to exclude any Koreans who might have favored trusteeship. From May 29–June 3, 1946, President Truman's personal envoy, Edwin W. Pauley, visited North Korea and reported that the Soviets had no intention of withdrawing from North Korea but were working to establish a Communist regime. In the autumn of 1946, the Russians conducted elections for local "People's Committees" and 93.3 percent of the voters approved a single slate of candidates. In January, 1947, General Hodge warned of civil war in Korea unless a joint Soviet-American solution could be found. On May 21, 1947, at Secretary Marshall's initiative, the joint commission met again in Seoul. At first, the Soviets appeared more open to hear all Koreans who had supported the Moscow agreements, but once again the discussions broke down. Following Soviet rejection of a seven-point proposal on August 26, 1947, calling for free elections in the two zones, the United States placed the issue of Korean reunification before the United Nations. The Russians countered with a proposal for the withdrawal of all occupation troops early in 1948.

At this point, the president instructed the State and Defense Departments to study the question of troop removal. In September, 1947, the Joint Chiefs of Staff reported that the United States had little strategic interest in maintaining its undermanned occupation units in Korea. (The Joint Chiefs of Staff included Admiral Leahy, General Eisenhower, Admiral Nimitz, and General Spaatz.) They noted: "In the event of hostilities in the Far East, our present forces in Korea would be a military liability and could not be maintained there without substantial reinforcement prior to the initiation of hostilities. Moreover, any offensive operation the United States might wish to conduct on the Asiatic continent most probably would bypass the Korea peninsula."[6] If the enemy established strong air and naval bases on Korea, they would be subject to neutralization by air action. The Joint Chiefs had before them a report by Lieutenant General Albert C. Wedemeyer which added a further dimension to the discussion. Following first-hand study in the summer of 1947, he concluded that as long as Soviet troops remained in occupation of North Korea, the United States should maintain troops in South

6. Quoted *ibid.*, 325.

Korea or admit before the world an "ideological retreat." Wedemeyer posed three possible courses of action: unilateral withdrawal by the Americans which would abandon South Korea to the Soviet Union; indefinite occupation, which, once Soviet troops were withdrawn, would be unacceptable to the American public and would subject America to international censure; and withdrawal concurrent with Soviet withdrawal. Wedemeyer recommended the third alternative.

The United States proposal placed before the General Assembly called for elections in the two zones before March 31, 1948, with U.N. supervision, as a first step in the establishment of a national government. A U.N. temporary commission on Korea would supervise the elections and speed the formation of a national government. The Soviet resolution for the immediate withdrawal of all occupation forces was defeated and the American proposal was adopted with only the Soviet Union abstaining. The U.N. temporary commission was refused entry into North Korea and the Interim Committee of the General Assembly (the Little Assembly) then instructed the temporary commission to hold elections wherever it could function. Elections were held in South Korea on May 10, 1948, and, despite Communist efforts to create disorders, four out of five eligible South Koreans registered to vote, and more than 90 percent of those registered cast their ballots. The U.N. commission reported that the first free election in Korean history was "a valid expression of the free will of the electorate." The elected National Assembly met on May 31, 1948, chose Syngman Rhee as chairman, and completed a constitution promulgated on July 17. On July 20, Rhee was elected president of the Republic of Korea. On August 15, the American military government came to an end. On September 9, the Democratic People's Republic of Korea was formed in North Korea and by the end of December, 1948, the Soviets withdrew all Soviet forces, leaving behind a People's Army. By June 29, 1949, the last of American troops left South Korea following recommendations by the National Security Council and General MacArthur. Only a small advisory group of five hundred army officers and men remained to assist in the training of a Republic of Korea Army of 65,000 troops.

The withdrawal of American forces was not the administration's sole responsibility and concern. The NSC recommendation for withdrawal had also called for substantial military and economic aid to the Republic of Korea. The Congress delayed action for four months on Truman's first request for $150 million and turned down a supplementary request for $60 million in the budget for 1950/51. A defense agreement between

Korea and the United States was signed on January 26, 1950. Truman had grave misgivings about the internal political and economic situation and wrote of President Rhee: "He attracted to himself men of extreme right-wing attitudes and disagreed sharply with the political leaders of more moderate views, and the removal of military government removed restraints that had prevented arbitrary actions against his opponents. I did not care for the methods used by Rhee's police to break up political meetings [nor his] . . . lack of concern about the serious inflation that swept the country. Yet we had no choice but to support Rhee."[7] The character of Rhee's government was to divide Americans between administration spokesmen, who insisted that no other leadership was possible in a country that had been overrun and kept down by the Japanese since 1905, and liberal and revisionist critics, who maintained that South Korea's democracy was an illusion. (The revisionists quoted the Canadian and Polish members of the U.N. commission as questioning whether a genuinely free election had been conducted on May 10, 1948.)

The crisis came in early summer of 1950. Truman acknowledged that intelligence reports from Korea in the spring of 1950 had pointed to a substantial buildup of North Korean forces and incursions by guerrilla elements into South Korea. The president had known as early as 1948 that Korea was one of the places where the Soviet-controlled Communist world might attack. In the minds of some officials, the Soviet Union sat at the switchboard and initiated the calls which set in motion Communist aggression. The attack might come in the area "from Norway through Berlin and Trieste to Greece, Turkey, and Iran; from the Kuriles in the North Pacific to Indo-China and Malaya."[8] There were growing signs of expanding North Korean capability for military action, but the president believed there were any number of other trouble spots in the world where the Russians were capable of attacking. The president believed that the North Korean invasion was Soviet-inspired and controlled and that the Russians were trying to gain Korea by default, gambling that the United States would be afraid of starting a third world war and would not resist. What happened in Korea was a repetition on a larger scale of what had happened in Berlin. The Reds were probing for weakness. The United States, in Truman's view, had to meet their thrust without getting embroiled in a world war.

Following the successful Inchon invasion, the United Nations forces moved north under MacArthur's command. The president, on return-

7. *Ibid.*, 329.
8. *Ibid.*, 331.

ing from his historic meeting with General MacArthur on Wake Island, spoke on October 17 at the San Francisco Opera House. He reviewed the situation in Korea, declaring: "We know now that the United Nations can create a system of international order with the authority to maintain peace." He revealed plans discussed with MacArthur "for establishing a 'unified, independent, and democratic' government in that country in accordance with the resolution of the General Assembly of the United Nations."[9] The change in administration objectives in Korea was born of idealism and of underestimating the enemy. MacArthur had told the president at Wake Island that North Korean Communists were no different from other Koreans and were happy when taken prisoner; that the Chinese had no air force and would not enter the war; that if they did and their 50,000 to 60,000 troops came as far as Pyongyang, they would be slaughtered. As for the idealism, Truman stated, "This is a tremendous step forward in the age-old struggle to establish the rule of law in the world." Administration military policy moved almost imperceptibly from a goal of reaching the 38th parallel to reunifying Korea.

With China's intervention in the Korean War, the differences between the administration and its commander in the field became increasingly clear. MacArthur ordered a bombing mission to take out the bridge across the Yalu River from Sinuiju (Korea) to Antung (Manchuria). Undersecretary of Defense Robert Lovett and Assistant Secretary of State Dean Rusk warned of the risks of bombing on the Manchurian side of the river. The Joint Chiefs of Staff concurred, saying that only if there were an immediate and serious threat to American troops (MacArthur had insisted that experienced American units should spearhead the drive to the north despite instructions that non-Korean forces should not operate near the Manchurian border) would such bombing be authorized. Predictably, MacArthur responded that Chinese troops were pouring across the bridges and said: "I deem it essential to execute the bombing of the targets under discussion as the only resource left to me to prevent a potential buildup of enemy strength to a point threatening the safety of the command."[10] The president turned to the Joint Chiefs of Staff, who urged that every effort should be made to settle the issue of Chinese intervention by political means, preferably through the United Nations. The State Department suggested a buffer area be established in northeast Korea, a twenty-mile demilitarized zone ten miles on each side

9. *Ibid.*, 369.
10. *Ibid.*, 337.

of the Yalu, under a United Nations commission. On November 24, General MacArthur initiated a major attack by the Eighth Army aimed at ending the war and sending the troops home by Christmas, thus contradicting his alarming messages of November 6 and 7 that justified the bombing of locations on both sides of the Yalu River. On November 28, MacArthur, through four different messages to political sources, publicized the fact that his losses in Korea were due to "extraordinary inhibitions . . . without precedent in military history." The truth was that his demand for authority to bomb bases in Manchuria and engage in "hot pursuit" of enemy planes returning from missions in Korea to Manchuria had been opposed by all United Nations countries with troops in Korea.

The administration had reached the point of grave decisions. MacArthur continued through press interviews and communiqués to dispute administration policy. Having confessed at Wake Island that he had been misguided in allowing himself to be drawn into domestic politics in 1948, he nevertheless pursued his cause politically with members of the Congress. The president had to view American foreign policy in a worldwide rather than regional context. The president observed that if MacArthur's "advice had been taken, then or later, and if we had gone ahead and bombed the Manchurian bases, we would have been openly at war with Red China and not improbably with Russia. World War III might very well have been on."[11] Truman, looking back, declared he should have dismissed MacArthur at this time but felt the effect would be damaging to the Korean effort and be linked with American military setbacks.

In discussions with its allies and particularly with the British, the administration sought to offer reassurances. One hundred Labor M.P.'s presented Prime Minister Attlee with a petition protesting the president's reference to possible use of the atomic bomb in Korea. The president replied that his reference had been quoted out of context. He had meant to say that the government necessarily had to consider the use of all available weapons but he fervently hoped the bomb would never be used anywhere because of its terrible destructiveness. In discussions between administration leaders and Attlee in Washington, the prime minister observed that opinions differed on whether the Chinese Communists were Russian satellites. General Marshall quoted Chou En-lai as having repudiated the idea that the Chinese were merely agrarian reformers. During his year as a mediator in China, they had made not the

11. *Ibid.*, 383.

slightest attempt to conceal their Moscow affiliations. Attlee believed the Chinese were ripe for "Titoism." Acheson warned that if the American people were led to believe the United States must accept Chinese aggression in Korea, they would turn to isolationism in Europe. He also seriously doubted that the Chinese, having succeeded in their intervention, would be prepared for negotiations which might serve American interests more than Chinese. Both Acheson and Truman argued that before the United States could negotiate with China, the Chinese would have to prove they were our friends. They and the Russians were less interested in their borders than in keeping American troops tied down in Korea. If the United States were to agree to the Chinese claim of a seat in the United Nations, we would be offering a reward for aggression.

It was obvious throughout the debate in the Congress and in the United Nations following China's intervention that the Truman administration was at odds with many of its allies on the relationship between power and diplomacy. Truman and Acheson were unwilling once American troops were in retreat to wind down the war, for various reasons. They believed Chinese demands were and would remain excessive, given the momentum of Chinese troops in Korea. There was a further reason for the administration's reluctance to negotiate. Americans felt betrayed by an old and trusted friend. As the president explained in a press conference of November 30: "Neither the United Nations nor the United States has any aggressive intentions toward China. Because of the historic friendship between the people of the United States and China, it is particularly shocking to us to think that Chinese are being forced into battle against our troops." At the United Nations, the Chinese had shown no willingness to negotiate. In international forums they had merely used the same violent and false rhetoric that Americans had come to expect of Soviet representatives. In their intervention, the Chinese had been "forced or deceived into serving the ends of Russian colonial policy in Asia." "If the Chinese people were free to speak they would denounce the aggression against the United Nations," the president declared.

In the war's last, critical phase, the Truman administration confronted fateful policy decisions which neither revisionists nor interpreters and critics of the Cold War had to face. Voices were raised which contradicted what the same people had been saying not long before. Segments of public opinion who had opposed a stengthened national defense and a sound military policy now urged a full-scale war against China. Others favored provoking a world war; still others urged a retreat to Fortress America. In a democracy where free expression of opinion prevails, the malcontents always have an advantage and differences of opinion make news compared with agreement. The Army Chief of Staff, General J. Lawton Collins, flew to Tokyo for meetings with General MacArthur.

The Far East commander had argued that he had three alternatives in Korea. One was to limit fighting to Korea and this would be the same as surrendering. A second course, which MacArthur favored, was to blockade the coast of China, bomb the China mainland, introduce Chiang Kai-shek's forces into South China through Hong Kong, and use other Chinese Nationalist troops in South Korea. A third alternative was to seek an armistice to be supervised by the U.N. with Chinese Communist forces remaining north of the 38th parallel. Truman was convinced that MacArthur as a seasoned soldier must have known that the actions proposed under the second course of action involved a risk of world war. Truman attributed MacArthur's black-and-white view on the need to extend the war into China to the differences of perspective growing out of military and presidential briefings. A military commander whose aides depend on his giving them favorable efficiency reports tends to receive reports that are tailored to his perspective. A president is more likely to hear a diversity of viewpoints from different advisers represented on his staff and is less likely to be served by "yes" men. Truman attributed many of his differences with MacArthur to the advising process for military and political leaders.

With respect to the pursuit of diplomatic initiatives in late 1950 and early 1951, Truman was no less skeptical than Acheson. He told the French prime minister, M. René Pleven, the United States would not negotiate at the price of collective security and national self-respect. The Chinese would be willing to accept a cease-fire only if the United States were willing to pay a price it was impossible to pay. Moreover, the administration saw successive negotiating efforts undertaken which proved to be failures. For example the General Assembly adopted a resolution on December 14 and assigned the task of exploring prospects for a cease-fire to three neutral leaders, Entezam of Iran, Pearson of Canada, and Rau of India. By January 2, the negotiators announced their effort had failed. In every approach to a cease-fire, troublesome technical issues arose, including the right to free inspection on both sides of the cease-fire line to observe military build-ups and the need for air reconnaissance and a naval presence by the Americans. If the United States reinforced its troops by replacing men whose tour of duty had come to an end, the Chinese would demand the right to increase their forces on an absolute numerical basis.

When Truman declared a national emergency, he did so on the basis of the best judgment of his military and civilian advisers. Defense requirements and military procurement necessitated the establishment of defense priorities over civilian needs. Congressional leaders were generally supportive, although some conservative senators like Taft and Wherry doubted the president needed additional powers. Other politicians and newspapers made noisy demands for a crash rearmament program and full wartime mobilization. As with every controversial issue, the administration had to steer a middle course between inaction and overreaction. For some senators, bipartisanship was a one-way street. A president was expected to consult with them and seek their approval for whatever he did. But they felt no responsibility of the type Arthur Vandenberg had manifested when he shared the administration's problems in discussions with Marshall and Lovett without trying to sabotage its policies.

Truman was deeply disturbed by the Congress' tendency to overstep its authority and violate the separation of powers. As a young man, he had read Montesquieu's *Spirit of the Laws* and the *Federalist Papers* and became imbued with the right of each branch of government to jealously guard its prerogatives. The president's solemn duty is to resist legislators who try to carry out fishing expeditions into his private files. Truman declared: "The President cannot function without advisers or without advice, written or oral. But just as soon as he is required to show what kind of advice he has had, who said what to him, or what kind of records he has, the advice he receives will become worthless."[12] This issue became crucial as the controversy over MacArthur reached its height.

As we have seen, MacArthur, late in 1950, had increased his demands for authority to bomb Chinese airfields in Manchuria, use troops from Formosa, and blockade the China coast. In response, the Joint Chiefs of Staff had proposed that the South Korean forces be increased by two to three hundred thousand men with the necessary small arms and submachine guns. MacArthur questioned the effectiveness of Koreans and urged instead that increased weapons and munitions be provided to the National Police Reserve of Japan. MacArthur insisted that without the strategic course he was proposing, all of Korea would have to be abandoned, a prediction that proved erroneous.

12. *Ibid.*, 454.

On January 1, the Communist forces launched a major attack on the Eighth Army, forcing the abandonment of Seoul. During January, the Eighth Army stemmed the tide and Generals Collins and Vandenberg, who visited MacArthur, reported that, barring Russia's intervention and massive Chinese involvement, the United Nations forces would hold South Korea. The Truman administration had from the earliest stages of the Korean War believed that Soviet strategy for weakening 'American leadership in the building-up of NATO was to draw it ever deeper into an Asian war. The president had to consider the effects of every military decision in Korea on the defense and unity of Europe and over-all American preparedness to meet Soviet challenges in the Cold War. There were numerous meetings between the president and officials of the State and Defense Departments in early 1951 to formulate policies that served the security needs of Korea, Europe, and the United States.

Meanwhile, the influence of Republicans in the Congress increased as a result of the mid-term elections. Through the winter of 1950/51, the mood of Congress grew increasingly bellicose, with resolutions in both Houses calling on the United Nations to declare Communist China an aggressor. In communications with Prime Minister Nehru of India in July of 1950, Stalin had seemed to say that the Communists would expect as a precondition for settlement the admission of Communist China to the United Nations (taking over China's seat in the Security Council) and the reunification of Korea under the North Koreans.

In March, 1951, the United Nations forces had regrouped, the military situation in Korea had been stabilized, and the conditions for a realistic cease-fire at or near the 38th parallel appeared to exist. On March 19, the Joint Chiefs and the secretaries of State and Defense met to consider a State Department draft on which a presidential statement would be based. On March 20, MacArthur was notified that a presidential announcement was contemplated which would call for diplomatic efforts toward settlement before U.N troops sought to advance beyond the 38th parallel, and that he was asked for his recommendations. MacArthur opposed any further restraints on his action. However the president, following extensive consultations within the administration and with representatives of nations who had troops in Korea, prepared a draft statement saying that, in accord with the Security Council resolution of June 27, 1950, the basis "for restoring peace and security in the area" now existed. Before the president could make his statement, MacArthur on March 24, released his own statement, the content of which was at cross-purposes with the president's plan. The general in effect threatened the enemy with bringing the full weight of allied power against Communist China even though offering to meet with the commander of the Communist forces "to find any military means" whereby the political objectives of the United Nations could be accomplished without further bloodshed.

The most likely explanation of MacArthur's move, according to orthodox historian John W. Spanier, must "be found in his desire to extend the war to China; for in MacArthur's judgment, such action was required by the highest interests of the United States."[13] In his statement, MacArthur asked Peking to admit it had lost the war, hardly a condition for a cease-fire. On April 5, the Republican minority leader, Congressman Joseph Martin, read a letter from MacArthur to Congress comprising a further challenge to President Truman's authority. The president concluded that if he allowed MacArthur to continue to defy civilian authority, he as president would be violating his oath to uphold and defend the Constitution. For over a year he had tried to win MacArthur over to his policy and failed. Following the Martin letter, the president announced on April 11, 1951, that MacArthur was dismissed from all his commands. He was dismissed for failure to submit his statements for clearance, for challenging the president's authority for foreign policy, and for opposing the administration's decision to limit the war in Korea. The substance of the administration's concerns was confirmed and amply demonstrated in MacArthur's testimony in the Senate hearings on his return.

The real issue between Truman and MacArthur concerned the nature of the response to the challenge of communism. The aim of the Truman administration was the containment of the Soviet Union and its satellites, not their destruction. The goal of the Truman Doctrine, the Marshall Plan, NATO, and the United Nations action in Korea was to erect "unassailable barriers" to Communist expansion. The means to this end was the building of "situations of strength," particularly in association with NATO allies. The military core of the containment policy was the nearly complete reliance on strategic air power to deter or win World War III, given the conventional military superiority of the Soviet army. Korea from the start presented American policy makers with a dilemma. Both Acheson and MacArthur had excluded it as being outside America's strategic defense perimeter and not to be defended in the event of an all-out war. At the same time, American failure to resist So-

13. John W. Spanier, *The Truman-MacArthur Controversy and the Korean War* (New York: W. W. Norton & Company, 1965), 201.

viet aggression in South Korea would only whet Soviet appetite for expansion elsewhere. Nonetheless, "the limited Soviet challenge in Korea
did not fit our strategic doctrine. South Korea was certainly not 'worth'
the price of total war; massive retaliation upon Moscow was not the answer to the shrewd Russian exploitation of the government's one-sided
concentration upon air-atomic striking power. A more limited response
was needed."[14]

For the administration, the Korean War was and remained a peripheral war. As a limited war, it was a means to teach the Soviets that aggression did not pay, but it had to be fought in such a way that the alliance of
the most powerful Western states not be destroyed. For MacArthur, Asia
and not Europe was the main theater in which the struggle with communism was being fought and would be decided. His troops were fighting
Europe's battles now and, from his viewpoint, ought not be limited. Since
MacArthur was convinced the Cold War would be decided in the war in
Asia, he was prepared to use any means to achieve this end. The administration saw the Korean War as a limited war; the general viewed it as a
total war in which he as commander should not be subject to constraints.

The differences between the president and his commander while serious might not have been critical except for two developments. The
first was the transformation of American objectives in Korea after Mac-
Arthur's brilliant Inchon victory. The objective had been resisting the
North Koreans and establishing the integrity of South Korea as it had
existed before June 25, 1950. "Once the United Nations force marched
across the 38th Parallel, however, the objective became the total elimination of the North Korean government and the unconditional surrender
of its armed forces. But Korean unification under United Nations control would have threatened Chinese security."[15] When the administration accepted the goal of unifying Korea by force, it ended the limited
character of the war and therefore the constraints on the enemy which
had kept China from direct intervention. It also legitimized MacArthur's view of the conflict rather than the view it brought to the struggle
and the one to which it was to return.

The second development came with the increasing influence of conservative Republicans in the Congress who aligned themselves with Mac-
Arthur. Under the best of circumstances, it has been difficult for any administration to justify a limited war. The greatest failures in postwar

14. *Ibid.*, 258–59.
15. *Ibid.*, 278.

American foreign policy have been in establishing the imperatives of a strategy for resisting limited aggression by limited means. Traditional habits of mind have prevailed; Americans have preferred to think in terms of unconditional surrender of the enemy and total victory. War is viewed as a purely military endeavor, not one with political objectives. According to Clausewitz, there was no area of military operations that was not related to political and diplomatic objectives, none that was unencumbered by "outside interference." The United States alone among great powers has tried to separate military action from underlying political objectives. "Not until military men as a whole accept the need for close political direction will they be less likely to issue public statements voicing their displeasure at the 'political interference' with their conduct of a limited war."[16] That displeasure having been expressed, political allies inevitably came forward as in MacArthur's case with senators like Taft, Wherry, Bridges, and Knowland opposing Truman. Having fought the liberal eastern wing of the Republican party unsuccessfully in the late 1940s, the middle-western conservatives used the MacArthur controversy to strengthen their claim that Democrats and heretics within their own party were destroying the American political and economic system. They coupled their criticism of New Dealers with attacks on those who had lost China and Eastern Europe and were now losing Korea. "The conspiratorial interpretation of American domestic and foreign politics could not have been advanced at a more appropriate moment in American postwar history."[17]

A feeling of frustration about endless conflicts was mounting. The American penchant for quick answers to problems clashed with the demands for patience and resolve. It would be difficult to prove that Truman and Acheson made concessions to conservative political pressures at various stages in the Korean War, for example, in accepting temporarily the goal of unifying all of Korea by force following the Inchon landings. What became evident in 1951 was that the political attacks from the right had weakened the administration's ability to achieve a political settlement, causing Walter Lippmann to write: Truman "was not able to make peace, because politically he was too weak at home. He was not able to make war because the risks were too great. This dilemma . . . was resolved by the election of Eisenhower."[18] Because he was a Republican and a victorious commander in World War II, Eisenhower

16. *Ibid.*, 275.
17. *Ibid.*, 268.
18. Walter Lippmann, New York *Herald Tribune*, August 24, 1956.

could accept the partition of Korea without being denounced as an appeaser. Truman and Acheson were never able to accept the only terms for peace the Chinese would accept. These terms only Eisenhower could carry out; his predecessors were vulnerable to attack from the followers of MacArthur, Senator Joseph McCarthy, and the conservative wing of the Republican party.

The gravest lesson of Korea is the high price paid when the nation lacks a sense of the objectives of warfare. It is sobering that the lesson could be even greater if military commanders reserved the right to decide on the use of tactical nuclear weapons in the field. Militarily, the argument for such weapons may be compelling. Politically, their use could bring on World War III and mutual annihilation. Essentially, two strategic doctrines exist to guide such discussions. The one is MacArthur's, that in war "there is no substitute for victory." The other is Clausewitz', in which "it is an unpermissible and even harmful distinction [that] . . . a great military event . . . should admit a purely military judgment; indeed, it is an unreasonable procedure to consult professional soldiers on the plan of war. . . . For war is an instrument of policy . . . it must measure with policy's measure."[19] The administration sought valiantly but inconsistently to follow the second doctrine in a nation that in considerable measure was wedded to the first approach. Not fully understanding all the implications of the differences between its objectives and prevailing American attitudes and more concerned with the promotion of transcendent and universalist ideas for a brave new world—ideas such as collective security—the Truman administration failed to educate the people in the realities of international politics and limited war. Its policies were oftentimes better than its explanations, but because it talked more about what ought to be than about what was, more about ultimate designs than its practical efforts, the government floundered and was plunged into an ever deepening national crisis. It would remain for a wartime hero, General Eisenhower, to help free the nation from its domestic trauma and neutralize the more strident critics of a national foreign policy.

The Cold War had been brought on by the failure of the United States to fight World War II for explicit and well-defined political and territorial objectives. The Korean War threw the nation into disarray because neither the public nor the principal commander in the field accepted the objectives for which that limited war was being fought. An

19. Karl von Clausewitz, *On War* (New York: Modern Library Edition, 1943), 599, 601.

administration which conducted the war with judgment and restraint must nonetheless be held responsible for the public's lack of understanding and for the permissiveness it showed toward its Far Eastern commander. The first phase of the Cold War ended, therefore, as it had begun with no clear theoretical understanding of the responsibilities and limitations of the United States as a world power, its responsibilities for containment and the limitations of containment in Asia.

Revisionism and Korea

For revisionists, the objective of American foreign policy was to free Korea of Russian influence as World War II had freed it of Japanese influence. In this, the United States was seeking to establish once again "the principle of the Open Door Policy and reap the benefits of benevolent and liberal empire."[20] The U.S. intervened suddenly and without public debate and, while Secretary Acheson spoke reassuringly of restoring Korea to the status quo ante bellum, President Truman within three months had approved military operations north of the 38th parallel. The new secretary of defense, George C. Marshall, who succeeded Louis Johnson, ordered MacArthur, following his dramatic Inchon landing, to proceed and "let action determine the matter." With MacArthur's advance, the political objectives of the Korean War changed both for the U.S. and the U.N. Washington was determined to avoid having to make an issue of the 38th parallel and on October 7, 1950, the United Nations General Assembly, responding to American leadership, approved a resolution providing that "all appropriate steps be taken to ensure conditions of stability throughout Korea."[21]

To emphasize MacArthur's clash with Truman in the autumn of 1950 is misleading. Americans in the first days of the Korean War assumed they would be successful in establishing a worldwide liberal economic order. Both at the grassroots and among the governing elite, Americans believed that Korea could be unified by force and doubted that Communist China would intervene. Revisionists looked back to the 1880s and 1890s to discover the origins of the American sense of omnipotence. Through preponderant power, the United States would be able to maintain free markets for itself and its friends in Asia. It would be illusory to

20. William Appleman Williams, *The Tragedy of American Diplomacy* (2nd ed.; New York: Dell, 1972), 295.
21. Quoted *ibid.*, 296.

suppose that MacArthur was not representative of a broad segment of American thinking, viewed from a revisionist perspective.

Some revisionists have discovered that even Secretary Acheson acknowledged that "a school of academic criticism has concluded that we overreacted to Stalin, which in turn caused him to overreact to policies of the United States. This may be true." Before concluding that Acheson had gone over to join his critics, it is important to read the sentence that follows: "Fortunately, perhaps, these authors were not called upon to analyze a situation in which the United States had not taken the action which it did take."[22] Nonetheless, revisionists make their case essentially on the grounds of American overreaction. Was it not true that the United States had demanded sole control over Japan at the end of the war to assure hegemony throughout the Pacific? Would China have emerged as a hostile power if the Americans involved, especially Patrick J. Hurley, Roosevelt's envoy, had possessed a clearer view of the forces at work in China's internal struggle? Both Roosevelt and Truman made mistakes in their assessments of Asian politics, but Roosevelt "was an experimenter, not much worried if things went wrong temporarily; something else could be tried until a tolerable situation had been achieved." Truman by contrast "considered any decision final" and saw this as a supreme virtue. The way he put it was that he slept well after it was done and woke up to something else. "For Roosevelt, nothing was ever quite done."[23] For him, public matters were always in ferment. Only the end had to be kept continuously in view.

For revisionists, one of Roosevelt's ends was friendship with China, and had Roosevelt lived he would never have rested until a solution was found to this objective, including the unthinkable solution of recognizing and supporting Mao. Truman pursued a policy of containment in Asia in defiance of geography. But "deployment thousands of miles from both coasts was simply an impossible logistical task." A reaction was inevitable as young men and taxpayers contemplated the results. "It had taken only two years after Roosevelt's death, and with Truman's management, to turn two great victorious allied powers into aggressive enemies." Russia and China overbalanced the United States in population—a billion to two hundred million. Neither had troops in combat but both had drawn American troops into war in Asia. No president ex-

22. Dean Acheson, *Present at the Creation: My Years in the State Department* (New York: W. W. Norton & Company, 1969), 753n.
23. Rexford G. Tugwell, *Off Course* (New York: Praeger Publishers, 1971), 201.

cept Buchanan, who had allowed the Civil War to develop, had presided over so far-reaching a political transformation as Truman did as wartime allies became enemies. Once begun, wars with Communists on the Asian mainland were inevitably enlarged by Kennedy and Johnson and finally liquidated in part by Nixon. If Truman was the architect, Acheson was the builder of policies that led to war with his "insistence that all disturbances, especially revolutionary ones, were instances of Communist aggression and that they must be met everywhere with military opposition. This was true in Germany, in Persia, in Greece, in Asia, and in the Near East."[24] Truman and Acheson were primarily responsible for the conflicts that threatened the maintenance of peace, as revisionists viewed the world.

For Korea, the critics pointed to domestic political forces that led to the crisis. Following the elections of 1946, Truman faced an increasingly hostile Congress. By 1948, the cost-of-living index had risen 25 percent over 1945. The interests of the people had been sacrificed to the mercies of big business and big labor and a "free market" that no longer existed. The transition from wartime controls had been so abrupt that adjustments could not be made. Despite his disabilities, including those of a former senator—"Senators have a singular immunity to the consequences of what they say and do; they have little difficulty in escaping blame and claiming credit"[25]—Truman was reelected by a narrow majority. In his inaugural, he placed greatest emphasis on the U.N., the Marshall Plan, NATO, and Point Four. His domestic proposals concerned welfare and education, but Congress ignored his requests as they opposed his military budgets.

Overnight, Korea changed the country's attitude toward military expenditures, but for revisionists, "There was something curious about the immediate undertaking." It followed close on the heels of Chiang Kai-shek's flight from China. Fighting broke out on the border of a hostile nation which had been considered one of the Big Five powers. "It was assumed that the attack was inspired by Russia, although this assumption later appeared to have been false."[26] The entire Korean affair conflicted with Soviet objectives, priorities, and military strategy. At the moment of the Korean crisis, the Soviet Union and the European Communist movements were deeply involved in a massive peace and coexistence propaganda campaign, which Korea was to shatter. Russian arms

24. *Ibid.*, 203, 206.
25. *Ibid.*, 209.
26. *Ibid.*, 212.

shipments were not sufficient to assure victory over the larger South Korean army, suggesting that the arms transfers were looked on more as a stabilizing than a destabilizing force in the region. Soviet leaders must have known that war in Korea would mobilize the Congress and narrow the gap between Soviet and American military power. The Russians not only had boycotted the Security Council and U.N. meetings since January but failed to return before August to veto full U.N. support of intervention in Korea.

The Soviets' first press accounts were quite distinctive, with the Russians printing objective accounts from Reuters, the Associated Press, and even the full text of an American diplomatic note with the official reply. They appeared to be avoiding statements which engaged their prestige too deeply. The revisionist historians Joyce and Gabriel Kolko wrote that Korea "conflicted not only with Soviet global political strategy but with their military strategy as well. Less than a month after the crisis began the former United States military governor of Seoul province during 1945–48, Colonel Maurice Lutwack, offered the view that the highly individualistic North Koreans had started the war themselves at the opening of the monsoon season, at precisely the time the Russians would have avoided had they had any responsibility for the affair."[27] Soviet strategy preferred the launching of military campaigns during winter months and chose to avoid direct attacks on cities. One revisionist writer concludes: "Korea . . . was a strategic mistake, ending in an occupation to be maintained for years. If it was not one of those Russian attempts to challenge the United States on the periphery of the American sphere of influence that became a fixed point of departure for American policy, then it was undertaken under a misapprehension still being paid for in 1970."[28]

General MacArthur's command in Tokyo and the Truman administration in Washington were said to have been taken utterly by surprise by the North Korean invasion. Yet MacArthur's chief of intelligence, Major General Charles A. Willoughby, maintained that his intelligence unit collected information which he relayed to Washington as early as March, three months before the invasion, which unmistakably pointed to a North Korean buildup for war. On May 10, the South Korean defense minister held a press conference in Seoul in which he declared that North Korean troops were moving in force toward the 38th parallel

27. Joyce and Gabriel Kolko, *The Limits of Power: The World & United States Foreign Policy, 1945–1954* (New York: Harper & Row, 1972), 586.
28. R. G. Tugwell, *Off Course*, 215–16.

and there was imminent danger of invasion from the North. All such reports were discounted in Tokyo and therefore in Washington as well. The revisionist I. F. Stone has asserted: "The hypothesis that invasion was encouraged politically by silence, invited militarily by defensive formations, and finally set off by some minor lunges across the border when all was ready should explain a great deal."[29] According to this version of revisionist thought, men like Louis Johnson, secretary of defense, and General MacArthur believed that war with China was inevitable and that an early war was better than war later. "MacArthur's whole subsequent course of behaviour (and that of his powerful supporters) was consistent with a strategy designed to provoke and then escalate a war in Asia."[30]

Not all revisionists go as far as Horowitz and Stone, who assert that the ideological views and political ambitions of certain American leaders brought on the Korean War. The majority insist that as the war progressed Washington and Tokyo divided not on the matter of goals but methods. The Joint Chiefs of Staff instructed MacArthur to go ahead in his attempt to liberate North Korea following his brilliant victory far up the Korean Peninsula at Inchon, provided there was "a reasonable chance of success." The government of the United States and not its commander in the field had changed the political objective of the war in the middle of the conflict. However, the Chinese sent a series of warnings, including a statement to India, that they would not sit back and allow the Americans to come to their border. On October 10 Chinese leaders publicly stated that if American troops continued north, they would enter the conflict. When American jet aircraft strafed a Soviet airfield a few miles from Vladivostok and the Russians protested, President Truman decided to fly to Wake Island for the memorable meeting with General MacArthur.

The details of that meeting, while shrouded in controversy, cannot obscure one broad area of agreement: the United States Air Force thereafter confined its activities to the Korean Peninsula. Beyond that, Truman gave one version and MacArthur another, but both hoped for the unification of Korea. For MacArthur this meant striking at Chinese bases across the Yalu, while the president, with responsibility for American policy in Europe and the world, urged more limited military operations. In the MacArthur Hearings which followed the firing of General Mac-

29. I. F. Stone, *The Hidden History of the Korean War* (New York: Monthly Review Press, 1952), 44.
30. David Horowitz, *A Free World Colossus* (New York: Hill and Wang, 1971), 119.

Arthur, Senator Brien McMahon complained that everybody who had anything to do with decisions on the last stage of the war had been wrong and Senator Saltonstall of Massachusetts evoked an affirmative answer from Secretary Acheson to the question "They really fooled us when it comes right down to it, didn't they?" To revisionists, this failure was attributable to the American sense of omnipotence and the drive to establish economic hegemony in Asia. To interpreters and critics like George F. Kennan and Walter Lippmann, it was due to American political blindness about China's vital interests and threats to those interests which would inevitably provoke a response.

The remaining military history of the Korean struggle is less subject to dispute. On October 25, MacArthur, having assured the president at Wake Island that the Chinese had not been seen, nor was it likely they would enter the war, advanced to the Yalu River at Chosan. On October 26, Chinese volunteer forces attacked South Korean and American troops near Chosin Reservoir driving them back. At this point, the Chinese withdrew, having warned they would resist American military action north of the Yalu but that, like the Americans, they wished to limit fighting in Korea, their main concern being Formosa. The Peking government accepted an invitation to come to the United Nations to discuss Formosa and presumably the Korean War. According to revisionist writers, neither Truman nor Acheson was ready to contemplate a negotiated settlement, particularly with congressional elections a few days off. They feared the political effects of a settlement, the wrath of the Republicans, the end to any hope of Korea's unification, and the damage to rearmament based on NSC 68. General MacArthur delayed a ground offensive scheduled for November 15, the date first announced for the arrival of the Chinese delegation at the United Nations, to the morning of November 24, the new date for their arrival. Europeans were incensed and Prime Minister Attlee flew to Washington for consultations. The Chinese delegation packed its bags and returned to Peking.

MacArthur advanced along two widely separated routes, leaving a wide gap in the middle. Masses of Chinese troops poured into the gap and in two weeks North Korea was largely cleared of American troops. MacArthur asked authority in "an entirely new war" to strike directly at China. Fearing Soviet intervention, American policy makers denied him that authority and returned to the pre-Inchon strategy of restoring the status quo ante bellum. President Truman spoke casually at his November 20 press conference of the use of the atomic bomb if authorized by the United Nations, but Prime Minister Attlee persuaded the administration to abandon this idea. (Truman was said to be merely cataloging alternatives.) Attlee failed, however, to convince Truman or Acheson to negotiate. The American leaders threatened that were the U.S. to abandon Korea, it would be forced to consider abandoning NATO.

Following the Yalu debacle, the Truman administration put the nation on an all-out Cold War footing. The president "got emergency powers from Congress to expedite war mobilization, made selective service a permanent feature of American life, submitted a $50 billion defense budget that followed the guidelines of NSC 68, sent two more divisions (a total of six) to Europe, doubled the number of air groups to ninety-five, obtained new bases in Morocco, Libya, and Saudi Arabia, increased the army by 50 percent to 3.5 million men, pushed forward the Japanese peace treaty, stepped up aid to the French in Indochina, initiated the process of adding Greece and Turkey to NATO, and began discussions with Franco which led to American aid to Fascist Spain in return for military bases there." In March, 1951, the Americans detonated a thermonuclear bomb. America acquired bases around the world, encircling both the Soviet Union and China. President Truman completed the task begun when he announced the Truman Doctrine on March 12, 1947, and by 1951 "he had made sure that if any communist showed his head on the free side of the line, someone—usually an American—would be there to shoot him."[31] Yet with all its military strength, with an enormously expanded military establishment never before contemplated in time of peace, analysts could describe the structure as "means without ends." The Truman administration, despite its accomplishments, failed to develop a policy structure capable of meeting the political and military problems that lay ahead.

This weakness was evident in the final days of the Korean War. In early 1951, MacArthur resumed the offensive and drove the Chinese and the North Koreans back to the 38th parallel. The administration saw the opportunity of constructive negotiations especially with the Chinese in retreat. MacArthur, in reckless disregard of his superiors, crossed the 38th parallel and demanded in effect unconditional surrender by the Chinese. Truman resolved to remove the general and found cause in a letter the general sent to Representative Joseph W. Martin, which was read in the House of Representatives. MacArthur urged the military reunification of Korea, unleashing Chiang Kai-shek to fight on the mainland, and the eradication of communism in Asia, declaring: "Here in

31. Stephen E. Ambrose, *Rise to Globalism* (London: Penguin, 1971), 210.

Asia is where the communist conspirators have elected to make their play for global conquest. . . . Here we fight Europe's war with arms while the diplomats there still fight it with words." General Bradley, in the congressional hearings that followed MacArthur's dismissal, spoke of an extension of the war into China as "fighting the wrong war at the wrong time in the wrong place against the wrong enemy." Three out of four Americans questioned in public opinion polls appeared to favor MacArthur over Truman. They appeared to favor the liberation of North Korea if not China over a policy of containment. Truman walked a narrow line seeking peace in Asia but rearmament in Europe.

A Soviet offer for a military armistice was rejected on June 23. It had removed the three conditions set by the Chinese and the North Koreans: withdrawal of American troops, return of Formosa to China, and the seating of Peking at the United Nations. On July 10, peace talks resumed, spearheaded by the United Nations and the NATO countries; they broke down, were resumed, faltered, and resumed again. Finally, General Eisenhower in his campaign for the presidency pledged to go to Korea to end the war. Summing up the Truman era, one revisionist wrote: "When he left the White House his legacy was an American presence on every continent of the world, an enormously expanded armaments industry, [and] American corporations in Europe and Latin America on a scale surpassing Herbert Hoover's wildest dreams."[32] And none of this would have been possible without the war in Korea.

Power and Its Limits

On Korea, as on other issues in the Cold War, the four interpreter-critics offer a different perspective. Particularly George F. Kennan, Walter Lippmann, and Hans J. Morgenthau differ from both the revisionist and the orthodox historians. Many writers in the postwar world have emphasized America's power. But what distinguished the writings of all four interpreters from that of others was their stress on limits. Having discussed national power in part 3 of *Politics Among Nations*, Morgenthau devoted parts 4, 5, and 6 to various forms of "Limitations of National Power." Writing of the American decision to intervene through the United Nations in Korea, Kennan explained: "I had approved from the start our decision to resist by force of arms the incursion by North Korea into South Korea that began on June 25, 1950. But I had done so on the

32. *Ibid.*, 216.

assumption and understanding that our action was only for a limited purpose: namely, the restoration of the *status quo ante* on the Korean peninsula, and that our forces would not, even if military successes permitted, advance beyond the former demarcation line along the 38th parallel." [33]

Lippmann, perhaps most consistently of all, warned of the risks for the United States of a land war on the mainland of Asia. Critics saw in such warnings a preoccupation with Europe and an obsession with Western civilization. Kennan and Lippmann, it was argued, had little understanding of Asia. (In the 1960s, President Johnson and Secretaries Rusk and McNamara in shaping Asian policy were to make this criticism again with telling effect and to silence opponents such as Kennan and Morgenthau on Vietnam.) What the experiences of the past quarter-century demonstrate, however, is the interpreter-critics' profound understanding of the limits of power, of the fallacy of doctrines of American omnipotence, and of the truth that the United States, while the most powerful of great powers, is yet powerless in a thermonuclear age to impose its will on others everywhere throughout the world. Because the four interpreter-critics have been at home with paradox, they understood that the United States could be both all-powerful among nation-states and powerless in much the same way the parent and the state are powerful and powerless at the same time within the family and the nation. As individuals, we learn to live within these constraints; as nations, we resist and push them aside.

The debate over the Cold War and its militarization in Korea came to a head over differences concerning the limitations of American power. The postwar architects of the policy of resisting aggression were children of Munich; the failure of England and France to resist the spread of nazism in Central Europe and its tragic consequences for Europe and the world were never far from their thinking. Collective security was their guide and the possibility of damaging effects to world peace and national power resulting from failure to use force was their overriding fear. In his memoirs, Secretary of State Dean Acheson wrote that the North Korean attack on South Korea on June 25, 1950, "was an open, undisguised challenge to our internationally accepted position as the protector of South Korea. . . . To back away from the challenge would have been highly destructive of the power and prestige of the United

33. George F. Kennan, *Memoirs, 1950–1963* (Boston: Little, Brown and Company, 1972), 23.

States."[34] On the issue of resisting expansion from the North, the American people, including at least three of the four interpreter-critics, were united. The strongest statement came from Kennan: "It was clear to me from the start that we would have to react with all necessary force to repel this attack and to expel the North Korean forces from the southern half of the peninsula."[35]

But Kennan's support extended only as far as the 38th parallel and the restoration of the status quo ante between South and North Korea. He wrote: "I made it clear as early as July 1950, in the internal discussions of our government, that I was opposed to any advance beyond the 38th parallel." On August 8, he warned in a Department of State memorandum: "When we begin to have military successes, that will be the time to watch out. Anything may then happen—entry of Soviet forces, entry of Chinese Communist forces, new strike for U.N. settlement, or all three together." He reiterated his views two weeks later in an off-the-record press conference and gave as his view "that the Russians will not be inclined to sit by if our forces or United Nations forces . . . push the North Koreans beyond the 38th parallel again. . . . They may . . . reoccupy North Korea, or they might introduce other forces which would be nominally Chinese Communist forces . . . (goodness knows who would be really controlling them). . . . Obviously, they are not going to leave the field free for us to sweep up the peninsula and place ourselves forty or fifty miles from Vladivostok."[36]

What is important in Kennan's statement is his sense of the limits of American interests and power, limits which had reality in themselves but also reflected the limitations imposed by the interests and power of others. No one would claim there was a total absence of this type of thinking in the Truman administration. The original instructions to General MacArthur were: "You are authorized to conduct military operations . . . north of the 38th parallel in Korea" but "as a matter of policy, no non-Korean Ground Forces will be used in the northeast provinces bordering the Soviet Union or in the area along the Manchurian border."[37] Yet the same day General Marshall sent General MacArthur a for-his-eyes-only telegram saying, "We want you to feel unhampered tactically and strategically to proceed north of the 38th parallel."[38]

34. Acheson, *Present at the Creation*, 405.
35. Kennan, *Memoirs, 1925–1950*, p. 486.
36. Kennan, *Memoirs, 1950–1963*, p. 23–24.
37. Department of State Bulletin, Vol. XXII, September 18, 1950, p. 468.
38. Acheson, *Present at the Creation*, 453.

Kennan's concern about this ambivalence in the position of the American government was heightened by his doubts that General Mac-Arthur was under effective control by anyone in Washington. It was this fact, and not personal differences with other administration leaders, which caused Kennan the deepest anguish. Leaving government for the Princeton Institute for Advanced Studies soon thereafter, he was to be out of touch with such events as the warning by the Chinese Communists through the Indian ambassador in Peking, K. M. Panikar, on October 3, 1950, that China would enter the war if American forces advanced beyond the 38th parallel, the arrival of American forces at the Manchurian border on November 21, General MacArthur's initiating on November 24 of a "win the war" offensive, and the Chinese entry in force on November 25 into the war. Nor did he know of the personal assurances given by General MacArthur to the president at Wake Island and his promise, in response to a direct inquiry from Washington in the first days of November, that a Russian or Chinese intervention was nothing to be feared. Nor is it important that Kennan underestimated the extent to which the Chinese would take direct action in the region based on their own interests and not in response to Russian dictation. What mattered was that Kennan's map of international politics enabled him to see that effective use of American power was limited at the borders of China both by the risk of overextending its own power and by the vital interests of the Chinese and the Russians.

No one is of course wholly right or wrong in measuring and evaluating power. As Henry Kissinger once observed, estimates of power are both the most central and most risky requirement of foreign policy. Any attempt to estimate and calculate power tends to be nine parts judgment to one part science. It may not be unfair to suggest, however, that two groups are particularly disposed to err in their estimates of power. The one group includes those for whom power is something essentially evil, associated with the behavior of greedy and selfish men and a passing phase of an old international order. The other group is composed of those for whom power, and in particular its military expression, becomes an end in itself. For Kennan, the first lesson of the conduct of our Korean policy is "the terrible danger of letting national policy be determined by military considerations alone. Had the military been given their head (and this goes for the entire combination of MacArthur and the Joint Chiefs of Staff in Washington)—had they not been restrained by the wise discipline exercised, in the face of unprecedentedly savage political opposition, by President Truman, Secretary of State Acheson, and General Marshall, disaster would almost certainly have ensued."[39] Yet Kennan's uncommonly generous praise of old friends ignores two important facts. First, it was the same men exercising "wise discipline" who by a policy of drift and indecision allowed the situation with General MacArthur to reach a point of no return. Second, the trend toward military thinking in policy making once war breaks out is inevitable if victory is seen as the only acceptable goal in war. What comes naturally to the military mind is also the prevailing mode of public thinking. It is instructive that in November, once United Nations troops were in retreat as Chinese Communist forces poured across the border, the same American public which had applauded our entry into the war called for total American withdrawal as rapidly as possible.

The idea of limitation runs counter to the American national character as it views the outside world. Our tendency has been to have everything or nothing to do with the world—and be chary of anything in between. The League of Nations was first supported as an American political invention and then rejected as a grave threat to national sovereignty. Americans fought one war to make the world safe for democracy and another for unconditional surrender. They dismantled a mighty army after World War II and conducted the last stages of the war without the guidance of clear political objectives which might have assured the formation of a postwar balance of power in Europe.

The concepts of limitation of power do not generally commend themselves to the wider public. They have about them an air of compromise and weakness; they require the use of language which has a flavor more European than American—detente, neutralization, spheres of influence, tacit agreements, and privileged sanctuaries. "The concept of limited warfare—of warfare conducted for limited objectives and ending with the achievement of those objectives by compromise with the existing enemy regime—was not only foreign but was deeply repugnant to the American military mind."[40] Korea illustrated the difficulty of conducting a limited war. Vietnam provided an even more decisive test and the irony of that troubled period in American history is that most of the debate involved not men such as Niebuhr and Kennan but the all-out critics opposed to those proclaiming that the only objective in war was victory.

39. Kennan, *Memoirs, 1950–1963*, p. 38.
40. *Ibid.*, 95.

Hans J. Morgenthau has contrasted the nonpolitical American approach to war and the British and Russian view, born of long experience, that wars are fought for political ends and military strategy must be shaped to these ends. In April, 1945, when the British urged that General Patton's army liberate Prague and as much of Czechoslovakia as possible, General Marshall said in a note to General Eisenhower: "Personally . . . I would be loath to hazard American lives for purely political reasons." To this Eisenhower replied the next day: "I shall not attempt any move I deem militarily unwise merely to gain a political advantage." When the British urged that the Americans capture Berlin before the Russians, General Bradley's reaction reported in his *Memoirs* was: "As soldiers we looked naively on this British inclination to complicate the war with political foresight and non-military objectives." Of this characteristic viewpoint, Morgenthau wrote: "This concentration on military objectives to the neglect of political considerations has one virtue: it is apt to win wars quickly, cheaply and thoroughly. Yet such victories may be short-lived, and an enormous political and military price may have to be paid for them later."[41] In Morgenthau's view, the tendency to shy away from defining the nation's political objectives was a major problem in our conduct of the war in Korea as it had been in World War II. Even before going to the defense of South Korea in the name of collective security, American policy makers should have asked four questions: First, what is our interest in the preservation of the independence of South Korea; second, what is our power to defend that independence against North Korea; third, what is our power to defend that independence against China and the Soviet Union; and fourth, what are the chances for preventing China and the Soviet Union from entering the Korean War.

The Truman administration was not unaware of these questions, but because it intervened in the name of the abstract and utopian concept of collective security, it did not keep them steadily and clearly in mind. It vacillated between the utopianism of collective security and the realistic requirements implicit in seeking answers to the four questions. For example, it allowed General MacArthur to advance to the Yalu River to achieve the reunification of Korea and then turned back when faced with the risk of a third world war. Morgenthau, in words reminiscent of Churchill's description of Baldwin's dilemma when, at the time of Italy's

41. Hans J. Morgenthau, *The Decline of Democratic Politics* (Chicago: University of Chicago Press, 1962), 330, Vol. I of *Politics in the Twentieth Century.*

attack on Ethiopia, Britain and the League weighed the possibility of sanctions, wrote: "Mr. Truman had declared that the effective prosecution of the Korean War meant the possibility of a third world war; he resolved that there must be no third world war; and he decided upon intervention in the Korean War."[42]

Finally, Morgenthau criticized the Korean War policy of the Truman administration on grounds of the over-militarization of our Asian policies since the war. The shock of the North Korean attack led to an over-emphasis on local military defenses. It gave rise to an interpretation of Asia's needs and problems as being primarily military in character. The North Korean attack was interpreted as having been planned by the Soviet Union as the opening move in a series of military aggressions likely to occur anywhere in Asia. It was argued that Soviet policy had shifted from subversion and political penetration to open warfare. Assuming this interpretation to be correct, a comparable shift in American policy was called for, placing far greater stress on the militarization of the Cold War.

Morgenthau, criticizing American policy, has maintained that such an interpretation was implausible at the time and has been wholly discredited by subsequent events. "The evidence, both intrinsic and explicit, points strongly toward a different interpretation. According to it, the Russian role in the outbreak of the Korean War was one of acquiescence rather than of instigation, resulting from a miscalculation of our intentions and capabilities."[43] The overemphasis on the military aspects of the crisis in Asia led to premature pressure on the Japanese to rearm, pressure that contradicted early postwar policy and brought together widely divergent Japanese groups in strongly anti-American demonstrations. The other consequence of the false perception of the origins of the Korean War was what some observers have called "pactomania." The United States has paid an enormous political price, for example in Iran, for "insignificant or illusory" military advantages. "Neither the Southeast Asia Treaty Organization (SEATO) nor the Bagdad Pact [both of which have since largely withered away]," wrote Professor Morgenthau in 1956, "adds anything material to the strength of the West. All the nations concerned, with the exception of Iran, Pakistan, and Thailand, were already members of one or the other Western military alignment

42. *Ibid.*, 103.
43. Morgenthau, *The Impasse of American Foreign Policy* (Chicago: University of Chicago Press, 1962), 257–58, Vol. II of *Politics in the Twentieth Century.*

before the conclusion of those pacts. . . . Iran and Thailand . . . would be liabilities rather than assets for whatever side they would join in case of actual war."[44]

In looking back on the judgments of interpreter-critics on Korea, it would be reassuring for the architects of American foreign policy as it evolved from 1943–1953 if they had been proved wrong. Yet from the Korean War to the present, the American approach has been to look first to military response, more often than not formulated for each successive crisis with little regard for the four central questions Morgenthau sought to raise about Korea. It seems fitting, therefore, to close our discussion of the period of the Cold War which comes to an end with the Korean War by suggesting that alongside orthodox and revisionist theories about the Cold War, the interpreter-critic perceptions deserve study and discussion as indeed may be the case for subsequent chapters in this fateful era of world history.

What George F. Kennan feared most in the development of an American policy for containment for Europe materialized in Asia, for it was in Asia that containment came to be viewed in largely military terms. It was also in Asia that containment was cast in universalist and indiscriminate terms without being measured by the historic foreign policy constraints of the interests and power of the nations most directly concerned. The driving force of containment in Asia was collective security and this invited disregard and contempt for a clear-eyed recognition of containment's limitations on the borders of China and the Soviet Union. Collective security had a chance of success when applied against a second-rank power such as North Korea. It could not succeed against one of the Great Powers.

Yet American policy makers who had accepted this limitation in giving each Great Power the veto on enforcement actions by the Security Council—a legal expression of a military and political reality—disregarded this fact in allowing United Nations troops to move to the Yalu. Moreover, not only was collective security beyond reach with regard to China and the Soviet Union but containment involving a change in the status of North Korea came up against the interests and power of the two most powerful communist states. At this point, a combination of force and suasion offered the one most hopeful course. The lack of a clear conception of the imperatives of foreign policy in the Cold War, especially for Asia, and of a viable American theory widely accepted by

44. *Ibid.*, 260.

the public and its representatives occasioned an American crisis of confidence. The nation recovered its sense of identity and purpose and its national consensus. Its faith was restored, however, less by agreement on principles of foreign policy in the Cold War than by trusting its hero-president. No one could be sure that a wartime hero would be available to save the nation from its faulty approach to some future grave crisis in the Cold War.

Index

Acheson, Dean, 75, 136–39, 156, 165, 175, 206
Alperovitz, Gar, 5, 6
American misperceptions, 71, 73
Atlantic Charter, 19, 33, 56
Atomic bomb, 5
Azerbaidjan occupation, Soviet, 124

Balance of power, 172
Berlin blockade, 160, 169
Bialystok settlement, 98
Bizonal Economic Union, 125
British imperialism, 22, 33
Brussels Treaty, 125
Bullitt, William C., 21
Burns, James MacGregor, 13
Butterfield, Herbert, 10, 11, 12

Casablanca Conference, 29
Causality: alternative view, 53; orthodox view, 23; revisionist view, 45
Chiang Kai-Shek, 134; defeat of, 175
Churchill, Winston S., 14
Clay, Lucius B., 65, 68, 69
Colonialism, 33; American view, 33
Comecon, 126
Cominform, Yugoslavian explosion, 125
Containment, 119; doctrine of, 125
Cordon sanitaire, 95
Country club complex, 8
Crimea Conference, 107
Curzon Line, 82, 84, 86, 94

Decline of American power, 43
Dulles, John Foster, 69, 70

Economic causes of the cold war, 7
European Coal and Steel Community, 170

Feis, Herbert, 16

Great Cycle theory, 120

Harriman, W. Averell, 3, 37
Historical interpretation, perennial problem of, 71
Hodge, General John R., 185
Horowitz, David, 202
Hull, Cordell, 54

International organization, 95
Interpreters: critics, 94
Interventionism, 49
Iron Curtain, 124, 126, 127, 128; speech, American reactions to, 127, 128; speech, Stalin's reactions to, 127

Jervis, Robert, 71

Katyn Forest massacre, 85
Kennan, George F., 37, 38, 60, 72, 114, 115, 205, 212
Kissinger, Henry, 75, 208
Kolko, Gabriel, 46, 47, 51
Korea, 126, 184–98, 191, 198–205, 205–13; cease fire effort, 126, 191; interpreter/critic view, 205–13; orthodox view, 184–98; revisionist view, 198–205
Korean Invasion (June 24, 1950), 126, 179
Korean War, Chinese intervention, 182, 188, 203

LaFeber, Walter, 39
Lend-Lease, 61
Limitation of power, 209
Lincoln, Abraham, 11
Lippmann, Walter, 43

Loan, to Russia, 61
London Conference, 157
London Poles, 84, 99
Lubin Poles, 93, 99, 106–107

MacArthur, Douglas, 183, 187, 188–95
Maddox, Robert J., 6
Marshall, George C., 3, 69, 134, 145, 174, 185; Harvard speech, 145; staff conferences, 134
Marshall Plan, 142, 145, 148, 149–53, 151, 153, 154; bipartisan foreign policy, 151; convergence of national interest, 154; discriminate response, 153; intellectual history, 142, 145; legislative history, 149–53; problem of Soviet acceptance, 148; Soviet satellites, 148
Masaryk, Jan, 125, 159
Mastny, Vojtech, 21
Mills, C. Wright, 50
Mikolajczyk, Stanislaw, 35, 85, 91
Missed opportunities, 93
Molotov, 17, 57, 184; Ribbentrop Pact, 17, 57
Morgenthau, Hans J., 114, 205
Morgenthau, Henry, 62
Morgenthau Plan, 63, 67
Mr. X article, 125, 141

Niebuhr, Reinhold, 73, 76–80
Nitze, Paul, 165
North Atlantic Treaty Organization, 121, 155
NSC 68 (National Security Council Policy Paper No. 68),'165, 166

Open Door Policy, 45
Optimist-pessimist dichotomy, 128
Orthodox view, 2

Pactomania, 211
Patterson, Thomas G., 5
Pauley, Edwin, 185
Polish home army, 91
Polish question, 83, 84, 91
Power politics, 27
Privileged sanctuaries, 209

Reparation, 62, 65, 67; Yalta, 65
Revisionist, 6, 9; inconsistency, 9; view, 6
Roosevelt, Franklin D., 13–22, 19, 22;

failures, 22; idealism, 19
Russian imperialism, 25

Schlesinger, Arthur, Jr., 2, 87, 88
Schuman Plan, 170
Schumpeter, Joseph, 38
Seabury, Paul, 1
Security Council, 180, 212
Shulman, Marshall D., 3
Soviet imperialism, 35, 128
Spanier, John W., 194
Sphere of influence, 209
Stalin, 28, 62, 63, 70, 82, 83, 86, 96, 101; Democratic election, 86, 101; military strategy, 28, 83, 96; Yalta objectives, 63, 82, 96
Stone, I. F., 202
Syngman Rhee, 186, 187

Taft, Robert A., 167
Teheran Conference, 28, 93, 97
Thirty-eighth parallel, 126, 193
Thucydides, 92
Tocqueville, de, 25
Toynbee, Arnold J., 39
Trotsky, 24
Truman Doctrine, 1, 130, 136, 137, 139, 141; legislative history of, 136, 137, 139; revolution in American policy, 130; root principle of, 141
Truman, Harry S., 40, 135

Unconditional surrender, 29
"Uniting for Peace" Resolution, 126, 181

Vandenberg, Arthur, 136, 160, 168; resolution, 160
Vietnam, 209

Wake Island Conference, 188
War, tradition American attitude, 197
Warsaw uprising, 91, 92
Williams, W. A., 44
Willoughby, Charles A., 201
Wilmot, Chester, 27

Yalta Conference, 59, 62, 82, 88, 89, 91–105, 109, 110, 114; orthodox interpretation, 89, 109; revisionist, 89, 90, 110; interpreter/critic, 114
Yergin, Daniel, 60, 65, 70

DATE DUE

FEB 25 '85			
GAYLORD			PRINTED IN U.S.A.